Riding by Torchlight

A Grass Roots Advocacy for Classical Horsemanship

from Arena to Savannah

Susannah West Cord

Xenophon Press

Available at www.XenophonPress.com

Copyright © 2019 by Xenophon Press LLC

All rights reserved. No part of this work may be reproduced or transmitted in any form or by any means, electronic or mechanical, including photocopying, or by any information storage or retrieval system except by a written permission from the publisher.

Published by Xenophon Press LLC
Nassawadox, Virginia 23413, U.S.A.
xenophonpress@gmail.com

Hardcover ISBN: 978-1948717168
ePub ISBN: 978-1948717175

For my Mum

*Who taught me to follow my bliss
(especially if it smelled like a horse)*

Publisher's Introduction

In an era when classical dressage is at risk of being pirated by charlatans and imitators, Susannah West Cord takes a strong stand advocating for true classical principles. These time-tested methods comprise the body of knowledge that we call classical horsemanship. They prove to work humanely with most horses, with most riders, most of the time. Classical horsemanship does not refer to show horses or non-show horses, it references a tradition of passing down the very best knowledge proven by trial and error, improved upon by generations of riding masters over centuries. Take the horse to a show when you have something of merit to show, or choose not to show if you please, but don't use the horse for self-aggrandizement or ego-driven pursuits.

Today in the name of dressage there is factionalism that includes groups that no longer have the horse's well-being or best interests at heart. Susannah West Cord takes a brave stance against pretenders and has the courage to talk about difficult topics that others avoid. She is willing to speak about the "elephant in the room" that makes some people uncomfortable. Susannah West Cord is breaking the ice on topics that are difficult to broach. Xenophon Press supports this writing because this subject matter must be aired if we are to preserve classical horsemanship.

We need more grassroots support of correct riding. Correct riding is not determined by discipline; it is demonstrated by attitude and how we approach and treat our equine partners. There is bad riding in all equestrian sports and one could also argue that it is possible to find good horsemanship across disciplines. Horses are no longer used for transportation, agriculture or 'horse-power.' The non-horse people of the world are watching equestrians with a view to animal rights. Therefore, we have an obligation to honor the nature of the equine partners that have played a huge part in the civilization of mankind. We need to honor horses' generosity by respecting their true nature and treating them with kindness. Horses provide us with so much learning, wisdom about life, adventure, physical activity, and therapeutic benefits.

Susannah West Cord is advocating for a kind approach by sharing her personal discoveries as a lifetime horsewoman and admonishing current trends that derail humankind's ethical obligation to the species. We hope this series of essays is thought-provoking and inspiring. We are grateful to both our devoted readers and dedicated authors. Together, we make Xenophon Press and the mission of preserving classical horsemanship possible.

Frances A. Williams, Acquisitions Editor
Richard F. Williams, Publisher
Xenophon Press LLC

Table of Contents

Publisher's Introduction v
Foreword xi
Preface xiii
1 Once Upon A Time 1
2 Life Lessons 11
3 Balance 19
4 Perspective 29
5 The Little Things 39
6 Freedom of Expression 43
7 Miss Manners 53
8 The Healing Power of Horses 61
9 Never Again 69
10 Two Fingers and a Noseband 75
11 Educate Yourself 83
12 Are Classical Dressage Riders From Mars? 91
13 To Show or No To Show… 99
14 Dressage Derailed 107
15 Gusto's Journey 117
16 Pretty is as Pretty Does 135
17 The Year of the Clinic 145

Bonus Materials

Equine Hoof in Mouth Syndrome 161
Dressage Cross Training and Other Mad Hat Ideas 165

East Meets West 175
First Day at School 182
When One Door Closes… 186
Classical Horsemanship from Arena to Savannah 187
Blood, Mud and Mayonnaise 190
A Window Opens… 193
About the Book 195
About the Author 197

Xenophon Press Library 199

Foreword

About a decade ago, right about the time I first met Susannah Cord, I came upon the term "ethological equitation" in an online article. The term was beginning to become widely used to refer to a type of horsemanship based on the science of ethology, the study of animal behavior in the natural environment, and how we can use that knowledge to achieve better harmony with our horses.

Once you have had the pleasure of reading *Riding by Torchlight*, I am sure you will understand why Susannah's name and that phrase remain forever linked in my recollection.

A lifelong horsewoman, Susannah was classically trained at an early age before moving to the wilds of Texas and embarking on a new phase of her career. In these days when everyone is patenting and trademarking everything in the equestrian world, not to mention reinventing the wheel, she remains refreshingly modest and self-effacing, as most true masters do. I had to press her to include the story of her impromptu jumping adventure with legendary Badminton winner Lucinda Green after they galloped with zebra and giraffe on safari in Africa, and I suspect few people are aware she organized the first "East Meets West" dressage clinic in Texas with Walter Zettl.

Susannah came of age as a writer during one of the most contentious times in modern equine sport, when many ethical riders and trainers began to stand up against the practice of Rollkur so prevalent at the time. She was on the front lines, as some of the chapters in this book will attest, and her voice and advocacy for the horse did not go unnoticed.

She found her most compelling voice with stories of several rescue horses she rehabilitated. While she is quick to warn against the dangers of anthropomorphism, stories told from a horse's point of view can be extremely educational and riveting. When it is done well—the classic *Black Beauty*, recent Xenophon Press release *I, Siglavy* by Lisbeth Asay, or Frederic Pignon's marvelous children's book *Templado 'The Whisperer'*—there is a poignancy about the horses' lives that cannot be matched by more traditional narrative voices. Susannah's heartfelt story, "Gusto's Journey," takes its place beside such moving works.

Susannah won't tell you, but during her work with Gusto she became extremely proficient with the classical work in hand, and she developed a lovely piaffe with this formerly troubled Weltmeyer son; relaxed, rhythmic, and beautifully collected. It was a pleasure to watch them, both obviously enjoying the moment, and in fact working with her beloved Gusto served me well when I went on later to help two more Weltmeyer offspring. Gusto leaves a legacy that will be remembered.

Susannah would be the first to tell you that we stand on the shoulders of giants. Methods that work to train a horse kindly and for his well-being and longevity, working with the laws of equine biomechanics, have been codified and passed down over generations. As she points out, we are part of a tradition handed down by many masters who are quick to credit their sources. I think what truly fascinates her about the work in hand is its modern evolution where trainers proficient in certain forms of equine bodywork are beginning to combine this with the work in hand. I find it a welcome evolution. Gone are the days when we must keep the horse at arm's length—literally—for the work in hand and touch only with the whip. Now a judicious use of a soft acupressure touch here, a careful muscle release there, is adding a further dimension to the classical work in hand, and Susannah is proving to be quite gifted at it.

As riders mature and become educated in various systems, it becomes clear where their hearts lie by the choices they make in methods and the masters who espouse them. With her vast exposure to riding on several continents, not to mention many diverse disciplines, Susannah has made her choice, and found her authentic writer's voice, truly with each horse's best interests in mind. This can be a hard choice for young professional trainers and instructors, and it comes with consequences. Susannah is part of that cadre.

Nowadays – I am not young, but in the mentoring days of my stewardship – I find my most cherished friends in the equestrian world are inevitably people who have made those same choices and walk that walk in their professional lives. I am proud to count such impeccable people as Holly Hansen, founder of the Foundation for Classical Horsemanship and organizer of three classical symposiums; Frederic Pignon and Magali Delgado, originally of *Cavalia* fame, now clinicians extraordinaire; equine biomechanics lecturer Jillian Kreinbring, and of course Susannah Cord as dear friends. When we get together over dinner, stories go around the table of what I started with, attempting to practice ethological equitation and maintain the highest standards. It is an honor to be among such people, and I am happy to observe there are many more whose names I could gladly include here; I merely mention a few cherished personal friends.

When Susannah's *Riding by Torchlight* column first appeared, her philosophical approach to sometimes difficult topics was a breath of fresh air. The chapters included here have stood the test of time and are still relevant today, in addition to providing a slice of history we lived through with our sport. As Susannah points out, if we do not keep our own house clean, others will step in to do it for us, so it benefits all of us, not to mention our beloved horses, to present the highest standards of horsemanship to the public. Since I have known her, Susannah has attempted to do just that. I think you will enjoy her journey, and we can always hope for future installments.

Stephanie Grant Millham
Author of *The Legacy of Master Nuno Oliveira*

Preface

It gives me a bit of a jolt to realize this, but the book you are holding in your hands has been in the making since late 2004 or early 2005. That was when I was invited to join an online Classical Dressage chat room and spent way too much time debating this and that. It wasn't long before I realized it was a great way to lose time and withdrew from the group again, but not before my posts had caught the eye of a certain Nadja King.

Nadja contacted me directly and asked me to consider contributing to a new online magazine she had just begun to publish. That magazine was *Horses For LIFE*, a magazine that would go on to be an extraordinary resource of both traditional and eclectic information on horsemanship and the state of the equestrian world at large, before vanishing off the internet under mysterious circumstances a decade later.

My initial contributions, some of which you will find in this book as bonus material, were sporadic and either off the top of my head like Quincy's extraordinary story of "Hoof and Mouth Disease," or the result of a great deal of thought and hard work like my articles on my September 2005 *East Meets West Clinic* taught by Walter Zettl. But it wasn't until late 2007 when Nadja continued to pester me to write regular articles that the idea for *Riding By Torchlight* was born.

Unwilling to write the technical articles Nadja had been suggesting, I countered with a rather outrageous suggestion, fully expecting to be rejected. That I write a philosophical column for each issue, on whatever I wanted to write about, as it pertained to my day to day life with my off-the-track Thoroughbred, Torchlight and his barn mates. The idea was a reflection of my many little musings as I went about in the quiet vacuum of training horses by myself, day after day.

To my great surprise and consternation, Nadja immediately accepted, and I went about sharing my thoughts with trepidation. I soon found I was far from alone in my wandering wonderings and my column was well received by a steadily building worldwide audience. Little did I know, as I wrote my first few exploratory columns, that *Riding By Torchlight* would be my own coming of age story as I found my voice and place in the equestrian world. It would also become a commentary on the controversies shaking the horse world with the advent of Rollkur and the extreme use of nosebands. Articles like the scathing and infamous "Dressage Derailed" earned me compliments from renowned horse people I could barely believe had bothered to read my work.

Some articles, like "Year of the Clinic," would find new homes in other publications as far away as New Zealand, and be translated into languages I never dreamed of. "Freedom of Expression" and "Educate Yourself" found new homes on horse trainer, author, and speaker Jean Luc Cornille's extensive website. But to my great surprise, the tongue-in-cheek-turned-experimental article, "Gusto's Journey" was probably the all-time favorite of many readers.

It has been fascinating for me now to review and edit my own work from as long ago as fourteen years. There is an obvious growth in my technical writing abilities as my column took on a life of its own, but even more so, what touches me deeply now is the leap into a newfound emotional depth exemplified in the columns following my mother's passing.

Ultimately, *Riding By Torchlight* became a vehicle for my own maturation as a writer and equestrian, and a stepping stone to my first full length book, *Each Wind That Blows*, a memoir sparked by a riding safari in Kenya that I was to chronicle for *Riding By Torchlight*. For this, and for much support and encouragement over the years, I will always be grateful to Nadja King and her brainchild, *Horses For LIFE*. She sensed the writer in me before I ever knew it myself. For those who wonder what became of the magazine and of Nadja herself, welcome to the club. I know no more than any of you. I am so sorry that so many of us enjoyed and supported the magazine only to be so disappointed in the end.

Over the years I wrote close to thirty columns and stories for *Horses For LIFE*, somewhat more than could fit in one book. I have done my best to edit them, searching for excellence and relevance while still maintaining a sense of continuity. At the end of each I have added a short retrospective, a few thoughts off the top of my head in regard to what memories or musings rereading the column in the spring of 2019 has sparked for me.

I hope you enjoy reading this collection as much as I have enjoyed living, writing and reviewing them.

I owe a great many thanks. The equestrian industry is fraught with pitfalls and disappointments. You can spend a decade developing a client base only to have someone ride your coattail to the finish line to harvest the fruits of your labor without a second thought or thanks. You can pour yourself into events that ultimately serve as catalysts to uplift and promote others, only to be sidelined yourself and demoted to less than a footnote in their histories. You can give a horse and owner everything you've got and still be deemed unworthy when a new and shiny trainer comes along…and so on, the list is endless. If it were not for the horses, I think many a trainer would quit.

But every so often, someone *will* come along and see the light and longing, the talent and the potential, burning for fulfillment and expression in you. And those rare people will stand by you, hold space for you, nurture you, support you and have your back, and open doors to untold opportunities. They will unknowingly say something you've been longing to hear, teach you something others wouldn't or couldn't. They will make the heartbreak and disappointment fade and dissolve, and they, along with the horses, will make it all worthwhile. They are a huge part of this book, for they informed the choices I made and eventually wrote about.

For being those rare people in my life, I gratefully give my special thanks to my first ever real dressage teacher, Christine Hermann, who picked me out of the crowd at ten and nurtured my talent and passion for the next few years until her life took her elsewhere.

To the late international dressage judge, Frederik Christian Obel, who judged me in my first (and so far only) international competition, found me worthy and gave me encouragement and assistance.

To German Olympic Silver Medallist, Karen Schlüter, who saw something in me and did her best to help me up the ladder at a time I was thinking only of getting off it. I decided not to take it further down the competitive and international route, no reflection upon her or her efforts on my behalf. This still warms my heart. My lesson on her Grand Prix mount, Ramazonas, still sings in my heart.

To Jane McLoud who gave me everything she had for the two years I worked for her, and showed me I could be the kind of trainer I wanted to be, a trainer who trained for the wellness of the horse, first and foremost.

To Eddo Hoekstra, and the five years of monthly four-day clinics on dozens of horses that taught me I could be the kind of trainer he already thought I was.

To Stephanie Grant Millham, who brought all the technique and feel together and wasn't shy about praise and recognition, giving me finally the affirmation I needed that I am not just imagining it when things, finally, go right. Really, really right.

To Carol McArdle and Holly Hansen, who each in their own fierce and particularly honest ways, have influenced, encouraged and supported me on my journey.

Thank you to Richard Williams of Xenophon Press for publishing this work and making it available worldwide to our community of like-minded riders.

Without all these friends and teachers, none of the stories herein would exist.

Last but not least, my profound gratitude for the hundreds of horses who have lent me their bodies on which to learn, their hearts to love and their minds to enjoy. My cup runneth over, but most especially, it runs over for a certain talented, sweet, neurotic, but oh-so-kind and clever OTTB named Torchlight. May he live forever, at the very least, in our hearts.

Susannah West Cord

1

Once Upon A Time...

First published in January 2008, this column was the first of the series.

I was looking for a horse. It was finally time. I had been riding and training for others for long enough, toppling over and over again into the usual pitfall of young and passionate horsewomen; the great no-no of falling in love with other people's horses. Working hard, bonding, gaining their trust and confidence, only to lose the client to any number of circumstances. A move out-of-state, a more experienced, bigger name trainer, or perhaps the horse was simply sold, owner's interest lost.

No, it was time for me to have a horse of my own, to train for me, and me alone, to love and develop for years to come. Luckily for me, my understanding and generous boyfriend (though maybe he was just weary enough of my crying over lost horses) put up a decent sum of money and I began the search. It soon led to a neighboring barn, where two lovely off-the-track thoroughbreds were said to be for sale. I never made it past the door. The sum demanded was exorbitant considering their circumstances, and more than double my actual funds. One overpriced and recovering from a bowed tendon, the other sound but still hugely overpriced for a horse fresh off-the-track, possibly in need of serious rehabilitation of every kind. I never even peeked at them.

My search eventually led to a horse of a different kind, but that is another story for another time. He pictures in this story mainly in his role in bringing me back to the same barn, where the two off-the-track Thoroughbreds still resided. It was the only barn offering stalls with runs, and that was what I wanted for my new and beloved steed, an oversized Clydesdale/Paint cross we named Banner. He was not at all what I had intended, but he stole my heart on contact, despite his lack of years for which he amply made up in his absurdly and overly generous size. A mere twelve by twelve stall would never do....

Soon after, on a warm and sunny day, I arrived at the barn to find my dream horse standing tensely in the cross ties. I am sorry to say that as his 16.3 HH blood-bay lanky frame shimmered in the sun, his finely shaped head and ears at rapt attention to some distant mirage, he filled my eyes, heart and soul and I forgot all about my own sweet Banner. In comparison to this wonder he was but a clunky, gawky and clumsy teenager.

Waves of regret washed over me when I realized this was one of the horses offered for sale a few months ago. He was now sold to a sweet, young, and inexperienced woman, of whom I will merely remark that she deemed it necessary to don white cotton gloves to groom her horse. The bay beauty and she seemed on somewhat tenuous terms, he pawed and she pouted, his attention and interest anywhere but here. Still recovering from a bowed tendon, Tommy, as he was known, was confined to his stall 24/7 except for his adventures in misbehavior when the beleaguered but faithful girl came to hand walk him every evening. This generally involved his levitating in every possible direction, detecting any number of God's abominations in the bushes and not letting up until he had reduced his meal ticket to tears.

I allowed myself a few moments to drink in his beautiful lines, the generous hip and sloping shoulder, short back and well-shaped legs. Then I set out to erase him from my mind; obviously he was never meant for me to begin with. And I did have my very own horse now, and a lovely horse it was. It was time to quit coveting what I could not have.

A few months of ignoring a serious crush, and the object of my determined lack of affections had finally worn his owner thin. To her great luck, the woman from whom she had bought him decided it had all been a mistake, and not only bought the horse back, with interest, but helped her find a lovely older schoolmaster perfectly suited to her needs, with whom she enjoyed a mutually loving relationship, all feet firmly planted on the ground.

To my great delight, a short time later Tommy was offered to me for training. The tendon had healed to perfection, he had begun some groundwork, his owner herself had been riding him, but felt he needed an experienced dressage trainer to put a solid foundation on him before he was to begin his career as a jumper. I was thrilled, my eye firmly on the ball. I would enjoy this great opportunity, and never wonder about what could have been.

Avoiding the pitfall of emotional attachment was an easy task. My first sensation on Tommy's back was a far cry from rapture. It was a mind-numbing, bone-crunching fear. His back a taut wire, his mind fluttering on the wings of a hummingbird, his eye on a different kind of ball. The kind bouncing off the fence next door, which happened to be a softball field. If we were really lucky, I thought, the ball might make it all the way into our public arena, and I might make it into their soft ball field in ways I'd rather not imagine, especially the part where I made my ungainly way over a twelve foot fence. This never actually happened. But in my chilled bones I was convinced the odds were against me.

Tommy felt every bit like a horse I had ridden shortly before, resulting in a serious fall, the kind that leaves the fear soaking your cells for months to come, a fear well out of your rational and reasoning reach. Like most serious horse people I have taken my share of falls, stood up, dusted myself off and gotten back in the saddle without a backward glance. But over the years three falls from various horses have left me with an irrational fear that took months to drain from my system, and that was one of them.

It was a young and beautiful thoroughbred, sworn to be broke, with whom we nonetheless spent a good hour on the ground before I ever put foot in the stirrup. We followed all the rules of both conventional and natural horsemanship. When I finally got into the saddle he was licking and chewing, carrying his tack with ease and contentment. Unfortunately, that did not apply also to riders. No sooner had I settled into the saddle than he reared straight up and in a tremendously athletic feat launched us vertically and forward into the air, finishing with a satisfyingly gravity-defeating buck. Needless to say, I hit the ground like a ton of bricks. We worked him some more, I finally rode him without trouble. I was bruised but uninjured. But the sensation of his body as he tensed into an upward soaring arc stayed with me, coated in glacial angst.

It just so happened that Tommy was built much like this young horse, and felt much like him in terms of tension. Were I presented with this set of circumstances today, I would insist on spending a great deal of time on groundwork, using all my skill and desire to win his trust and ensure confidence in me and in the ridden state before I ever sat on him and rode with expectations. But I was young and I was proud, I needed the ride, I needed the work. And I wanted to ride this horse.

It took six months before my stomach quit fluttering at the thought of riding Tommy. If it weren't for his owner relentlessly presenting me with a tacked-up horse three times a week, I might have chickened out any number of times. It wasn't that he was scary. Other than being generally a tense and excitable horse, he was not in the least bit dangerous. It was just the way he presented himself under saddle, uphill and drawn to a fine line by tension; it felt like I was riding a Russian roulette game. I was never sure in which chamber he had hidden the bullet. Fortunately, I never found out. And by now I think he has thrown the gun away. Or, more probably, there really never was one.

Seven years on, Tommy remains my greatest challenge. I renamed him Torchlight. His track name was Tom the Torch, and that just wouldn't do. I still mostly call him Tom. My fear is long gone, but in its place I have found an understanding that his has not. As his physical training progressed, slowly but surely, it became apparent that the race track had left many a fear imprinted on his every cell, with deep roots.

As we began to unravel the tangled threads of his racetrack existence, we found an extremely sweet and earnest horse, with great passion and desire to please, who had been raced too often and too hard. Doomed to never recover between races, winning was obviously precluded.

In its wake this handling left a horse who was eager to please but desperately afraid he would not succeed. His cover-up was a complete lack of attention. But once you showed him a simple thing he could do with ease, he was all yours and at full attention. It was easily lost; the steps had to be small and within easy reach, with a great deal of backtracking. He required, and requires to this day, careful and sensitive handling. As trainers and riders around us ridiculed our slow and less-than-impressive outward progress, I felt him slowly begin a healing process on the inside. Little by little the outside has come to reflect the healing that occurred and continues to occur on the inside.

When they called for draw reins, side reins, gag bits, flash nosebands and tougher riding, I looked to Tom and all he asked for was more patience. It has become my secret weapon, this patience that has sometimes been my only useful tool on this journey with a great but injured soul.

I had been working with Tom for a few years when my boyfriend-turned-husband and I decided to make the move to our own thirty acre horse property in a different state. In those years it had become apparent that Tom was not mentally cut out to be a jumper. My resolve to avoid falling in love with this particular horse had weakened beyond repair. It simply always felt like he was meant to be with me. It had from the first day I saw him, however impossible it had then appeared.

The thought of leaving him behind was hard to bear. I was able to work a complicated deal that involved a horse we had retrained as a jumper, on which I was owed a great deal of money, which also happened to be a horse coveted by Tommy's owner. With that and my husband coming to the rescue once again, to my joy and slight disbelief, Tom made the move with us. I thought I was bringing with me a lovely dressage prospect, my dream horse that finally became my very own, at least on paper. I was, but more importantly, I was bringing with me a life-changing, mind-expanding, soul-challenging mentor extraordinaire.

As Tom's life changed dramatically, from a stalled life to the option of a twenty-five acre pasture in a herd, he changed. He dropped copious amounts of weight as he appointed himself herd manager, intent upon constantly ensuring everyone's wellbeing, in the process traveling miles a day. His once blossoming frame became gaunt with hollow shades, his exquisite head bony and angular. He lost his shoes as his feet crumpled in the new climate. His fluid trot stuttered and sputtered across the hard ground. Being ridden was now not only a distraction from his new responsibilities, barely to be endured, it became impossible. Whatever progress we had made seemed lost to the winds.

We started over from scratch. Unbeknownst to me, I was starting on an entirely new phase of my life as a horsewoman, courtesy of Torchlight Training. It's an old cliché, but had I known then what I know now, how challenging would be the road ahead, I might well have bailed and run for my life. I was about to have to relearn the most basic facets of horsemanship from the bottom up. Put all ambitions on hold, my burgeoning show horse taking me back to basics I didn't even know were missing. How could I? I didn't know they wouldn't just develop like they had with any other horse I had ever worked with. Trust and affection with horses had always come easily for me. Tom was about to make me work harder for that than I had ever worked for anything in my life.

Before our move, my focus, as with all horses in training with me, had been intent upon developing Tom under saddle, worrying about top line, conditioning, was he reaching into the bridle, was he releasing his back, in balance, happy under saddle, did he trust my hand, search for it. The relationship part I took for granted, as always it came with the handling and the work, didn't it? He was friendly, affectionate even, in a sort of distracted and offhand manner.

We went to a few shows, and he did well enough, though green and excitable, he trusted and allowed me to be in relative command, emphasis being on relative. After some discussion on the subject of the necessity of staying in the arena for the entirety of the test, we even came to terms on that. For a non-jumper, he was showing some promise in terms of scaling dressage rings. All in all, we were moving along the training scale in fine, if excruciatingly slow form.

With the move, his life took on a whole new dimension wherein I mattered not a lick. I was purely a distracting and frustrating entity that took him away from his newly found social life in which he reveled. No longer was I a welcome relief from the confinement of his stall. With absolute doggedness, Tom took me down a road that allowed only one real focus. How well did I know him, and more importantly, how well did he trust me. As it turns out, not nearly well enough.

Everything had changed, nothing was as it had been, all I took for granted, absolutely all of it, now had to be reevaluated. In the process, I was reeducated in all things 'horse'.

It started from the ground up.

I learnt about horse boots and he developed iron feet and remains barefoot today. Because of him, my husband and I began seriously studying hoof health, and though we are not fanatics or experts, with the aid of an experienced barefoot trimmer, eventually all our current horses successfully transitioned to barefoot. Tom in particular, ever the challenge, has shown a huge improvement in the biomechanics of his hind legs and haunches. Somewhat cow hocked and due to past trims not well in command of his heels, he had always 'wobbled' in his hocks, making engagement increasingly challenging as his hocks deteriorated to the grinding. Today, he moves almost cleanly and places his feet, heels first, well and firmly under his body. This alone has made him infinitely more rideable.

I became an ardent student of equine nutrition. As Tom gained his weight back, I not only gained knowledge but developed a keener and more inquisitive interest in the feeding of horses. Moving from a boarding facility to a ranch where your horses now spend the better part of day and night out in all weather, seriously challenges a feeding program previously taken for granted with little to challenge it in terms of wind and weather, sun and rain. It took a few years, but I think we have it down now….At least he no longer turns a crackling burnt orange in the summer!

As I experimented with different configurations of horses in different pastures, I learned to read individual horses and temperaments better. One development in that regard, however, took me completely by surprise. To our great amusement, the handsome and dashing Torchlight fell irrevocably in love with a then twenty-seven year old, swaybacked and cantankerous Saddlebred mare, who sports a tangerine sized calcification on one cheek. Nicknamed Mama after she possessively took over the mothering of a weanling burro I brought home on a whim, she was a fixture of the ranch when we bought it, and her relationship with Tortilla the burro has brought hours of amusement since. Tom moved into their smaller pasture where he settled down, as long as he was with his own true love, warts and all.

Inevitably, the next point on Torchlight's agenda required me to learn how to handle herd separation issues. Leaving his Juliet was worse than leaving the herd by a long stretch. Neighing, pawing, eyes rolling hysterically, fishtailing on the lead line, his conviction strong that they surely would all perish in his absence, or at least suffer as he did.

Old Mama did, I must say, put up a halfhearted display of missing him, but his ardor was largely unequalled. The burro just stared at this extravagant waste of energy. I only wished he'd feel that way about me, the one who loved and cared for him, paid his bills, and had whisked him away from a jailed life to one of freedom. Right? Who was this ungrateful beast and what did he do with my Tommy? I found myself giving into the very kind of frustration that I patiently addressed in my clients, all the while reminding them "It's a horse, not a human. They don't appreciate the same things we do. They are usually smarter than that." Ah, the joys of backseat horse handling.

By demand, I became more involved with groundwork, with the psychology of horsemanship, not just trusting my feel but complementing it with techniques gleaned from various schools of natural horsemanship—it took time, but today Tom moves easily between pastures and different herds. My reward is not confined to my relationship with Tom. I now move easily from 'conversations' with one horse to the next. And he's just plain happy next to me. Halters are barely used anymore. I may even be considered his new Juliet, though the now thirty-two year old Mama still holds a soft spot in his heart.

Finally he allowed that it was time to ride again. Our ridden work has taken many twists and turns, some unconventional, though classical dressage remains at the heart of it. Perhaps those very twists and turns brought me back to that heart.

Whether it was pursuing the teachings of Klaus Ferdinand Hempfling, riding primarily in a halter for weeks, taking reining lessons with a professional reiner, or attending a Parelli course on Riding with Fluidity, they have all served to highlight the beauty and pragmatism of 'Form and Function' that Classical Dressage has perfected. We have taken much away from those experiences, but nothing so poignant as that with every return to dressage I fell deeper in love with the ideals and the tenets of our masters, past and present. No other discipline enhances, preserves and reveres the horse, not just his virtues and usefulness but the horse itself, as does Classical Dressage.

The road has been slow and arduous. It has taken hours of contemplation, days of frustration, weeks of soul searching and months of dejection, not to mention humiliation. It's a tough pill to swallow when you can easily ride everything but your own horse. Or when you just told an interested party at a clinic away from home that he is Second Level and how far he has come, only to have him revert to a histrionic giraffe barely capable of Intro, never mind a straight line or exhibiting any remembrance of ever having been ridden before in his life. That is complete news to him, if not to you, and you are left feeling like the girl who told everyone Prince Charming was taking her to the prom, only to have him show up with another girl. At least Tom didn't bring old Mama to further my humiliation. I will remain grateful for small favors.

But, it's back to the drawing board, knowing you haven't done enough for the relationship. And leave the ego at the door.

I have learned to put ambitions aside to a degree never known to me before, and put Tom's wellbeing always at the fore. I thought I always had, but he has shown me new definitions of that belief. Unlike so many forgiving and infinitely patient horses that can allow you some illusion of perfect harmony, with Tom there's no gray area. It's black and white. He's content to be involved and relaxed in the work, or he is not.

I can *make* him do just about anything, he is willing and kind enough, but if I want lightness, ease and accord, to look my horse confidently in the eye after a session, I have to be ready to put it all aside and work on his trust at the drop of a hat. That means backing off the lesson and the whole curriculum. It means going back to groundwork, a bareback trail ride, a hand walk around the land. Or maybe a few days of just being together, grooming and doing bodywork like the *SENSE Method*.

But in between those times have been moments of pure exhilaration, of sheer joy, of a love felt purely as it flowed between species. Moments that confirm and define me as a rider, trainer, but above all, a lover and friend of horses. Moments such as the first time Tom let himself show me unequivocal affection.

After years of patiently and aloofly accepting my attempts at affection, he demanded my presence at his head as I attempted to groom his body. When I responded and placed myself at his neck, he stunned me when he turned and laid his head across my shoulder and simply stood there for several minutes, blowing softly in my ear. I am not ashamed to admit that tears ran freely down my face as this introverted, locked away horse handed me the keys to his heart. Since then, this practice has become part of our required routine as per Tom, and he would happily stand thus for hours if I could only carry him so long. Displays of physical affection have become commonplace with him, but I never take them for granted. I worked too hard to gain them.

There have been highlights in our work, too, of course, though none as dear to me as the one above. Tom recently offered to free lunge, a state I thought we'd never achieve, his love of freedom always translating into a complete lack of attention once out of the round pen. But one day, as I turned him loose in a large arena, he simply…longed himself. Languidly and with full attention, he flowed around me, occasionally glancing at me as if to say, "Get it? Do you get it? It's the next level, missy. You're finally ready. Try to keep up now!" We went through all our usual practices without the benefit of walls or lunge-lines, just working off one another, in mutual inspiration, and it was a dream. Another dream not to be taken for granted, as he has since reminded me!

Tom has offered me any number of small triumphs along the way, on many levels. The first time he freely came galloping across the pasture to greet me, his first temper tantrum when I chose to work another horse before him. Every time he chooses to touch me first. The way his face changes when he sees me, his alertness melting into a soft focus and a rumbling nicker. The pleasure of trusting him to carry me safely, bareback in a halter. The first time we jumped, however small the jump, it was a huge victory to have him calmly jump under saddle, and repeat the exercise without reservations or a meltdown.

To have him seek my company, to the point of hanging out outside my window, waiting at the fence till I come out to play. Being able to perform well at a recent Walter Zettl clinic, especially after our previous clinics with Herr Zettl had mainly involved trying to keep Tom from swinging from the chandeliers, so to speak. Herr Zettl's pride in the improvement in Tom's overall state of being seemed to transcend my own, and turned previous humiliations to dust in the light of his appreciation and understanding of the hard work that went into Tom's transformation. Not to mention my own. And yes, it was a clinic far from home.

My dream horse turned out to be a hard taskmaster who has motivated and inspired me, forced me to reach higher and search deeper. There have been no easy rules, no pat answers. Every horse I ride from now on may thank Tom for his instruction. I do, because every other horse is a relative piece of cake compared to him. We all benefit from his hardships and challenges. As my mentor, Eddo Hoekstra, said recently upon riding Tom: "It's like riding ten different horses in one." At least they are all friendly, if not all in agreement.

Plans to show have fallen by the wayside as our journey became far more interesting than making the next level. I still think we might one day, if for no other reason than my belief that the world of competitive dressage needs more classical riders and horses. But it will be up to Tom. There may be other horses better suited for that endeavor. His strong suit is without a doubt to be my ever-demanding tutor. His teachings will endure for my lifetime and every horse I encounter on my journey.

The road rambles on, and it is mostly dark and winding, the only step clearly viewed the one at our very feet. The rest drop away, out of sight, till our passage brings us close, very close. Tom keeps me guessing, and the rewards are better than ever for getting it right. With a steady hand—or is it hoof—he keeps me on the straight and narrow, easily letting me know when I have strayed from the path on which he has set us. The path he requires for optimum results, or rather, optimum harmony. Sometimes I am a little thick, and slow to get the message.

Onwards in this dark I wander, my guiding light the soft shimmer of his spirit illuminating the way. It is in turns unnerving and enchanting, like riding by torchlight through a strange forest in the murky twilight of a late summer's eve.

In Retrospect, 2019

…My journey with Tom was but the tip of the iceberg, the door that opened the way to another thousand. Before my journey with Tom came to a close, I had learned to use the concepts of Natural Horsemanship, round pens and barefoot with caution and a great deal of pragmatism and common sense. There is always more to be learned, from anything and anyone, but sometimes it turns out to be lessons in what we'd rather not, than in what we must.

I learned that my built in understanding of biomechanics and the necessity of trust and relaxation, imparted to me through years of Classical Dressage, saved me from making any number of mistakes in my application of Natural Horsemanship concepts and in the round pen, but also limited my understanding of the many pitfalls others fell into.

I learned I'd rather work my horse at liberty in a square pen, because the corners provide him an opportunity to hide from excessive pressure and provide feedback about my attempts at communication. I learned that a horse can be just as miserable barefoot, bareback and 'all natural' as a horse shod and locked in a stall, and that the wellbeing and soundness of the horse can be exceedingly subjective and limited to an owner's understanding thereof.

I learned that much like some spices, just a pinch of some techniques and tenets go a very long way.

2 Life Lessons

February 2008

A funny thing happens when you buy a horse. First of all, people have all kinds of reasons for doing so. They usually go something like this:

- Horses are therapy (and more fun/warm/loving/fuzzy than an hour on the couch).
- They give me a sense of freedom.
- I saw My Friend, Flicka and realized I couldn't live another day without horses.
- They provide good exercise out in the open air.
- I enjoy the relationship and the connection to nature.
- I was looking for a new hobby and this looked like fun, and less money than a speedboat (or so I thought).
- I grew up riding and can't imagine a day without horses.
- I bought a horse for my daughter to keep her out of trouble. Now I am riding the horse and she is taking piano lessons. Or is it singing lessons? …Or…belly dancing…no, computer lessons. No, that was last month. Piano lessons.
- They are so pretty I just *had* to have one, and I really like the whole top hat and coattails look.
- I always wanted a pony and now I can finally have my own (forty years, eighteen inches and fifty pounds later and usually in the form of a four year old, 13 HH barely halter-broke Arab stud. Doesn't he look JUST like the Black Stallion?)

Of course there are plenty more reasons, of all sorts, but in my personal experience, never has anyone, myself included, listed:

- I am looking for life lessons from an extraordinary companion.

But the funny thing is, that's often exactly what you get. Life lessons in a really cute and sometimes, even magnificent, package. Now whether or not people decide to accept and work with this part of the package is entirely up to them. It's kind of like the whole *Mission Impossible* thing. Should you *choose* to accept this mission and so on. Except in the movies they always accept, and in real life horses get a very mixed set of responses. Oh, and this package generally does not self-destruct in ten-seconds whether you accept or not, although I know people who might argue with that. And they have the vet bills to back it up. But I digress.

Some people do choose *not* to accept that offer. There are people who have been in the horse business for decades, their entire lives, who still maintain that horses are slow, dimwitted, stupid animals that don't actually feel pain, and have no wisdom of their own to impart.

One renowned trainer I had the uneven pleasure of working around for several years, took every opportunity to tell me how imbecilic horses are, with a brain no bigger than a chicken's. Or was it a peach pit, I can't remember now. You could inflict pain on them, it didn't really matter, because they didn't feel it the way we do, it was more of a *mechanical* reflex. Trainers should use these mechanical reflexes to their advantage. I'd wonder how big a part of his comparably huge brain he was using, because if he was using the scientifically proclaimed 10%, and the horse was using the better part of his, then they'd be on equal footing, more or less. Maybe the horse would have an edge if the trainer didn't have all the 'tools'.

Next time I'd see him, he'd be terrorizing a horse, muttering about how this horse knew exactly what was expected of him and was simply defying him. Hmm, that sure goes with a dumb, mute chicken brained animal. Dumb enough to not feel pain, smart enough to outwit an experienced horseman at every turn, and all in spite of the extreme discomfort and pain it would bring him. Oh, but he didn't feel pain. Right. No, wait, I'm confused.

So let me start again. Smart enough to outwit him and defy him, but too dumb to feel the pain then inflicted on him. I think that says it? At the time, I didn't have the courage to mention this paradox to him. I doubt I would have made a dent, but it'd be nice to be able to say I tried. I could feel heroic.

He was an otherwise nice man, even a kind man, and when we weren't talking horses, I enjoyed his company immensely. But he was not willing to learn the life lessons the horses could teach him. Instead he bullied those lessons to dust, shouting louder and louder till the horses gave up. It was business, a business he grew up in, and horses would never be anything else to him.

The only thing I can take away from experiences such as these is that some things haven't changed over the centuries, they have simply shifted around.

Dumb, soulless, devoid of self-awareness and consciousness, unable to feel pain of any kind. These were all labels once applied to slaves. It's what the slave master has to tell himself to account for and justify his actions. Humanity has a ways to go.

On the other hand, there are many experienced horsemen and women out there who all have stories of the horses that changed their lives, of the horses that taught them to see, really see, and really listen. Paul Belasik writes about such an experience in his book *Riding Towards The Light*, Pat Parelli has his Casper, Klaus Ferdinand Hempfling his little gelding Janosch. I have my Torchlight, who better than any other horse has taught me to keep my inner ears wide open. The Cherokees have a saying: *"Listen, or your tongue will make you deaf."* That ought to be on every barn wall, and quite possibly Torchlight would like it tattooed on my forehead.

As riders and trainers, we have many 'tongues'. Our hands, legs, seat, weight, spurs, whips. Auxiliary aids, lunge lines, long-lines, nose-chains, the list goes on. Pick up any horse related catalog and the amount of equipment available is truly astounding and all too often horrifying. All instruments supposed to help us *communicate* with our horses, implying a two way street, but very often they shut up the horse and allow us to chatter more loudly, forcefully and incessantly.

And we have our mind. Who doesn't have an incessant voice in their head talking on and off or even nonstop about what is, should be or is *not* happening? (Everybody does, right? *Right!?* My inner voice wants to know.) As an instructor, I often find myself having to negotiate with and around people's inner voice, never mind my own.

All of those *tongues* need to be willing to lay dormant, even if just for a stride now and then, just be still, and *listen*. Or better yet, they could learn to mostly speak only when spoken to.

Listening to our horses brings on another paradox. For most people, listening requires control, the *self*-control to be quiet and allow the empty space to unfold within which another being's voice may be heard. In my experience, for a majority of people, gaining this control, and it really has to be gained in most cases, requires a *relinquishing* of control first. Relinquishing the control they believe is necessary in that moment to present the correct picture. The control to be *right*. Or simply the control that allows them to *feel* in control. And today's dressage riders are notorious control freaks.

Personally, I think it is the willingness to listen that separates the great trainers from the good ones. Of course, to be fair, relinquishing any amount of control can induce a sense of severe vulnerability, especially in the presence of a 1200-1500lb. animal. No matter how cute, warm and fuzzy he may be.

Now add to that a rider hung up on what the picture is supposed to look like, as dressage riders often are. Because that's what the books say, that's what my trainer looks like on her horses, that's what I saw on the cover of *Dressage Today*. They begin to ride the *product*, not the *process*. It is the basic existential lesson of living in the Now, being circumvented for a hoped for Future. They forget to ride where they are and try to ride where they wish they were, not understanding and in some cases not caring what goes *before* the pretty picture. They do not understand that creating the *look* does not automatically create the required underlying training and physiological development. Listening to the horse goes out the window in the quest for the image. Enter control and micromanagement of the horse. Enter bigger bits, auxiliary reins, sharper spurs....

Enter opportunity for choice. Take the road the horse offers, and the many positive and a few negative lessons to be learnt, or bring force and excessive control to the training game, and learn lessons the hard(er) way. Either way, the horse still offers lessons about life, but they go unheard when the rider manages to convince himself it's really all just about the training, the ride, the horse and *his* issues, issues that increase in direct proportion to the amount of force and gimmicks applied. This choice alone, or temptation of choice, could tell an aware rider a great deal about him or herself. How one justifies these choices tells us even more.

The way in which a horse teaches is personal and manifold. It depends upon the horse and the person involved. Some horses teach through gentle repetition, some through forceful negation, and some any variation in between. But their lessons all seem to me to be variations on a single theme.

Balance

In all of life we need balance. There are entire bookshelves in the bookstores with books devoted to helping you find balance and 'live happier, healthier lives'. But once you get involved with horses, you could put all those books away and simply study your horse. And then study yourself *with* your horse. Through his eyes you will see a clear view of yourself, starkly honest and yet often sublimely compassionate, as close to a mirror of the soul as you will ever find.

In my case, with Torchlight refusing to follow any of the usual pathways, he forced me to constantly rebalance my ambitions for conventional success with my very real but often circumvented ambitions for personal and spiritual success. He exercised and tested, again and again, the strength of my convictions and the fiber of my integrity. In effect, he helped mold my character over the past seven years. He has spoken to me in any way he could find, using any and all available avenues. Most of all, he has been very effective in letting me know when he was unhappy about something. And because I so very much need my horses to be happy, I listened as best I could.

It can be difficult to listen. At first you can feel like a fool, you can feel deaf and dumb. There have been numerous occasions when I threw my hands up in disgust, in tears, frustrated beyond despair that I just didn't understand what he was trying to tell me with whatever bizarre behavior he was now exhibiting. On more than one occasion I declared myself too feeble, too inexperienced, too plain stupid to do this horse justice. I knew he was talking to me and I wasn't getting it.

For the first time I felt the shoe on the other foot. I really knew what it must be like to be a horse living in the world of humans and trying to learn 'human talk'. To understand what was being said and what was expected of you, that numb feeling of watching someone speak to you as if you should get it while not understanding a word. It was like signing up for Beginners Chinese classes, and attending the Advanced course instead. Unfortunately, a great many horses find themselves in this situation and are punished for it, the teacher 'rapping their fingers' again and again, shouting with spittle flying in their faces in a language of which they have not even begun to grasp the basics.

I had placed myself in the barn of Torchlight Training and I was having a lot of trouble keeping up. Lucky for me, he wasn't into abusive or overly coercive training methods. He simply repeated himself with varying intonations and inflections, sighing loudly or acting out when his pupil continued to appear clueless. One of his favorite messages is simply weaving. He knows that gets my attention every time. For me, weaving is like nails on a blackboard. If he weaves, I am all ears, and sometimes the other messages get through. That is, if I can simultaneously shut up long enough to listen.

Often it is just a feeling, like a sudden inspiration. Sometimes it's a guess, a stab at a multiple choice question, where I keep checking off answers till it seems I get the right one. Now and then it's a 'knowing,' and I get an extra snuggle and a gold star for getting it right. Plus he quits that damn weaving.

But the main thing is I keep listening, I keep trying. Besides, I cannot take anything for granted around Sir Thomas Torchlight himself. Oh no, he is swift and merciless in his reproach. Weave, weave, weave, or a punishingly tense and bouncy trot that leaves me fantasizing about a kidney transplant. Being an addict to a soft and relaxed ride furthers his cause, he has a willing enough student, and like the weaving, any restriction gets my attention, *pronto*. In this way, he has trained me well and I am a better horsewoman on all levels for it.

It wasn't that I wasn't already trying to listen, but I have become a more skilled and imaginative listener, for imagination along with intuition are essential when talking with horses. Apart from anything else, first you have to be willing to imagine that they are indeed talking to you, that they do have a voice of their own, not to mention desires and wishes, even dreams and ambitions. I know. The Anthropomorphism Police will be knocking on my door in a minute. Well, let them come. Torchlight will set them straight or at the very least weave them into oblivion.

Other horses through the years have spoken loudly in the silence I relinquished to their domain, loudly enough for me to hear, and well enough for me to understand. There was Lucky, a thirteen year old Thoroughbred gelding, who had been trying for years to tell anyone who would listen that dressage was really not his game. He was a funny looking horse, with a low set neck, short back and long straight hind legs, and, probably at least partly due to his indifference to the demands on his time, he was endowed with a healthy dose of ADD. As a trainer, I did my best to help him get comfortable and focused so he might please his owner. But he was right. Dressage was really not his game, and he spooked and twirled his way through every session. When poor health finally forced the owner to sell, I asked the one question that Lucky had been trying to get me to ask for months. Would she mind if I jumped him, and if he showed talent, sold him as a jumper?

My jumper training partner thought I was nuts. Jump this spooky, cantankerous, unreliable and badly conformed horse? But when he saw the first jump, the transformation was swift and complete. His ears came up, his body gathered itself like he never would or could for dressage, and his first jump was perfection in bascule. Agile, smooth, perfectly distanced and with the grace of a cat. My only regret was that I had not asked sooner. He soon sold…to my jumper training partner.

Lucky went on to have a successful and happy career as an eventer, and when his legs gave out after years of carrying himself badly, he spent a year as a retiree here at our ranch. But pretty soon he was speaking loudly again, and once again the complaint was boredom. He just didn't seem happy. We organized a trial month at a therapeutic riding facility and Lucky never looked back. This once spooky and unreliable soul has become a solid citizen, carrying ill and troubled children into their dreams.

I have had some fun in the last many years finding new and often surprising careers for horses. There was Jesse, a burnt out cutting horse who measured like a pony and felt like a big horse jumper to me. Today he shows successfully on the Hunter Jumper circuit where he cleans up with his nine year old rider. He never met a jump he didn't like, and no amount of horse show hustle and bustle phases him.

Jewel, a little 14.2 HH Quarter Horse mare of no particular breeding and little training, carried me safely and with aplomb through a season of fox hunting, jumping anything I pointed her at. An undiagnosable lameness sidelined her, and today she, like Lucky, takes care of specially challenged children.

Cloud, a nervous wreck who had suffered some abuse, just needed a loving hand and someone to believe in him. My husband Alex was that believer, and with some time and training he transformed Cloud into what he is today, the perfect babysitter and gentleman for his new beginner owner.

And Valentino, a grade Quarter Horse with bedroom eyes (hence the name) who initially felt like an amateur dressage prospect, ultimately just wanted to be someone's fun horse and number one guy. He got his wish.

When I am asked how I knew that is where that horse's talent lay, I can honestly and without pretense say: "because he told me so." Horses like Torchlight and Lucky were clear in their intentions and needs, and because of them I gained confidence in my gut instincts.

But first I had to be *willing* to listen. To hear the soft whisper of my feelings or an outside influence even when they seemed irrational and against the order of the day. Even when it went against what I wished to hear, and that can be a 'toughie,' as I well know. But other than acting out, it's the only way horses can reach us - through our gut feelings. And when that doesn't work, and they are forced to act out, it is our responsibility to question whether they are simply naughty, or desperately trying to communicate with us, the only way they can, through resistance.

Like Walter Zettl always says of rearing and dangerous horses: "*It's the stupid horses that put up with all manner of treatment; it's the smart ones that fight back.*" It's simply not enough anymore to be a good enough horseman or woman that you can *make* a horse do anything, although it can certainly come in handy. The real standard is can we find a way to have the horse *want* to do it, happily. And if not, are we willing to accept that our dream for the horse is not his own, and he has others?

My dream for Torchlight was always that he would show, a classically trained horse in a world of modern dressage. That, apparently, is not of interest to the gentleman, and I have had to regroup and be content with the lessons and opportunities he does hold for me. There will be other horses for me to show, horses that do share the dream and enjoy the spectacle.

In the meantime, Torchlight is doing a bang up job of shaping me up for *their* future. Perhaps down the road he will come around to my point of view, but so far, his personal agenda has been his own version of *A Course in Miracles*, the miracle usually involving me waking up to *his* reality. And although I never consciously asked for it, there is no doubt he has become the epitome of that one elusive reason for owning a horse:

- I am looking for life lessons from an extraordinary companion.

He *is* that. Bloody weaving and all.

In Retrospect, 2019

…That was perhaps the most important thing that Tom taught me. To really, deeply, sincerely, listen to the horse, to turn a deaf ear to ambition and hopes, distance myself from the intense yearnings of me or a client, and in that space, truly listen to what the horse thought was possible, however vague, disappointing or fantastical it might be. Finally, to be bare-bones honest with myself and my client, no matter how discouraging it might first appear, for acting according to the underlying truth is always better than fumbling along in the fog of unrequited dreams and illusions.

3 Balance

March 2008

Just the other day, to ease the burden of laundry duty, I turned on the television just in time to catch the gruesome and yet awe inspiring chariot race of the old movie, *Ben-Hur*. As I tuned in, Charlton Heston was congratulating his four lovely white steeds on a good pre-race workout, speaking to each individual horse with great affection, addressing their strengths and weaknesses. It was a convincing performance, and each horse was distinct and charming in his personality.

They were congratulated on their heart and courage, their stamina and speed. One horse was the rock, on whom Ben-Hur depended to bring it all together. He accepted the caresses and instructions with a stoic stance, eyes far off. Another, fussy and intense, needed reminding that the race was won in the last go-round, not the first. The third had to butt in on the conversation and gain the attention, and I smiled, thinking of Torchlight. Always needing to be in the spotlight, always busying himself with everyone else's business. But mostly, it was nice to see man's relationship with horses portrayed so personably.

Race day arrived and it was thrilling even as I ached for the hardships that surely were to follow. The horses reared and pawed, fighting in the harnesses, eager for the mad dash they knew was about to commence. Teams of gleaming bay, black, white, gray and chestnut filled the stadium, all exquisite in their own right. I worked hard at attaining the 'ignorance is bliss' state of grace, hoping it wouldn't be as bad as some of the old westerns where it seemed horses tumbled and fell, never to walk again. Like many horse lovers, I've never held my breath for the rider, but one horse tumbles and I'm a blubbering mess. Perhaps it's their innocence, their lack of choice in taking that life and limb threatening tumble.

Yet I couldn't take my eyes off the screen or reach for the off button, mesmerized by this little window into the past lives of our horse's ancestors. Not just the movie horses, but the horses that actually lived such a life as the one portrayed on the screen, many moons ago.

Sure enough, chariots turned over, wrenching the harnesses, bringing horses tumbling and stumbling to the ground, scrambling to their feet. All seemed to walk off in one piece. It made me wonder about the animal protection laws in place at the time. These days they are strict and enforced, animal rights agents attending any scene in which an animal performs.

Now here were these vulnerable yet somehow fierce creatures, taking part in this possibly murderous scene, not just for the sport and pride of man, but for his entertainment. The entertainment of generations to come who could watch them again and again, as they run for the laurel wreath but even more so, and seemingly very much for real, for their very lives. Who spoke for them then? Perhaps only the innate love and regard mankind as a whole and with few exceptions holds for the equine race, with a little moral musing and general conscience thrown in.

Laundry seemed to take forever (perhaps pausing frequently to catch up on the movie had something to do with it) and *Ben-Hur* was followed by another great classic, *Lawrence of Arabia*. Soon scores of flashy and fiery head-tossing Arabs burned their tracks across the screen, inspiring awe and wonder that such spindly legs and slim bodies could carry their riders through the deep sands, up and down heavy dunes, without injury, without the wretched sound of snapping bones.

And mostly completely inverted, a dressage queen's worst nightmare. How do they survive, never mind thrive? And what on earth do they feed horses out there in the desert? As adaptable as horses are, surely even they cannot glean nourishment from sand and thorn bushes?

Glowing in the sun and adorned in fine regalia, they buzzed like glittering hummingbirds among the more sedate camels. And although camels strike an impressive pose of ungainly majesty as they stride out over the desert, they pale in comparison to the beauty and splendor of a spirited horse. Even at a standstill, a horse draws the eye like few other creatures on earth. Is it that their spirit is so close to the surface, so near in their eyes?

In contrast to the camels, I was reminded of the unique nature of horses, where spirit, pride and passion meet, devoid of animosity, the desire to please and willingness to perform. Camels on the other hand, seem to be of service, if not service minded, their tenure accompanied by grunts, groans and moans, bellowing and spittle. The spittle did me in. Let's stick to horses.

As in *Lawrence of Arabia*, where wars were fought from the backs of horses and sheiks valued their Arabian steeds as revered family members, in ancient times, and up to just a hundred years ago, horses were warriors on a par with their human partners. They were irreplaceable, valued by their owners as their own flesh and blood, and often considered as a beloved friend. They were buried with honors, and their memory enhanced by bards and storytellers embellishing their finest moments with impossible feats of bravery. Loved and revered as they were, they were trained to be in the direct path of harm, and were as dispensable as they were irreplaceable. Only in death would they be spoken for, and then only to raise up in glory their feats of bravura.

As one looks down the tiers of the ages, we find horses being fiercely loved and tragically destroyed, all in one breath, all at the hand of one master. Today we see this pattern still, racehorses breaking a leg in mid race, jumpers injured beyond repair, dressage horses worn down by the very training that should preserve them. Yet they are nearly all revered and adored by the people that surround them. Still, despite the genetic memories that science now finds may well exist, memories that, however faint and subconscious, surely include cruelty, sacrifice, suffering and terror, still they continue to willingly serve us, to seek us out, to live and die at our hands. Only now it is for sport and for pleasure, a hobby, a passion, a holiday excursion, amusement, show and ego gratification.

It begs the question, how often do we, as a whole, balance the scale of those negative experiences with positive ones? Enough to leave them happy to be back for more? I like to think on a whole we do, on a whole we're not a bad lot. I like to think there are more horses leading happy lives than not.

Or do they serve a much greater purpose in which that scale is not of vital importance? The paths they forge through our personal wilderness have been and continue to be documented and told, in books and in videos, in movies and in articles, in prisons, at self-help seminars and personal growth workshops involving horses as sounding boards. More than ever, they have a voice of their own, more than ever they are heard as more than a useful hunk of powerful flesh, as they act as catalysts for personal discovery and epiphanies, helping us heal and evolve, one person at a time.

But what about on a larger scale. What about the global effect of the equine race and spirit? Do they have a voice and are they heard? Will anyone speak for them today? And what do they show us, what global epiphanies can be experienced by the horse community, in part or as a whole?

Today, on a much larger scale than the individual relationship, we find horses teaching us very real and very serious lessons, about power, prestige, money and politics, and the integrity of humanity as a whole. They do this with the mental dexterity and elegance of an enlightened guru, with placid eyes and mute faces they cause *us* to ask *ourselves*.

Then we raise the question with our friends, next within the community, and before we know it, they have easily proven the Law of Physics that, *"Every Action will have an equal and opposite Reaction.*" As will every opinion. And questions breed opinions like mice.

In the dressage world this is easily and fascinatingly if painfully exemplified by the current state of affairs at the top levels. With the increasingly widespread and accepted use of the horrific technique known as Rollkur, or Hyper-flexion of the neck, the sport of dressage has hit a low point since its baby steps as an everyman's sport in the early twentieth century.

Furthermore, 'Relaxation' has mysteriously disappeared from the Training Pyramid in the latest FEI Rule Book, removing not only one of the main building blocks but perhaps more importantly, one of the built-in mechanisms of thoughtful training philosophy that *protect* the horse from overly ambitious and fast-paced training. After all, one cannot find relaxation in a horse in any kind of distress.

Remove 'Relaxation' and ta-daa…Rollkur is one step closer to justified, the inherent painful tension caused by this technique now a necessary and acceptable component of the 'ground tension' they stress is essential to the big mechanical movement, wherein the horse is forced to *push* laboriously *off* the ground rather than dance on it in an effortless lightness supported by the gravity defying pull of powerful and gymnastically stabilized hindquarters.

This mechanical and laborious movement was painfully exemplified in a recent video that made the internet rounds to great acclaim, in which a beautiful and talented gray mare heaved from side to side as she endlessly twisted and churned her tail, expressing the tension in her spine and attempts at rebalancing the only way she could, with the one part of her spine that was not restricted beyond expression.

The effort that went into her flashy if irregular movement was tangible as she faltered again and again in transitions, highlighting this lack of balance. Yet this is the movement that draws applause, and is justified by the claim that this draws spectators and money to competition dressage. So now not only owners, riders, trainers and judges but also spectators and sponsors must ask themselves—what is more important, the grand show or the wellbeing of the exhibitor?

In response to the mad march of Rollkur, distinguished horsemen and women like Olympic rider and trainer Klaus Balkenhol, classical trainers Walter Zettl and Anja Beran and Veterinarian and trainer Dr. Gerd Heuschmann, have spoken out in defense of the horse and the classical training system, and books and articles surface almost daily to counteract the hollow promises of 'modern dressage'. The debate is now openly fought in mainstream magazines and forums, involving all manner of rhetoric and sometimes a great deal of venom.

But the dissent and outrage within the community has found its most controversial and aggressive spokesperson in the shape of Russian horseman, Alexander Nevzorov, who denies and decries not just Rollkur, but just about everything we have come to accept as conventional horsemanship, even the classical, even that considered benign and beneficial. After centuries of speaking quietly and often futilely for itself, the horse has been found by a loud defender, a protector not afraid to be in the fray of opinions and debate. And he goes far beyond the obvious tortures of Rollkur and the like. He blankets hundreds of years of experience and hard earned wisdom under one heading: shameful.

So where are the horses taking us now? They are masters of going with the flow, yet we are still under their subtle influence even as we like to think we steer the boat. And now that Nevzorov has brought his considerable intellect and personal power to their aid, those quiet little questions will be increasingly difficult to ignore.

As the scales tipped deeply towards an inhumane and distressingly brutal form of horsemanship, the opposite and equal reaction took on form in the mind and heart of a deeply committed and passionate man, apparently with the background and ability to back up his opposition to the conventional sport horse world as a whole, never mind Rollkur. Whatever one may think of his assertions, the interesting fact that he has appeared at a time when the horse world desperately needs a counterpoint to Rollkur is inescapable. At one end of the scales we find Rollkur, possibly defined now as 'Show Dressage,' legitimizing it as a separate entity from 'real' dressage. Weighing in heavily and oppressively, Rollkur is passionately defended by its propagators, heavy-handed in their bullying, the end always justifying the means.

On the other end, we find Nevzorov, equally as passionate if not even more so, fueled by a higher moral purpose that Rollkur lacks in its entirety. He has the courage to call it as he sees it, often as heavy-handed and intimidating as the very people he despises. Like them, he weighs down his cause with incendiary verbiage, scientific studies and withering disdain and insults for those that oppose or question his views and conclusions.

Both parties send people into emotional orbit, their personal convictions, horsemanship and behavior thus challenged, judged harshly and found lacking by people they will never even meet.

But perhaps if we put aside our personal and emotional conflicts with either party and take a 'world view,' we will find the Universe is simply once again acting out a law of physics. Possibly, like the horse, Nevzorov's purpose is more subtle and mysterious than even he realizes. Could it be that the purpose of Nevzorov isn't so much to reach people directly—it is hard to reach people when you insist upon first insulting and belittling them—as it is to weigh down the other arm of the teeter-totter that is the horse world.

Perhaps by his very existence and willingness to fight and fight loudly, fight dirty, fight hard and to the last drop, he will be the opposing and equal reaction that will help bring some measure of balance and harmony back to our world.

Could it be we are in the middle of the greatest assignment the horses have given us yet, to find the balance between pleasure and high performance, money and mindfulness, pride and priority, power and persecution, art and its caricature. It's a tall order, but by the looks of the horse world today, a necessary and sorely required one.

The majority of us find ourselves somewhere in the middle of this teeter-totter, and though we may well prefer it to be a level and stable (no pun intended) playing field, that is hardly ever the case. But I know if it has to lean more in one direction, I'd rather find it leaning towards Nevzorov's camp. I'd rather see Rollkur fighting the uphill battle. (Through six feet of snow, ice and mud in a downhill wind of hurricane strength.)

Though I find myself doubting the 'one on one' effect Nevzorov's teachings will have, I trust in his overall effect, the blanketing effect he will undoubtedly have on the community as a whole, as an uncompromising and stern presence, the 'conscience of the horse world' if you will. Perhaps we *need* someone to take it all the way away from Rollkur and 'Show Dressage'. Or any type of bastardized show riding, for that matter. As far as it will go to the other far extreme, just to show us the view, and that it is *possible*.

Having said that, very few of us will be able to live up to his ideals, and he himself lays claim to an extraordinary talent. By leave of this talent he sets standards previously unheard of, and sometimes I wonder if people may not get hurt in the quest to live up to his ideals, the ideals of a very gifted man. They are ideals that likely embody everyone's horse dreams, but for how many are they, realistically, attainable in real life? We don't all have this extraordinary talent. Few do.

And so he starts off his relationship with the horse world by declaring more or less *all* of us incompetent and abusive. Oh well, so much for spending my life steering clear of auxiliary aids, gimmicks, gadgets and bits bigger than a simple snaffle. In 'my' world, I have been the subject of ridicule for babying my horses. In Nevzorov's, I am still an abusive parasite who terrorizes my horses on a daily basis. It's a tough crowd, people.

The old saying: *"You catch more flies with a drop of honey than a gallon of gall…"* seems to hold no water for Nevzorov, who is heavy-handed in the gall department. Instead he appears to hold his very talents and achievements against those of us of lesser stature, who still resort to more conventional forms of horsemanship, however gently we endeavor to do so. As such, he will likely alienate more than he will befriend, and more minds will shut than open.

Dale Carnegie, author of the hugely successful book *How to Win Friends and Influence People* put it this way: *"If a man's heart is rankling with discord and ill feeling toward you, you can't win him to your way of thinking with all the logic in Christendom…."* If you ever rode a horse in the conventional way, and if you ride with a bit, it can be difficult to not feel dressed down by his rancor, and it is easy to feel discord and ill-feeling towards him. Easier still, then, to ignore the very real value of his studies, his personal achievements and his principles.

Yet we do so at our peril. We cannot ignore what this man is brave enough to say, regardless of consequence and public opinion. His achievements in horsemanship speak for themselves, and perhaps speak better for him than his own words. As such I grieve for lost opportunities in communication, lost to the winds of his arrogance and rampant condemnation of the very world he wishes to improve.

But then again, perhaps that is not the straightforward role that he is here to play. Perhaps he is not here so much to teach as to *show*, to cause us to challenge our beliefs ourselves, as horses do. To provide a stark backdrop to the mindless and even heartless riding proclaimed victorious today, and to weigh down the other arm with all his proof, that Rollkur and its general population of brutish riders may *not* own the day, the decade or the century.

With his studies we are all put on notice that the status quo of 'modern dressage' will not long prosper. Autopsy upon autopsy proves his point. The scales tip again, and this time perhaps, we may hope, they remain in his favor if not entirely in his court. We may be many then that would have to give up riding as we know it, and for far too many that would mean giving up riding altogether. But perhaps we can temper what we *think* we know, with what he shows us. Perhaps not every horse ridden in a bit suffers, but far too many do.

Let's be inspired by his candor and even his rancor, take its sour juice, drink it down and let it revitalize our personal efforts as riders. Let's take note of his studies and learn to be lighter, kinder and give the horse the benefit of the doubt. Perhaps by exploring bit-less riding more riders will find alternative answers, answers applicable even when back in a bit.

If a grain of salt be called for to further digestion and acceptance, let it fall in Nevzorov's favor rather than those of Rollkur fame. Their pictures and bizarre statements of defense speak for themselves anyhow. Nevzorov is here and he is here to stay, the most ardent defender our equine friends have ever had. And a defender they need as much as ever, a White Knight to Rollkur's Black.

In the final analysis, we must all judge for ourselves, using our horses as a guide. And if Nevzorov's gall burns, we can take a closer look and find out why. If the shoe fits, consider lopping off the foot and grow a new one. Hey now, in the world of thought and personal growth, anything is possible, but all right, start small, maybe just a toe or two. But he *is* the closest thing we have to a catch-all communal conscience, and as such is worth considering, however far-flung and judgmental his allegations may seem.

If Torchlight has taught me anything, it's that horses are vehicles for change, and every day I can redefine myself and my horsemanship through his eyes. As much as Nevzorov aligns himself with the horse, there are two things horses offer in abundance that Nevzorov denies all of us. Non-judgment and forgiveness. Every day Torchlight grants me a brand new slate. I try to be honest, to reexamine things I took for granted just yesterday. I have made and continue to make mistakes on a daily basis, but despite the many commandments of Nevzorov I have managed to unwittingly break or warp, that doesn't negate the overall positive effect that *I* have had on Torchlight's life. The river runs both ways.

Not only is this past aloof introvert today an affectionate extrovert, but far more intriguing to me, Torchlight's idea of *'play'* has changed. It used to mean simply running madly, flat out, back and forth. Now, it means rearing, bucking, prancing, and tossing out the occasional natural *levade*, *capriole* and *courbette*. And if my presence in his life, and my attempts at 'training' have helped him rediscover *'play'* and physical and mental agility, then I, though a mere mortal who does ride in a snaffle, can't be all bad. There is comfort in that under the onslaught of Nevzorov's self-righteous if often justified anger.

The other day I sat on our deck on an unseasonably warm afternoon, and looked out over the pasture. Our small herd of horses grazed peacefully on the hillside, Torchlight softly shining his blood bay mark, on the land and on my life. I thought about all the changes he has made in his life and in mine. I thought about all the lessons he has taught and continues to teach me, and I wondered what else he has in store for me. One thing I know. Around him we are always in the process of *some* assignment, and he is always helping me define my horsemanship for the future.

And I am not alone. Today, if you're involved with horses, you're in the throes of something bigger than yourself. It's hard to hide in your backyard anymore. Today, the stakes are higher than ever, it involves all of us, it is taught by all the horses of the world and a few people, and the outcome of the lesson will define horsemanship for years to come. It may even determine our right to ride.

In Retrospect, 2019

…This was the first time I mention the possibility that our very right to ride might come under attack. It was a theme to which I would return on several occasions as I watched the competitive horse world mire itself ever deeper in the chaos brought on by the rewarding of abusive techniques that lead to spectacular, if decidedly bizarre, performances by some of the most athletic dressage horses this world has ever seen.

One website, just one page devoted to the extraordinary Totilas, declared him 'The World's Greatest, Gaited Dressage Horse,' and posted the pictures that suggested it was not far from the truth, and it was not a compliment.

Constant controversy continues to dog the perpetrators of Rollkur, which in varying degrees of extremism is also known as hyper-flexion and LDR (Low, Deep, Round). The technique has been discussed, defended and redefined ad nauseam, but at heart remains the same. An abusive technique that forces submission leading to what Dr. Andrew McLean calls 'learned helplessness,' while over-exerting particular muscles, the overdevelopment of which creates this spectacular, if wholly unnatural, movement in the horse.

This, along with the extreme over-tightening of nosebands now becoming a common focus of further controversy, means the horse world is frequently drawing the attention of non-equestrian animal lovers, for whom there is little room for the subtleties in the use of tack and technique. It's black or it's white. It's good or it's bad. It's right or it's wrong.

And so I will say again what I first hinted at all those years ago. If we ourselves do not begin to better manage and stop rewarding the abuse so apparent in our equestrian sports, we may not like who does, or how it ends up affecting all of us, even those of us who feel we wear the white hats.

4 Perspective

April 2008

Every once in a while, I hear someone say: *"Perspective is everything."* It's one of those old clichés that is based on a core truth. The thing that makes it very interesting in my estimation is that perspective is largely unreliable, as prone as it is to the subjectivity of the narrow viewfinder of our personal experience. Three people can attend the same event and you'll hear three very different versions of the same story. Ask any trial lawyer, he'll tell you.

One friend of mine came back from World Cup raving about Salinero and Anky's fantastic rides. Another told me only about Salinero's spectacular escapades during the medal ceremony and the ensuing chaos and screaming. Another was dismayed and appalled at his lengthy and head curling warm up, but amazed to see his apparent recovery for the actual test.

If I look up perspective in the dictionary, it uses phrases such as; *the appearance of objects as determined by their relative distance and positions, a sense of proportion, a specific point of view in understanding things or events* and *the ability to see things in a true relationship.*

Seems to me that finding perspective in today's Equine "Gigantorama" (not in the dictionary) is becomingly increasingly difficult and confusing. *Things and events* easily become overstated or simply misunderstood and twisted in the endless warped chain of re-telling. Bias and personal interpretation adds its own distinct shades and is regurgitated as honest to goodness fact and truth. The further the distance and the altered position of the viewer, the more the appearance is adapted to their position.

As for a *sense of proportion*, anyone who has ever boarded at a horse care facility will know that no one is better at losing a sense of proportion than a group of horse owners. Once upon a time, I could get quite incensed about the chunks missing from the neck of my horse, to be found between his neighbor's teeth. Then we moved to a ranch and pasture herd living and I found a new perspective, shaped by new experience. No chunks missing today? Well, paint me yellow and call me happy.

How many of us can honestly say that we speak with complete objectivity when it comes to our equine experience? How many of us can claim to have the *ability to see things in a true relationship*? And who defines the *true relationship?*

My personal experience and perspective on my relationship with Torchlight has changed tremendously over the years. It has gone from 'what a talent, can't wait to show him' to 'what a teacher, but yikes, don't think he's a show horse.' My outlook now is an understanding and acceptance that he is here to teach and to heal, and that I am here to learn…whatever he has to teach.

Someone else looking in may simply see someone too scared to go show, and dismiss me as one of those 'classical' types. We don't ask much of our horses, you know. (Torchlight might disagree.)

When I first got my draft cross Banner, I spent several months just on groundwork. Other boarders at the barn laughed at me and accused me of being afraid of riding my own horse. Actually, I was afraid of being trampled by a 17 HH three-year-old with no ground manners. I figured it was more important to stay in one piece long enough to actually get to ride him. Perspective.

My Thoroughbred colt Curly who we didn't start till he was five because he was so slow in maturing physically, has had some people congratulating me on my patience and foresight in preserving him for the future, and others shaking their heads at my overly cautious approach and waste of time. For some he is the dream Thoroughbred who wasn't started too young, never raced and is without wear and tear. For others, he is over the hill with nothing to show for it. Either way he is for sale, since my perspective on where I am going and how I am getting there has changed.

I host dressage clinician Eddo Hoekstra here once every few months and his approach gets different responses. It's been very interesting to observe over time.

Eddo's system is based on balance and gymnastics with little concern for head placement other than the way in which it helps place the neck in alignment with the body to allow for relative engagement. In other words, the head is never forced but allowed to be well in front of the vertical if necessary while exercises reorganize and rebalance the horse until he himself attempts to come into vertical flexion, roundness and *on the aids.*

Those that stick with it find the horse coming into a softness and lightness they may have only hoped to be possible, with the horse seeking their hand in an exquisite and intimate conversation. The bit becomes merely one balance point amongst others, subordinate of the seat and the balance of the horse in movement, the cusp that outlines the margins of the horse.

But to some people it appears we are all riding around singing kumbaya and feeding our horses lollipops while they lumber along like cows chewing cud. Or do cows lie down for that? Well, you get my point. I can assure you we don't go so far as to lumber them lying down. Though it would be an interesting trick.

A few have not recognized it when the change in their horse occurred. Accustomed to a tight and heavy 'feel' in their hands labeled as 'on the bit,' the lightness never registered as a positive change, but as a loss of control.

There is yet another way to interpret our lessons. To someone who believes riding with a bit is inherently cruel, our lessons are all an exercise in abuse, no matter the relaxed and comfortable appearance of our horses that point to another possibility. But then, I watch an Olympic ride and want to weep with despair, but hundreds of thousands see poetry in motion, a happy and dancing horse keeping terrific time with its twisting tail. It's a subjective filter we all look through.

To someone who has never had a positive experience with riding in a bit, it is easy to see why it would become an *object non grata*. And unfortunately there are a great many people and horses with nothing but 'Bad Bit Experiences'. Trainers like Eddo Hoekstra, Walter Zettl and Anja Beran who have the knowhow, integrity and a 'non hand' oriented game plan are hard to come by. But simply because a person has not experienced it does not mean it is not possible. Of course, having said that, no doubt some people feel they have experienced it and still prefer bit-less. More power to them.

I find the controversy regarding bit versus bit-less absolutely fascinating and educational. I have respect and regard for both sides of the fence and I practice both approaches. Some of you may already be chucking me over your shoulder because obviously I am an idiot and/or have not seen the light. This is always a possibility.

I can only speak from my personal experience, which involves the re-schooling of everything from abused horses through various breeds and many disciplines including old rope horses ad nauseam (I know, rope horses and dressage? It helped them be better athletes and it helped me pay the bills.) I have many fond memories of that high headed giraffe with the muscular plasticity of a steroid popping heavy weight lifter finding relaxation, grace and connection through gymnastics.

I achieved this not by draw reins, seesawing and pulling on the mouth, but through gentle placement in the horizontal plane and soft support for a mouth seeking the hand all the while reorganizing the rest of the horse.

There is great sweetness and artistry in such a connection, but if you've never felt it and haven't seen it, it's probably like believing in Unicorns. I haven't seen one, but I know someone who has. No, really! I don't dismiss the possibility, because who knows? They are discovering new species every day, and then there is the whole 'other dimension' hypothesis.

Point is, there will never be a study to disprove the existence of Unicorns - why bother, have you seen one lately - just like there will never be a study to disprove that bits harm horses. Because we have ample evidence that they do, every day, *in the wrong hands.* And oh boy there are a lot of wrong and ignorant hands. Not to mention just plain wrong bits, no matter what hands they are in. Which is one reason I consider bit-less bridles as a superb alternative. But does that mean I claim to know Unicorns cannot possibly exist or that bits are always bad, and bit-less bridles always good?

Uh-oh, I'm in hot water now. I'm an idiot *and* a monster. Some feel that if it can cause harm, it should be banned, period. Studies prove they do harm, period. But how many horses were involved in those studies, and what kind of riding were they really subjected to? This is not explained, only that they were ridden in bits. The examples we see of bad bitted riding on Nevzorov's DVD, for example, are horrifying and deplorable, but is that the everyday reality of every horse ridden in a bit? I would willingly eat rat poison, bathe in sulphuric acid and otherwise torture myself to death if I ever rode like that.

Isn't it kind of unfair that only really terrible examples are presented as partial evidence that all horses suffer in a mouthpiece? How about showing riders from the old Spanish Riding School, Nuno Oliveira, Klaus Balkenhol, or Reiner Klimke? It's a very different picture then. I'm not quick to judge, having seen various versions of bit-less bridles rub noses raw, dent the fragile nasal cartilage, and fitted tight enough to impede breathing and handled with such brutality it wouldn't matter what was on the horse's head, it hurt and it terrified. But that doesn't mean I judge all bit-less bridles to be bad, just acknowledge that even they can be misused and abusive.

Were the horses in the study ridden in a curb or a snaffle, twisted or blunt? With or without tight nosebands? In draw reins, German martingales, side reins?

Were they all ridden softly and kindly, in which case it does prove that bits however well used are instruments of torture, or were they all victims of the kind of riding we know as Rollkur? Were they yanked on every day or did it 'only' happen once or twice in their lifetime? So many questions to which only the horse knows the answer.

What qualifies as a soft feel for one person may mean a hard pull to another. Is it a pound of feathers or a pound of lead? We are swimming in very tricky and deceptive currents here. Other studies talk about the shapes, the breathing, the saliva, the chewing, all interesting but none conclusive as far as I can tell, yet. Maybe I am dumb as a rock, or maybe there are just too many buts, ifs and exceptions in my personal experience, like my observation that horses yawn, chew and even produce saliva when worked at liberty, no tack whatsoever. As far as I can tell, it's a natural part of them processing information.

Many of my horses have been 'mouthy,' deliberately and consistently taking things in their mouth to chew, almost obsessively. How does that relate to the information that states, as I have understood it, that it is unnatural for them to do so when moving? I just don't know, I am no scientist, simply trying to make sense of all the new, often subjective, information coming our way in the light of my own observations.

I have never in my own practice had a blue tongue, a slack tongue, a bleeding mouth. I have only ever seen two bleeding mouths, and that's two too many that will never be forgotten. The first time I almost got myself in a fist fight by bringing it to the rider's attention. They were taking bets and doing the odds in the background as we orally duked it out. The other horse we bought and gave a new lease on life.

But I can barely imagine what it would take to make that happen. I have had plenty of horses that liked to suck on the bit long after I took the bridle off, leaving me standing there holding the bridle like a hand maiden. Does that mean they love the bit and to be ridden in it? I don't know. It's subjective and anecdotal evidence and certainly in no way scientific.

But call it scientific and we are all agog. Sweeping statements and conclusions are made on narrow slats of often biased evidence, fueled by torrid emotion. Guilty as charged, right here in the writer's chair. But for once I am trying to be objective.

So what made sense and seemed reasonable is under renewed attack. Studies throw more black ink in the embryonic fluid of a fledgling world of dressage and horsemanship struggling to be reborn in the twenty-first century, and in the process, riding with a bit could well become the baby thrown out with the murky bathwater of any abusive and/or Rollkur type riding.

Am I arguing against bit-less riding, or the evidence of the studies, or out and out for bitted riding? No, I guess I am arguing for inclusion and temperance.

Because when it comes to riding horses, we *all* live in glass houses. Where ever we look we can find bad examples of horsemanship, even terrible and awful.

Riding in bits can be harmful. It can also be harmful to a horse simply to have a human in their life or on their back, period. I watch many a 'natural horseman' ride their horse in kindly halters, bosals or bit-less bridles but have no clue whatsoever about how to post the trot, how to engage their horse to protect his spine, the center of the horse's nervous system, and around the arena or down the trail they go for hours at a time, bumping along in a 40-50 lb. western saddle, but bumping "naturally."

All I see is a dead weight pounding a fragile concave back, retracted neck, high, pressure laden croup, joints wearing down, internal organs compressed, the likelihood of 'kissing spine' dizzying my dressage and biomechanics infused and conditioned brain. But hey, they are not hurting their mouth. There is much to be said for that.

You can be as natural as you like and still cause harm. You can be barefoot but have the wrong trim and you'll cripple your horse for months, possibly for life. Being a proponent of natural horsemanship does not immunize you against bad horsemanship, just as being a dressage rider does not automatically mean you have great hands or know what you are doing, or why.

There is a propensity for starting horses around eighteen months to two years old and though I find it horrifying, the majority of western riders and more and more English as well as Natural Horsemanship have no trouble with that. How 'natural' is it for an unfinished back and joints to carry such weight, and carry it badly? The above scenario now plays out on a spine unfinished and terribly vulnerable.

Speaking of Natural Horsemanship and perspective, Linda Parelli was known to trash dressage, in which she had once partaken, apparently not under very good instruction to judge by her description of it, until she was introduced to the dressage of Walter Zettl by yours truly. Now Walter Zettl is helping define Parelli Horsemanship for the future, Parelli's 'refinement' being based on real dressage. Perspective changes with open-minded experience.

Western riders have jeered at me about bridle dependence and hanging on the dressage horse's mouth, yet tie-downs, martingales and 'running reins' are perfectly acceptable forms of tools to them. I have observed some (please note I say *some*) go to yanking and snatching at their horse's mouth filled with a thin twisted wire, shanked snaffle in order to create 'lightness and non-dependency'.

Self-professed trail riders, endurance riders and 'backyard riders' scoff at dressage but go for long distance rides on a horse that couldn't be carrying their rider any more terribly should they try to make it so, bit-less bridle or not. Jumpers can't be bothered with boring dressage so they tear around the course, ensconced in martingales and fast and furious bits and complain their horse won't turn on a dime, costing them precious time.

I'm not trying to pick on anyone in particular but rather on *everybody*. Every discipline, philosophy and conviction has one fatal and permanent flaw that leaves it open to failure, delusion and attack: the human element. Even bit-less has to have a human there to make it bit-less riding, and humans make all kinds of mistakes, no matter how good their intentions. So if we are going to point fingers, let's point them all around, shall we? I like to think everybody is doing their best except from my *perspective* it's often not enough. But then I am a Perfectionist Dressage Queen.

My overall perspective on all of this? A little twenty-four year old Arab gelding who we'll call Pluto, recently helped shape my perspective on that.

Pluto is the much beloved steed of a very lovely and sweet young woman who started out with him just a few short years ago. To her credit she is very well versed and proficient in various natural horsemanship methods and has great command of her horse on the ground, and under saddle for that matter. There is clearly a great deal of love and regard on both sides of this relationship.

But when she came to me for lessons a little over a year ago, Pluto's top-line was upside down and at twenty-four seemed doomed and calcified in this state. His croup was as high as the cantle of her saddle, his tail stuck out and his back was horribly sunken, her view from his back the flat of his forehead. I really wasn't sure what could be done for them. He was defensive about contact of any kind, and not surprisingly given his physical condition, would kick out as soon as canter.

We started out with very basic exercises at the walk with only very slow and short trot and canter breaks, since his owner was unable to post or two point in her saddle. Despite this shortcoming, little by little, on a very soft to loose rein, Pluto began to give, to reach and to relax his top line.

Eventually, Pluto's owner acquired a new and better fitting saddle that allowed me to teach her to two-point the canter and post the trot. Pluto improved exponentially. His stride doubled, his frame lengthened and magically, the years have melted away.

Today, Pluto's frame and face is that of a much younger horse. His back rising, his croup lowering, his tail now drops gracefully, and his rider can no longer observe the whorls on his forehead from the saddle because he is choosing roundness and vertical flexion. He is seeking a light contact with the hand, using it to leverage the reaching of his once frozen top line as best he can, when he can.

Pluto and others like him have convinced me so far that the bit is not necessarily the pure evil we are now told it is. If any horse could have convinced me he could never find peace with it, he is that horse. But he chooses to use it to his advantage, as the answer to the multiple choice questions we ask of him.

At the end of their last lesson, Pluto welcomed me to his side with a repetitive soft, throaty nicker. I'm a sucker for a nicker. I have never given him treats. It felt like the greatest compliment I could ever receive.

I like to think he thanked me for helping them find a better way to be together, or maybe he was just saying, "Don't you think it's high time I got a treat?" or "Don't you think I look ten years younger?" or "Does this saddle make me look fat?" Whatever it was, it wasn't the sound of a horse just tortured by the object in his mouth.

So I have to question the righteous conclusions and passionate pleas for I have experienced the gentle reaching into and voluntary quiet mouthing of the bit by too many and very different horses. I have felt them seek my hand and look for me if I 'go away'. I have known horses that sometimes reach out and take the bit themselves when the bridle is still hanging on the wall. Does all this prove anything? Not in scientific terms it doesn't. But it does suggest it's not all black and white.

It can be argued that they are stoic, and they are, and don't let on just how much pain they are in, but wouldn't you see it in their eyes, in their bodies, their tail? As important as the TMJ is to their overall relaxation how can they perform as beautifully and comfortably as they do if their mouth is so very impeded by even a well handled bit?

The eyes are the windows to the soul of the horse, and what my students and I have seen over the years is how their eyes become softer and clearer and more present with the work we do. I have seen the face of a horse change so much in one session, people have questioned if it's the same horse. Could this really take place if they were in constant pain?

I don't know. I just know for now I leave the options open and try to give it all a fair shake. I will let each individual horse tell me what is right and what is wrong. Torchlight did not care for the bit-less bridle we tried, supposed to be the best and most researched, perhaps because he is hyper claustrophobic. On the other hand he is great in a rope halter. He likes some bits but not others, and is very particular about saddle fit.

I don't have all the answers. But one thing I think is pretty true for now. Horsemanship is an open book of which many pages are still unwritten, and no one person has the complete picture and authority. Every time something is called an absolute truth, someone else has an experience to put a crack in the perfect picture.

I guess what I am wishing for is for the believers of 'no bit under any circumstances' to be a little less aggressive about their 'absolute truth'. They define us by its use, accuse us of idiocy and mindless abuse and deny the great accomplishments in horsemanship by masters who have only the wellbeing of the horse at heart. Look at the horses in a Reiner Klimke book, or in Anja Beran's DVD, and tell me how those horses suffer as they move calmly, gymnastically, gracefully, beautifully, tails swinging quietly, eyes soft as they go through some of the most difficult exercises possible on the softest of contacts.

Any abuse is deplorable. But it is also present in many different guises in our equestrian world. I would leave you with these questions:

Is the abuse of the mouth of a horse less bad, equal to or worse than:

- The abuse of his back by bad riding and bad saddle fit (as common and pervasive as that of his mouth, and just as often a result of laziness and ignorance, not ill will)?
- The physical and mental suffering of a horse started too young, and shown too hard?
- The boredom and pain of separation of a horse by keeping him in a stall 24/7 with a twenty by twenty foot dirt turnout for twenty minutes a day?
- Is it as bad as a horse that never works outside of the arena, whose life can equal that of a factory worker?
- Or is shod instead of barefoot?
- Is barefoot but never sound, always in pain, but is kept this way because of his owner's stout belief in bare-footing although his feet are too far gone to selfheal, his life is not conducive to developing a strong foot and shoeing just might leave him pain free?
- Is it as bad as a horse that is kept alive for his owner's sake long after his desire to live has left him due to the interminable pain of severe founder?
- Is it as bad as a horse that is lunged ceaselessly, too fast and on too small a circle? (This last is a Natural Horsemanship pitfall, ironic because of their harsh criticism of lunging. They don't allow for the word lunge but they *will* 'circle' their horse for sometimes long periods of time on a twelve foot rope at trot and canter, with a horse with no balance.)
- A horse that never gets to graze?

- Is fed big meals of concentrated feed twice a day when his entire system is geared towards endless small meals?

I could go on and on. The pitfalls of modern horse keeping are countless and manifold. These are scenarios we see every day, regardless of the owner's beliefs and faith in their own moral high ground.

Point a finger and one will point right back at you. Horses are forgiving and make room for our mistakes and differences. Can't we do the same? And I am looking in the mirror as I speak.

In Retrospect, 2019

…Nothing much has changed. Or has it?

More and more, allowances are being made for bit-less bridles, even in competition, and top level competitors are riding their horses in bit and bridle-less exhibitions. German rider Uta Graf, and French Alizée Froment, both Grand Prix riders on the international scene, are crowd favorites.

My favorite thing about them both is not just the high standard of training with relaxation their horses exemplify, but that they show it's not about the bit, or the bit-less bridle, or the bridle-less. They show in snaffles and doubles, they exhibit in bit-less and bridle-less. Froment also shows her horses at liberty. And the horses go in the same proud and beautiful way, regardless of tack or lack thereof.

Conversely, lately I've been seeing a Facebook ad for a man touting his equestrian skills. The ad features drone video of him on his horse, bareback and bridle-less, riding figures in an open field. The music suggests I am watching something amazing and inspirational, poetic, even, and for some, it will be just that. Because their main focus will be the freedom of the open fields, the absence of tack. For me, while I appreciate all of the above, the overriding feeling is one of lack of harmony, ease of movement and balance. The horse is completely on his forehand, and more inverted than not, meaning his rider's weight is bearing down on his shoulders and forehand, compressing his spine. This is clear in his movements; they are ungainly and completely lacking in grace. His face appears strained and there is no joy or pride in the face of this little horse, only the expression of a horse trying his best under less than optimal circumstances.

It was never about the bit or the bridle, or lack thereof. It was always, and always will be, about the relationship and the manner in which the horse is treated, trained, and learns to optimize his bio-mechanical potential to carry and use his entire being, mind, body, and soul, in cooperation with his rider and his tack… or lack thereof.

5 The Little Things

May 2008

Appreciating the little things can be hard to do when reaching for lofty goals. It's one of the challenges for the aspiring dressage rider. Few people enter into the realm of this ancient training practice because the twenty meter circles are irresistible and deeply enticing. More likely, passage, piaffe, tempi changes and floating half passes beckon like mermaids in the waves. But in the real world, while dreaming of passage, a decent working trot may have to suffice. You may have to settle for a correct canter depart with a minimum of 'baubles' while fantasizing about tempi changes. That's life and that's dressage. Inspiration is easy; accomplishment requires steadfastness and hard work.

We build, step by step, the staircase to the heaven we envision. Along the way, we have to be content with the nuts and bolts of building new skills and painstakingly improving upon our craftsmanship, however pedantic the process may seem and feel at times. And just as important as our attention to detail, is our recognition of the little things our horses do to help us along.

Training the dressage horse means creating an exquisitely balanced and gymnastically organized horse, a horse easily mobilized by the rider's aids. When we watch a superbly trained and ridden horse, we see this taken to the full extent of its meaning, and it can be deeply moving and enthralling. What we don't see are the hours and days and years of quiet practice, months of unimpressive exploration, and perhaps countless moments of frustration laced with perplexity as unforeseen challenges rise to thwart the progress. Hopefully, there were also an infinite number of occasions of praise and acknowledgement of the accomplishments of the horse, however insignificant they may have seemed.

While a simple turn on the forehand may be a piece of cake to one horse, to another it could mean an occasion for resistance and even panic. For this second horse, just the slightest movement of the haunches would then need appreciation, in light of the hurdles he overcame to make the effort, and in anticipation of the doors this effort now opened to bigger and better things. Flying changes may come naturally to one horse, but be a source of mystification to another, in which case perhaps a simple change well performed would be the source of great delight and gratitude on the part of the rider, acting on the knowledge that a building block of the lead change was now well in place, having helped create part of the strength, balance, coordination and skill required for the flying change.

Rarely does a horse train by the book and we have to think outside of the box, again and again. At times like this, only the recognition of the smallest of changes, the tiniest of improvements, and the willingness to explore and build on these while temporarily forsaking the ultimate goal, may provide some light to illuminate the way.

The masters know this, and try to pass this on to us in books, but the experience of the day to day work with a horse and the many choices and decisions made in the course of one session; the questions of when to reward, when to carry on, when to be happy with what seems like next to nothing and end on the only positive note you found all day, are hard to distill and pass on in one short book. Luckily for us, in more recent times, we also get the information on DVDs, in clinics and symposiums, and may be able to increase our sense of importance and timing with regard to recognition of the horse's efforts, however insignificant the effort appears.

Watching a master like Walter Zettl teach is revealing of such wisdom in appreciation. From relative beginners to advanced riders, on superlative warmbloods or kindly schoolmasters of various breeds, every effort and minuscule change is applauded. Sometimes you have to watch very closely to discern, as he does, even the slightest alteration in the movement of the horse. It may be just a softening of the jaw, a slight reach of the neck, the deeper bend of a joint, the lessening of a defensive stance. Nothing goes unnoticed, and nothing is met with less than delight and gratitude for the horse's attempt at cooperation.

Every horse is found and greeted with sincere joy at the level of its best effort. The result is often surprising breakthroughs and leaps in ability, as both horse and rider gain confidence upon reaping praise for what to others might have meant next to nothing, and could easily have gone unacknowledged and unrewarded.

Observing the choices and heedfulness of an experienced horseman is an excellent affirmation, and a reminder that Rome was not built in one day, that horses more likely than not, do not lie awake dreaming of piaffe, and that a little attention to the tentative tries and appreciation thereof goes a long, long way. After all, every advanced exercise is merely a composite of many small basic skills. The more attention we pay to the little steps, the details of how we ride that walk-trot transition, how we create bend, how we better our aids, and how we reward the horse for every tiny attempt, the more likely we are to be building a solid and unshakeable staircase to our own little heaven; a well-trained and confident horse.

With little confidence in himself or me, Torchlight not only highlighted the need for such attention to detail and appreciation of negligible changes in his responses under saddle or on line, he has gone quite a bit further and carried the suggestion over from the arena to the barn, the trailer to the pasture, through grooming and simply 'hanging out'. He has taught me the value of living in the here and now with him, finding gratitude not only for the dreams he awakens in me, some of which he has expediently shot down in flames, but more so for the gifts he brings me in the present. The very real and very valuable attempts he makes at coordinating his efforts with my wishes, and when this is too difficult for him, then the alternatives he suggests, sometimes to my consternation, sometimes to my delight and amusement.

I once taught Torchlight to move up and down in a ditch, and stop at odd moments, rather than jumping willy-nilly in and out. This incidentally helped out with trailer loading and got him over his fear of backing off ledges. He liked it so well he would walk himself into ditches and stop with his front feet up, hind feet down, looking at me expectantly. Praise is in order, right?

I carried this over to having him place his front feet on a tree stump, an exercise simply in communication and confidence building, not to mention a nice stretch over his back. Enjoying the praise he received for this relatively insignificant event, he now wanted to place his feet on everything, including barrels and trot poles, insidious devices that had once caused him to throw momentous temper tantrums at the very suggestion he go near and, worse, step over them.

He had now learned to use them well at all three gaits, so apparently he decided putting them to use at a standstill was also in order. This of course presented something of a technical problem, with the poles being round and plastic and slippery, but he never tired of trying. I finally took pity upon him and presented him with wooden octagonal poles, upon which he triumphantly poses. I can now point at anything and he will place his feet on it, however best he can, and 'shake hands'. But it started with about a week of rewarding the unimpressive walking in and out of ditches, and a simple slight lifting of a front leg when I tapped it.

Every tiny give, every gesture of try, every overture of affection has meaning to me now. And more importantly, I have come to realize, they very much have meaning to him. The more I am present and respond in real time to what he is actually offering me, rather than living in my mind and criticizing his shortcomings in what I am asking and wishing for, the more he tries to give me, and the more I can accept.

So while I may dream of tempi changes and passage, he reminds me of the value of good basics and his training progresses the better for it. He reminds me to be appreciative of his friendship and of his willingness to try again, day after day. He inspires me to nurture the ever expanding vocabulary between us—a combination of gestures, words and expressions, developed through trial and error, his and mine—and to be grateful for his deepening interest in being around me.

I take joy in his little jokes. Gently pulling on my hat or hair; pretending to catch and then veering away and flouncing off while obviously throwing me a laugh over his shoulder, only to turn around and trot right back to me, wasn't that funny and you know the joke's on you, right?

I take note of his ears pricking when he hears my voice, his head swinging around to face me and the different tones of his nicker depending upon what he would like to see happen next. A workout, a nice cool bath when it's hot and sticky outside, an early retirement to his stall when the flies are a pestilence, a carrot or a snuggle. It gives me that warm feeling in my belly, a deeply comforting sense that although our 'career' didn't quite work out the way I so eagerly anticipated, he has taught me lessons of much greater value that go beyond our dressage training.

To remember that insignificant changes can accumulate and lead to big results. That seemingly unrelated experiments in training can build bridges between exercises, challenges, myself and the horse, and if nothing else, build confidence and mutual awareness and regard through the instigation and reward of *try*. To shine a light of appreciation on what my horse does bring to the table that day, even if it is not what I had hoped he was packing. To graciously shelve Plan A and savor Plan B for I may well be pleasantly surprised. To pay attention to *try* no matter what form it takes, often unexpected.

And to not sweat the small stuff, but sincerely appreciate the little things.

In Retrospect, 2019

…What wonderful lessons Torchlight taught me, and what a trip down memory lane to re-read this, all these years later. A nostalgic reminder of all the fun I had with Torchlight, exploring so many ideas and concepts. Makes me miss him all the more, though I know he is in a good place and absolutely adored. For now, I will just enjoy a million little memories of lessons I had all but forgotten, and pledge once more to honor them with every horse that crosses my path.

# Freedom of Expression

July 2008

Lately, I have been ruminating on the word, *expression*. It started with an article in *Dressage Today* by Michael Klimke, son of the late Reiner Klimke, and a trainer and competitor in his own right. The article is titled 'A Horse That Goes On His Own,' but on the cover it is represented as 'Allow the Horse Freedom of Expression.' That got my attention. How often does one hear that? We hear a great deal about expressive movement and expressive gaits, but how often do we hear about allowing the horse the one thing all of us in the free world take for granted? Freedom of individual expression.

Very early on in the article, Klimke reminds us that the horse needs to find the balance to be "*on the seat,*" and to "*...carry himself and go on his own.*" As riders and trainers, we have to develop the horse to move freely "*...without too much pressure from our legs and rein aids...*" and that this allows the horse to "*...work more freely in self-carriage.*" But most interestingly to me, he states: "*...the most important benefit is the often overlooked development of the horse's personality.*" He goes on to say: "*...it is easy for trainers to forget about this interior aspect of the horse's growth, but it pays to concentrate on each horse's individuality.*"

Somebody buy this guy a beer. Make it a case. In a dressage world increasingly in danger of churning out mechanical puppet, cookie cutter dressage horses, in a world still largely concerned with the deadly evils of the anthropomorphizing of animals, he speaks of the individuality of horses. Of learning to ride better from our seats to allow them to develop their own personal expression. And how this relates to their inner growth and development.

At the very end of the article, Klimke suggests: "*...in your daily riding, don't think the horse must learn your way. Concentrate on riding primarily with your seat, and you will succeed in learning your horse's way...*"

This reminds me of a tenet in movement therapy that I learned from Feldenkrais practitioner and SENSE Method creator, Mary Debono. When I asked her about the effects of Rollkur on the inner systems and biomechanics of the horse, she simply replied "*Movement benefits from choice.*"

In other words, put a body in a straitjacket and you severely limit that body's options in how to answer any question asked of it. More often than not, this means that while you may get an apparently acceptable answer, it is rarely, if ever, the correct or most desirable answer for that body, its individual biomechanics and conformational eccentricities. I think of this kind of training as drinking grape juice and calling it wine.

When our aids become a closed prison cell for the horse, we deny him any number of choices that would lead to his optimum means of expression, physical and otherwise. We also deny ourselves the pleasure of surprises and outright miracles in our mount's responses.

I often get a good giggle or two out of my training sessions. It's just plain fun to see what a horse will come up with when given a little 'wiggle room' in answering my multiple choice questions. With his innate fear of falling down, a horse will always seek balance, and with his natural pride and playfulness, if you open the door to a response that includes both these answers, chances are, he will take to it like a duck to water.

Torchlight has been a prime example of this philosophy. Initially, his responses arose from a very narrow field, survival techniques gleaned from the racetrack. Though the best he could muster at the time, they were barely acceptable even in my liberal school of dressage.

But by systematically closing doors while always leaving better options open, he progressively made better and better choices for himself under saddle and in groundwork. I never forced anything on him—other than in moments of acute self-preservation of which we thankfully, have had very few, in which I enforced some general principles involving gravity, the correct order of descent between me and the ground, and ETC; 'Earth to Torchlight Communications.' But by setting up avenues leading to correct answers implemented to the best of his ability at the time, he came to own his conclusions and as such, it has carried over into everything he does.

Eddo Hoekstra calls this skill building, using your position and the building blocks of gymnastic exercises to better yourself and the horse; always accepting and praising the best your horse has to offer that day, trusting that tomorrow will build on today.

This has opened a great many doors in Torchlight's world of communication. Today, Torchlight exercises his freedom of expression to show off his magnificent physique with a very creative and ever changing gymnastic repertoire; to choose a better way through the creek, to let me know cuddle time is not over, or hasn't begun, that he remembers what we practiced the day before, and that if I can't get the left canter, he'll just do it without me.

At times he practices his freedom of expression to clearly let me know his opinion on absolutely everything, from breakfast to my incompetence at grooming just so, to when he should be let out to when he should be brought in, to how much power should be in the hose that bathes him to how I should towel, or not towel, his face. The order of work, bathing and carrot stretches and if he has not been offered the opportunity to greet a visitor, now would be the time….to the point of triggering a dear daydream of mine, one in which he is just a little less in need of expressing himself fully and at all times. That said, I wouldn't trade this extrovert for anything, and certainly not for the mute extremist he used to be.

Speaking of mute, the American Museum of Natural History is currently boasting an exhibit called *The Horse – How Nature's Most Majestic Creature Has Shaped Our World*.

This was thrilling to me until I looked at the picture used to represent this exhibition. If ever a picture represented mute resignation, this is it. The head of a perfectly braided gray dressage horse in a badly adjusted, overly tight, crank flash noseband, veins popping, nose behind the vertical, eyes half shut with a world weary air permeating the photo. It is the picture not of majesty, but of enslavement. How this photo was chosen to represent *Nature's most majestic creature* is a mystery to me, and begs a few questions. Out of surely thousands of photos available, of spirited, trained or wild, proud and definitely majestic horses, who would chose a picture that exemplifies the very opposite? It makes me wonder if the horse belongs to someone related to the exhibition.

But it gets more interesting, to me anyway. Because, as exemplified by the Fédération Equestre Internationale rule relating to 'happy horses', happy and now majestic are in the eyes of the beholder, and as subjective adjectives, leave a great deal of room for interpretation. The July 2008 issue of *USDF Connection*, mentions not only the exhibit, but in parenthesis, discusses the picture.

However, the writer sees not dejection and resignation in the horse's expression, as I did, but a horse that looks a little sleepy in a noseband that could've been fitted better. My only consolation is that anyone to whom I have shown the picture, horse people or not, have mirrored my reaction without my encouragement.

So how do we define, encourage and regulate freedom of expression in horses? For starters, a great many people have told me no such thing exists; animals have no consciousness, no personal wishes or ambition. They scoff at people like me, being nonscientific, presenting only anecdotal evidence, being apt to emotionalize issues, and obviously terribly anthropomorphic (Horrors!)

But even science is now taking a closer look and rewriting animal science. These days, science is second guessing the motivation and tenures of the past centuries of horrors in animal experimentation, a period that can be traced to the famous statement *"I think, therefore I am."* by the French philosopher, Descartes. Somewhere, somehow, it was decided that animals do not think, they are pure instinct, and thus, without feeling, and fair game for any number of bizarre and unmentionable experiments performed in the name of research.

But perhaps the day is coming when animals are no longer considered dumb if cute machines. A recent *National Geographic* magazine features a wise looking border collie on its cover with the words 'Inside Animal Minds'. Inside the publication, they devote twenty-five pages to the studies that are now confirming what most animal lovers have always known. That animals are *not "…robots programmed to react to stimuli, but lacking the ability to think or feel."* Research now shows anything from an octopus to a crow exhibiting signs of higher mental abilities, "*…good memory, a grasp of grammar and symbols, self-awareness, understanding others' motives, imitating others, and being creative…"* as per the individual species.

A sheep was proven to recognize individual faces and remember them long term. The border collie on the cover has a vocabulary of over 340 words and counting. Dolphins were taught a sign for 'create' and would go off together and come back a few minutes later with a new routine they invented together. A *synchronized* routine, no less. Crows that invent tools. Monkeys that acquire sign language spontaneously. An octopus displayed playfulness bordering on a sense of humor. Scrub jays that return to move food if another jay watches them stash it, implying "*…the ability to recall a specific past event,*" something until recently considered a *"…uniquely human skill".* Yet other scientists continue to insist all animals are stuck in time, devoid of individuality and consciousness.

Torchlight would differ. Like most horses, he has a very acute sense of time and the order of things. Recently I fed him his hay, grain and daily treat of Blackstrap Molasses in a slightly out of order manner. The molasses usually comes last, after all else is in order. This day, due to other concerns, I fed the splash of molasses before the grain. He eagerly licked it up and then ate his grain with his usual attention to detail.

However, as I stood holding a horse for the farrier outside Torchlight's stall, next to the molasses bucket on the other side of the wall, I felt a soft blowing in my ear. Torchlight was politely campaigning for my attention through the bars, and as soon as he got it, nudged his molasses bucket, then looked at me expectantly.

"You already got it, mister." I said and returned to my horse holding duties. Another soft blow, another nudge.

When I reiterated my response, Torchlight stomped to the door opening, hung his head out, looked at me rather pointedly, then returned to his bucket, now giving it a rather harder nudge. As I enjoyed the show, he repeated his request, with increasing fervor, three more times before I took pity upon him and gave him another splash.

This is the only time Torchlight has ever demanded (and I do mean demanded, Torchlight does not beg) more. My only conclusion can be, that the molasses came at the wrong time, he was very much aware of my disorderly conduct and so the first serving just didn't count in his estimation.

But it's an uphill battle facing animal cognitive research. They speak of goal posts moving as new evidence smacks into the middle of the defense of skeptics and through the posts. Clive Wynne of the University of Florida says simply *"We're glimpsing intelligence throughout the animal kingdom, which is what we should expect..."* The article goes on to state that some of these discoveries have led to such signs of intelligence that we should blush for ever having thought any animal a mere machine.

But it's not what many want to hear. They do not want to hear the larger lesson of animal cognitive research, because as the article states, it humbles us. *"It proves we are not alone in our ability to invent or plan."*

One generally held concept that blocks acceptance of such discoveries, is the idea that only verbal beings are capable of feeling and thought. For some reason that continues to elude me, despite my earnest efforts at research, animal ethicists cling to this obscure definition. The idea that only if a creature can talk about its ideas and intentions is it capable of self-awareness. Well, I have met quite a few people who will talk about themselves, their ideas and intentions ad nauseam, and frankly, they seem no more self-aware than the next creature on the evolutionary scale. Joking aside, though, it makes me wonder. If a person is born mute, and never taught sign language, does that make them any less self-aware than you or I, just because they can't blab on about themselves? It reminds me of the T-shirt sported by some men that says: *"If I am talking, and my wife isn't here to hear me, am I still wrong?"*

Isn't it more likely that we find animals mute and dumb because we haven't explored *their* languages? Yet horses have gotten along with us for centuries, carrying out complicated tasks and demands, most of which go against their very nature. Perhaps, they are far more linguistically adept than we are.

Temple Grandin, one of the most accomplished and interesting animal researchers of our time, is severely autistic, yet has become an excellent communicator and author. In her book, *Animals In Translation*, she compares her relationship, and that of autistics, to the world around them as similar to the way animals relate, based upon extensive research in how brains work, human and animal, as well as research in countless related fields, and plentiful anecdotal evidence.

She tells the story of how a professor in her college days stated that animals were not conscious because they did not have words to think in. This was rather shocking to her, since she herself did not think in words, but in pictures. When she is hungry, she sees pictures of food, when she is thirsty, she sees a picture of water, etc.

She also states that the EEG of animals—monitoring mental activity—is not that different from ours. She believes they have conscious thoughts of smells, touch and taste, and their thought process is probably mostly made up of pictures and even sounds.

Jaak Panksepp, touted as a leading American neuroscientist, states that there is no doubt that both animal and human brains are wired for dreaming, anticipation, the pleasures of eating, anger, fear, love and lust, maternal acceptance, grief, play and joy and, here's the real kicker, *"...even those that represent 'the self' as a coherent entity within the brain."*

Anthropomorphizers, Unite!

Don't get me wrong. I don't think my horse thinks or feels exactly like me, or should be handled the way I 'handle' my human cohorts. He is still a horse, and as such I try to respect his inherent traits and instincts that differ from mine. But nor do I think he has no self-awareness, desires or dreams, opinions or is devoid of thought.

I remember a story about a horse in the nineteenth century who became famous for solving math problems and so on. His owner was very proud of his horse, until experiments proved the horse was not solving the equations on his own, but reading extremely fine variations in his owner's posture and body language to give the answers. The sad thing was, rather than being astounded at the ability of the horse to focus on and read people, and himself in particular, the owner was saddened and disillusioned and the public ridiculed them both.

So who and what define language and thus, self-expression? Maybe we have to meet them halfway, as Klimke suggests when he says to let the horse show us his way.

I am currently working with a very gifted horse named Blue, a nine or so year old Quarter Horse, who is teaching me a thing or two about expression, its freedom or lack thereof. His grandsire was the famous and wonderful Rugged Lark, a horse whose accomplishments in disciplines across the board were truly astounding. Rugged Lark was also famous for his intelligence and willing temperament, his playfulness and his ability to pass these traits on to his progeny.

But when I first met Blue, I thought it had to have skipped a generation. I had rarely met a less expressive, or more dull and uninteresting horse. I appreciated his dutiful show of support in attending his owner's lessons, but he always appeared to be 'phoning it in' as they say in the movie business of a less than inspired performance. His face was blank, his movements robotic, his head hanging low from the withers. I had to ask myself what had happened to this horse before his owner acquired him.

As our lessons progressed and we asked more and more of Blue, his stalwartly dull but obedient behavior changed, starting with sudden changes of direction, refusal to go forward, until one day he was unruly to the point of being unrideable by his owner and I found it necessary to take over. I almost regretted my decision as a very tough and difficult ride ensued.

Blue was no longer phoning it in, but was now exercising all his power to let us know he was no longer comfortable participating in our weekly sessions. He was screaming, crying and yelling at something, and I had no idea what he was saying. There was nothing we were doing then and there that was in any way insulting or offensive, and I finished the session at the first positive development. I felt like he was shadowboxing and I was in the wrong place at the wrong time.

I asked to take him in training for a few months. Initially, he withdrew to that same faraway place and responded to my overtures with a blank stare, going through groundwork and ridden exercises with stiff, jerky motions. It was not so much that I felt he was not paying attention, as that I felt he had no attention, to anything. He was completely withdrawn and introverted, a very dangerous horse.

Indeed, before long, a monster emerged. This one was called 'extremely herd bound'. His only safe place became the herd. Anything outside of the pasture was a place of terror. But instead of denying him the comfort of the herd, I continued to turn him out and decided they were at least causing some response in Blue. Groundwork would have to make the difference on our side of the fence. After a few sessions, he decided groundwork was fine, and that I was a safe place, too. Until we added the saddle. It all started over. Then that was all right, until I put foot in the stirrup.

This was worse than starting a horse from scratch. With a young horse, you get a clean slate. With Blue, it had been blacked out with a magic marker, scratched and torn, and attempting to clean it up caused him severe anxiety. Anything that brought him out of his self-imposed mental exile brought on extreme temper tantrums. But day by day, the tantrums subsided and just lately, it feels like he not only shows up, but assists in the sessions.

What has emerged over the past few months is a spirited and opinionated, extremely gifted wannabe mini warmblood. Rugged Lark is shining through at last, with an attention seeking, demonstrative grandson.

As opposed to his former self, this horse is very forward, with three huge gaits and a desire to be up and engaged in a very proud self-carriage. He is easily frightened, self-blocked, prone to overcorrection and extremely sensitive to the rein aids, but also increasingly willing to trust my corrections and requests. In a word, he is fun.

All I can surmise, as he opens to me more and more and begins to show affection and *try*, is that he was more horse, more expressive than someone bargained for in his past. He must have been crammed and jammed, physically and mentally, denied all self-expression and beaten for what little he tried, till he hid away in some dark corner of his mind, which is where we found him. He created a very narrow comfort zone within which he could function, but any challenge to the boundaries of that zone brought on extreme discomfort witnessed by us as severe temper tantrums and acting out as we unwittingly asked him to step outside in the sunshine.

Through allowing positive self-expression and as clearly and kindly as possible correcting the negative outbursts, Blue and I continue to navigate the rocky waters of his past, and stretch his boundaries.

Getting over a fear isn't the same as forgetting a fear. It's new learning that contradicts old learning. Day by day, I contradict all he thought he knew.

Blue is exemplifying what Michael Klimke taught in his article. Allowing positive self-expression brings about the best the horse can offer, willingly and with confidence. And he will be happy, majestic, and expressive.

In Retrospect, 2019

…Blue was one of those horses that broke my heart. He came from a western barn where the trainer was highly revered for his understanding of dressage. What I found was a horse that had been forced into a simile of straightness and a contracted vertical flexion with no understanding of alignment, engagement or suppleness, never mind relaxation or collection.

As he broke free from the physical and mental constraints of previous training, his mind finally revolted in full against what had been done to him. He needed three years, not the three months I was given with him, to fully recover.

Often in the sphere of rehabilitating horses we find ourselves opening Pandora's Box; a quiet horse finally releasing the fury, pain and terror he has held inside so long, an apparently sound horse suddenly exhibiting the lameness he has braced against. In my experience, strange and unreasonable behavior not based on current, but reflective of past, environments, usually blast forth in full force in the second month of rehabilitation, but take ever so much longer to heal and redirect consistently. When Blue left, we had barely passed through the first phase of him showing up in his own life, warts and all.

Soon after he left, I got word that he had exploded for no apparent reason, bucking his owner off and leaving her bruised and battered. I never heard what became of him after that, and I hardly dared ask.

Blue left me with an aching heart, a healthy dose of frustration, and memories of his first tentative steps towards a freedom of expression regained, danced in the dust of a sunny arena, ears pricked and eyes aglow once more, even if only for the briefest of instants.

7 Miss Manners

September 2008

My August contribution to *Horses For LIFE* was well under way. I was in Denmark vacationing with my family, but I still grabbed a few minutes here and there to write a few words. The article was going to be about the necessity of manners and discipline in relationship with our horses, in but especially, out of the saddle.

The subject and setting had me reflecting on my parents and my childhood at length. My mother, herself an avid equestrian, had always been my greatest fan and supporter, and had never let me give up on my passion for horses no matter what challenges we faced along the way. When a riding instructor thoroughly demoralized me at the tender age of eleven, it was my mother who reminded me of my great love of horses. She asked me for courage, and taught me never to let anyone take that love away from me.

Good manners and work ethic had always been emphasized in my upbringing. Until I was about nine years old I still curtsied as I shook hands, firmly of course, with strangers. I knew how to set a table with multiple forks, spoons and knives, which glass went with which wine, and how to fold a napkin. I could arrange flowers and carry the tray with finger food. My elbows were off the table, I chewed with my mouth shut and I knew better than to talk with my mouth full.

With a few days and a few paragraphs to go till the magazine deadline I boarded the plane to return to my home in the US. However, once in the US, I had not made it from the airport to the front door before my brother called with the devastating news. An hour after dropping me off at the airport, my mother was struck by a massive brain hemorrhage and now lay in a coma. I needed to come straight home.

Twelve hours later I was on my way back to Denmark. Fate struck again, this time kindly, and out of 300 passengers, I found myself sitting next to a young man headed home to Ireland for the exact same reason I was heading back to Denmark.

Our stories were almost identical. Our conversation kept us both sane on the long flight home. We vowed to keep in touch.

The similarities ended as we parted in the Danish airport, he boarding a flight to Dublin, me met by my sister-in-law to be rushed to the hospital. His mother is making a solid recovery, and my mother passed on five days later. But the lessons she imparted to me, by word, teaching and example live on in me.

Though I have long since stopped curtsying, I have come to be profoundly grateful for the manners that my parents insisted I learn and apply in my life. Some past acquaintances of mine have spoken derisively of good manners, as some ancient relic unnecessary to modern life. Take what you want, get what you need, however you can. Don't waste time and energy on customs and pleasantries.

But I have found that my by now unconsciously held mien has smoothed my way through a life lived in many different places and cultures, and sometimes decidedly odd circumstances. Where others have come away with horror stories, I have been surprisingly well met. Initially, I thought nothing of it, deciding I was just lucky. Well, I was lucky, but I have to come to realize that my luck was in the example and training set and insisted upon by my parents, not some random lucky star shining on me wee bonny head.

Manners can smooth a rough personality, positively contain an overly boisterous one, make up for lack of confidence, ease one's way over troubled waters, and as I have recently learned, fill the cracks and bolster the stays if you're crumbling. Manners add grace and dignity to a life led in a fast paced world that today often lacks the first and denies the other. I find it adds a sweetness and romance where the everyday is often anything but.

In terms of horses, the most important effect of instilling good manners is that they create a safe horse.

How often do we see that highly trained, high powered and high profile dressage horse dragging its human through the show grounds, while the human dances a maniacal tango to avoid getting their feet crushed? How often do chains tug ineffectually on their noses while the groom yells "Whoa, dammit," and then runs to catch up? And how often does the suggestion of teaching ground manners bring the response "Oh, that's just the way *Grandengutengemyten* is, and I don't want to beat it out of him."

Way too often, in my measured experience. The ultimate irony is that under saddle it's all or nothing. Under saddle these same people who so innocently want to preserve the spirit of their horse, will spur them till they bleed, and think nothing of pulling, cranking and tying them into any number of configurations with the latest gadget. Apart from anything else, it supposedly keeps them safe. That is, if they survive the hand walking part to the arena.

But expect anything resembling that same blind obedience on the ground and you're trying to break the spirit of the horse. But I have to ask. If you expect your horse to understand flying changes, piaffe and passage and any number of complicated lateral maneuvers from the lightest aid, many of which resemble one another closely, why not expect your horse to walk quietly and obediently at your side? To stop on command, tie and stand serenely? After all, like dressage, it's only a matter of training.

Very often when a new horse shows up at my barn, it is excitable and, as one client put it, leading them is like 'flying a kite,' a 1200lb. kite. Yet many of these airborne, barely controllable monsters become well behaved kittens as soon as the rider gets in the saddle, or at least the weight in the saddle seems to trigger some modicum of self-control.

If only a little time is spent teaching some basic ingredients of self-control and collaborative rule on the ground, as it is in the saddle, you neither abuse nor break a horse, but actually gain a safer and more trusting, willing companion.

When my parents instilled certain codes of behavior in me, it by no means crushed my spirit, as my life can attest to (sometimes to their chagrin, no doubt.) It gave me guidelines and rules, showed up boundaries and markers that provided insurance and assurance when I was in doubt as to how to handle myself in a new situation.

The same is very much true of horses. Spending time with your dressage horse on the ground in purposely unusual situations teaches the horse to look to you for guidance and hints as to how he should behave at this time. As opposed to him swiftly giving in to fear, claustrophobia and his keenly developed flight instinct.

Indeed, the ground work that lays down these rules and teaches manners instills confidence in their handler, creates a trust that paves the way for obedience, and teaches a two way communication that ensures safety, rather than the one way street the human invariably gets lugged along.

There are plenty of systems out there today that teach ground work and manners. My personal favorite would be Hempfling, whose work first impressed me when his book came out in Danish in 1996. His connection with the energetic and spiritual side of training was one I had been seeking confirmation and understanding of in myself, and his understanding of real dressage and how the groundwork with body language connects with the ridden work filled gaps in my understanding that had been frustrating me. His is still the book I return to whenever I need inspiration and reassurance.

To give credit where credit is due, Parelli has also taught me well, and if that is not your cup of tea, I can only say that for every person there is a teacher out there today, just take your pick, but pick carefully. As always, there are plenty of fast-talking charlatans who may skillfully rip off their contemporaries, but often their technique lacks compassion and empathy for their equine subject, or any true understanding for that matter. Whatever you do, don't fall for the accent. An accent does not a horseman make. I always tell my students that if it feels wrong, it probably is wrong. And it's YOUR horse. You and your horse can walk away.

But the training of groundwork and the manners it imbues isn't just for the sake of the horse. The more you study the horse from the ground and learn to communicate with him from your own two feet, the more you learn about how he works. The better you understand the psyche of a horse, the better you can ride him and glean from apparent bizarre behavior some understanding of his personal quirks and eccentricities. You also have a go-to if the ridden work is failing, or becomes untenable due to circumstances beyond your control.

It doesn't necessarily require months or years of ones time to achieve good ground manners, and often it requires only correct body language and precious little enforcement. Sometimes it takes as little as minutes to see a miraculous change in the horse and sometimes a few hours, sometimes more. Always, the groundwork softens and gentles, and more often than not, the horse looks outright relieved to be assured of who is leading and who is being led. The scariest place for a horse is the place where there is no clear leader, only a rope with a screaming human on the other end preventing him from leading fully. Or escaping if need be.

Few horses resent being the follower. But not knowing if they or you are in charge, if they can trust your leadership, is an ambiguous existence in which they never know if they are safe or not. This leads to any number of unwanted behaviors as they try to take charge of their life and create some sense of control, measure of safety and understanding of the world around them.

Torchlight's idea of ground manners was pretty much limited to cross tying politely and prancing prettily. Stressful situations led to explosions and his favorite move, the whirligig. That's the one where they whirl around you and teach you to run in circles. An instant smash hit with most horses. They have thereby proved that they really are the leader, (settling that niggling concern of theirs,) you are clearly following them, and you are every bit as terrified as they are. Just listen to you yelling "whoa, whoa, whoa." Which Torchlight apparently thought meant "look, look, look at the scary hairy place we've landed in," which he did, enthusiastically. Left, right, left, right, nicker piercingly, hop, prance, pull, look again.

Something had to change. We spent some concentrated time on groundwork in and out of a round pen, and he emerged a lovely pleasant horse who looks to me to solve his inner conflicts when nervous, and I, a more educated, feeling and aware of my responsibilities, team leader.

I really learned one very important lesson fully with Torchlight the Tremendous Teacher. That horses not only can, but are absolutely willing, to take responsibility for themselves. As long as the responsibility makes sense to them. He showed me that he could take responsibility for his behavior as long as I helped him down from the peaks of terror, with studied moves on the lead line like disengaging hindquarters and standing quietly for as long as he could stand it, giving him the opportunity to simmer down as long as I timed the intervals right. In other words, not asking him to stand beyond his limit. Which stretched with every experience as he learned to take charge of his body till his emotions could catch up.

Instead of ignoring me and expecting me to keep up, he has taken it upon himself to control his emotions for long enough periods of time to take his cues from me, until his instinctive terror takes a bow. His confidence in me has led to a much greater confidence in his surroundings, and in his ability to cope with new experiences. And when in doubt, he gauges the situation by my behavior, and looks to me for suggestions as to how to handle that rustle in the bushes.

A horse doesn't know he is behaving badly unless he is shown an alternative: *behaving well*. A little thoughtful and educated discipline and higher expectations of manners can change a horse's life with humans instantaneously. It can save limbs and lives, and ease the journey of a horse through his life with humans. And as a lovely side effect, it can bring dignity and grace to your relationship, leading to sincere affection and companionship.

Or perhaps obedience is the true side effect of a type of training that gives birth to a relationship grounded in mutual respect, understanding and appreciation.

My mother would have liked that idea. Plants and animals thrived in her tender hands. She loved nature, and nature loved her. Her house and garden were always full to overflowing, a magical place of blooms and fruit, stones and crystals. All thoughtfully and precisely placed for full effect and optimum harmony. It was a place of peace and healing. Except for a certain type of garden devouring snail. They met with no mercy and sudden death.

The tile with her house number on it fell off the house the day after her passing, shattered in a dozen pieces. The flowers all faded. The snails began to move in. Mom had definitely moved on.

My mom lived a full, sometimes painful, often challenging life. She left a legacy of Love, Dignity and Courage, along with a healthy set of manners and a measure of grace. All qualities I aspire to as a teacher, trainer and horsewoman. Through my horses, I see the wisdom of her teachings borne out, and as I continue to grow and learn with my equine passion, I hope I live up to her faith in me.

Otherwise, Torchlight might have to put me in the round pen and teach me a thing or two.

In Retrospect, 2019

…I can still second almost every word I wrote all those years ago. Only today, I would not speak of disengaging hindquarters, for I have seen too often how this disconnects the horse over time, creating a horse that knows only how to hop on his forehand, over time creating tremendous blockages and strain in the lumbar and sacroiliac regions. Even when I did use the technique referred to as disengaging the hindquarters, I took great care to keep my horse flowing and moving *within* his gait, allowing him to come gracefully and with balance to a gentle halt. In effect, I never truly disengaged my horses, I simply used the term while modifying it for my own use, but I did not at the time realize how important a distinction that would turn out to be.

I never let him swing violently to a stop with braced joints, pivoting on his shoulders while relinquishing his hindquarters to centrifugal force. With my lifelong training in biomechanics, I instinctively knew it was a move I had better use on my own terms, an instinct I have since had confirmed by the many disconnected, strangely blocked horses that have come my way.

When I started learning the classical in-hand work from my mentor Stephanie Grant Millham, I finally understood this instinct in technical terms and found the replacement I had been looking for in the in-hand shoulder-in. Today, I would apply the in-hand techniques I have since learned from Stephanie, to rather *engage* the horse in shoulder-in and put all that energy to good use.

Nor would I use a round pen unless I had no other option, and in that case, I would still proceed as if I were lunging, foregoing rollbacks for transitions, and suppling in-hand work for focus.

Even in the days when I still round penned, it was never at high speeds, and I always sought the relaxation and comfort of the horse first and foremost. I used the round pen mainly as an alternative to longing that allowed me to leave the horse at liberty, not as a means to chase and overwhelm the horse, as sadly is so often seen.

I read this column and I feel still the shock and emotional distance I was maintaining to the subject of my mother's death. It was a distance I could not maintain for long.

 The Healing Power of Horses

October 2008

It never rains but it pours. I've been hearing that expression all my life and always thought it a sad, resigned and pessimistic cliché, one I would never resort to. Queen Polly Anna of the Silver Lining, I would never admit defeat for long, optimism and positive thinking always just a choice and a breath away.

Life, like horses, has a way of putting your beliefs about yourself to the test. Lately I have had to admit, it's pouring, it's raining calamity. I am soaking wet and shivering, beat down and rebuffed, my silver lining subjugated to the steamroller of circumstances beyond my control. What, pessimistic? Me? Yes, *me*.

Jokes and laughter makes problems smaller and that has always stood me in good stead. But laughing off my mother's recent passing has not come easy, never mind how inappropriate it seems to the innocent bystander who may mistake it for cynicism and not an attempt at lightening and de-dramatizing a heavy load.

Then, after years of not so much as a whisper of it, in the past few weeks we've struggled repeatedly with colic. Three cases in three weeks, all in young and healthy horses. One serious, one requiring hospitalization, and one fatal, all of them terrifying, a horse owner's worst nightmare. It didn't help that the lovely young mare we lost after a long battle through a desperate night, belonged to a dear friend, the second horse in a few years I have had to euthanize on her behalf. Making that call never gets any easier. How many times can you say: "I'm sorry?" As I found out, repetition does not result in added effect. I think I cried more than her owner, grief and regret and what ifs mingling in a toxic and ultimately useless, cocktail.

Colic is a frightening and notoriously abstruse illness. Unless an autopsy is performed, we are usually left to wonder, till the end of time, what and how of this or that colic. That is the case with every one of these three colics. Because of their close proximity to one another, both in space and time - they all three lived together 24/7 in a twenty-five acre pasture with a good variety of native grasses and water accessibility - one would think we could gain a good idea of their causes. But all three followed their own pattern.

The first, in Curly, came on suddenly and with evidence of much manure. We happened to have brought him in a few hours before to be stalled till I had time to work him that afternoon. My new ranch hand, somewhat inexperienced, had left him by himself in the barn with no room mates. I was riding and hadn't paid close enough attention. When I returned to the barn, I found Curly on his knees, in a sweat, crashing to the floor only to jump to his feet, turn around and start over again. There were multiple piles of fresh manure mixing in the shavings.

My immediate belief was that he was having a fit at being left by himself in the barn, though this was completely out of character for him. He is a cool dude who hangs about quite happily. Obviously, after a moment's thought, this was not the case at all. I brought him out and turned him loose in a small paddock to see what he would do. He continued to roll and thrash about, periodically trotting wildly, entirely out of touch with his surroundings. I had never seen him act like this before for any reason. There were some gut sounds but they were erratic. There was no doubt we appeared to have a nasty colic on our hands.

As I called the vet I prepared a syringe of Banamine for an IV injection, and a large tube of Probi for oral application. Both administered, the vet asked me to give Curly twenty minutes to respond. Soon, Curly lay quietly in the sand, his breathing slowing, his eye softening. Half an hour later he got up and walked calmly off in search of grass and buddies. We had weathered a storm whose bark was worse than its bite, and we gave sincere and prolific thanks to all appropriate horse gods.

The following week we were not so lucky. Paisley started out around four in the afternoon, the same way Curly had, as most colics do, sweating and rolling, but soon her case took a very different turn. After immediately administering the Banamine and Probi, she seemed to be calmed and more comfortable. She walked and stood quietly, her breathing and heart rate slowed, she almost stopped sweating. It wasn't long, though, before it became apparent it was not enough.

Twenty minutes later she lay down again, then stood, but stood unnaturally placidly, her head hanging. For the next hour, as we waited for the vet, already out on two emergency calls and our other vet out of town, she never moved, was extremely reluctant to do so, except to express a desire to urinate which repeatedly failed but for once. We gave her more Banamine, more Probi. I performed several of the energy and nervous system related treatments I knew of. I wished fervently I knew more.

By the time our vet arrived, her belly was silent as a grave in all four quadrants. She was oiled and medicated, though we had more or less maxed her out on Banamine already. A small dose of Rompun was administered to aid in relaxation. All we could do was wait, our best hope a bowel movement sometime the next morning.

The vet waited with us for a good forty-five minutes till we could determine some gut sounds coming from one quadrant. I pointed out a slight beginning sweat but we felt it could well be caused by the medicine. Her vital signs were all excellent except for the lack of gut sounds. Our vet left, feeling assured there was a good chance we were on the right path, but also making it clear he was on call and on his way should we need him. I worked on her some more, trying to stimulate her nervous system. Lo and behold, shortly after she delivered a small pile of manure. Hope took wing.

A few hours later, we were trying to load her to go to the hospital, but she was incapable of moving. The vet was called back again. In the meantime, the slight sheen of sweat had surreptitiously developed into a soaking cold perspiration, Paisley drenching three sweat sheets including a wool cooler before the end of an increasingly dire night. In spite of the balmy night air she was ice cold and shivering, her hooves frozen to the ground or taking small, faltering steps. Her heart rate and respiration had skyrocketed and her gums were now turning an ominous purple. Another small dose of Rompun gave her a paltry fifteen or so minutes of relief. We knew Paisley had taken a sharp turn for the worse and was in deep trouble before the vet arrived.

Somehow, somewhere, despite our best efforts, our nonstop attention, and all our combined know how, something went terribly, terribly wrong. The vet confirmed that Paisley had become toxic, her bloodstream poisoned, the exact reason unknown, the possible causes numerous. Paisley's chances were now slim to none, but a 10% chance at a literally miraculous recovery held us back from the final injection. Phone call after phone call to her owner gave her the blow by blow, and they fell harder and deeper with every call, on both ends of the line. The ultimate decision was clear. We were ready with the lethal injection.

The final hours will remain burned into my memory despite my earnest desire to erase them forever. The vet napping in his truck. My husband and I bundled up in chairs in Paisley's little paddock, our ranch hand bringing us coffee and tea. A flashlight on hand to shine on her and check on her condition, which never seemed to change from simply awful, leaving us a sliver of hope until the last minute when it became lethal.

But worst is the memory of her three-year-old frame aging within a few hours to that of an old and feeble horse. Only that morning she had been a vibrant and spirited filly, kicking up her heels in the cool morning dawn. Now she dragged along with her head hanging off of a drooping neck.

Worst was the feeling of utter helplessness as we watched her continue on with nonstop but tiny and faltering steps, her stubborn shuffling along the perimeter, stopping only to paw with pathetic determination, as if pawing the ground dug a hole in which she could pour all her pain and discomfort.

Worst was the not knowing what was the right thing to do, or when. Swinging from despair to a slight flutter of hope, and back to despair. When was the right time to make a decision that could end her suffering but never be recalled, perhaps to leave a wake of what ifs, always to be regretted. To not be able to connect with her, comfort her. Where Paisley had always been an overtly affectionate and attention seeking horse, now any attempt at consolation was met with an empty stare and left behind by her shuffling walk.

The vet did all he could, administering painkillers at regular intervals, but nothing seemed to alleviate her suffering for long. The sweat collected on the outside of her wool cooler, leaving a silver shimmer on the red sheet. But at least it seemed to give her some semblance of warmth still.

Paisley left our world behind still dressed in that red cooler. Around three in the morning she suddenly stopped and lay down heavily. The vet checked her and shook his head sadly as Paisley lay softly groaning, her beautiful head so cold and still in my hands, her eyes rolling, seeking mine. All I could offer in response to her plea was a soft and repetitive apology. I made yet another call to her owner, more useless apologies. The vet prepared the final injections.

Then, abruptly, Paisley bolted to her feet and commenced her interminable pacing, as if the threat of her impending termination had penetrated the deep fog of her pain and filled her with new determination to beat the grim reaper. Like my mother, she fought till the last, and like my mother, we teetered between hope and the knowledge that there was none. Undaunted, the diminutive butterfly of fool's paradise fluttered once more, we gave her one more chance, one more shot of pain relievers. I made one more phone call. Up and down the roller coaster went in a maniacal whir that denied any sense of one's true north.

But the reprieve lasted less than a few minutes. Her shuffling changed explosively to a rampage that had her falling and banging against the fence, grunting and flinging herself off blindly in any direction until she crashed once more to the ground. Although horrified, I was almost thankful for the clarity with which our decision was now afforded. I knelt at her head and stroked the clammy skin as the vet ended her suffering, my husband standing over me, holding my shoulders. I looked and looked into her eyes and told her it was over, all over, she should let go and suffer no more, there was nothing to fight for. I thought of my mother and how I had told her the very same thing, using the exact same words only weeks before.

And I wept for them both as my husband and vet stood like sentinels over our bodies in the dark of a cold and unfeeling morning, stars twinkling cheerfully like so many oblivious idiots above us.

Only a week passed before the dreaded C word struck again. This time, my husband's young Lusitano, Tazo, was at risk. We found him early in the morning, and the resemblance to Paisley, before the cold sweat, thankfully, struck icy fear in our hearts. He stood still as a statue, only moving to paw listlessly at intervals. His abdomen emitted no sounds whatsoever. But unlike both Curly and Paisley, there was no sweating whether hot or cold, no rolling. He simply stood there, obviously miserable, his eyes dull.

We took no chances. Initial colic response meds administered, we rushed him in the trailer and hustled straight to the clinic. Twelve hours, oiling, interminable hand walking and plentiful shots later, Tazo produced gut sounds and a pile of horse apples that were met with such glee a newborn baby boy, long awaited and born to the throne of all Christendom, would have been jealous. He was applauded and congratulated, and probably mildly confused at all the fuss over a plain old mound of manure.

We were left wondering at our sudden misfortune, as well as grateful for all the years we went free of this affliction. And praying our three strikes are up and we're out of that game for a long time. Since colic has been unusually prolific in our area lately, it has been discussed at length with fellow horse-people. Our best guess leads to the unseasonal rain we received this summer, leading to far more grass than is normal for this time of year, now all and quite suddenly, dried up. Instead of nibbling at short dry stems and digging at roots, the horses have been tearing off mouthful after mouthful of dry grass, and perhaps not matching it with long drinks at the trough.

Or maybe unusual amounts of a summer plant or grass rode high on the summer rain and threw off their guts. Or maybe the colic fairy took a road trip through Texas this year and had a quota to make up before heading home.

We'll never know. And that is the dastardly legacy of colic. You can catch it immediately, do it all right and still lose the horse. You can do it all wrong or not know at all and the horse is peacefully eating his supper that night. You can get him to the hospital, commit to surgery, see him successfully through the wee hours of the morning and lose him the next day to founder or another, worse case of colic.

Our vet lost another young horse in a similar fashion the day after Paisley. Curious at their similarities, he performed an autopsy and found a two foot long piece of small intestine, black as coal and rotting. The veins leading to the intestine were all blocked by an odd rock hard material, possibly dead parasites. The intestine had died-off slowly as blood supply was cut off. Who would have thought? Who could have known? Only the colic fairy and a few friends.

Somewhere in there the world economy crashed, burying dreams in its rubble, but much closer to home, all we can do is carry on with the carrying on, while Polly Anna has left the building….for now.

Because that's life, and that's life with horses. As the song says, *Sometimes you're the windshield and sometimes you're the bug.* Am I all bugged out? Oh yes, and I am not sure I even know what that means. But it's a popular phrase and I do feel "bugged out" and flattened on the windshield of human existence. But who knows, this may be when I peel myself off the cold glass and turn around and become the butterfly and all that jazz. Polly Anna peeks through the door, weighing her options.

Torchlight was best buddies with Paisley, the young mare who succumbed to colic. They went everywhere together in their twenty-five acre pasture and spent many an afternoon dozing in the shade, nose to nose, tails swishing at pesky flies. When torrential downpours left a pool of water in their favorite grove, Torchlight would paw and churn it to a muddy pit of delight while Paisley waited impatiently at the water's edge. Then the two of them would revel in the liquid mud, like kids in a pool, taking turns rolling and snorting, gleefully filthy. Slick and slippery with mud they would bounce out, shake like dogs, drops of murky brown splattering anyone who came too close. I swear I could hear them hoot, holler and giggle, though Torchlight always managed somehow to hang on to some semblance of dignity.

In the days following Paisley's death, Torchlight sought out their favorite haunts, eschewing the comfort of the herd for the bittersweet warmth of memories. I had shown him her still body, upholding my belief that they need to know what became of their friend. I wanted him to know she didn't just disappear on a trailer down the road without a chance at goodbye. He walked tentatively to her side, sniffed her once or twice, paused, sniffed again, then turned and with a hollow glance my way, walked slowly away.

The next few days he was his usual friendly and affectionate self, but with an air of detachment, a faraway gaze emptying his usually alert face. A gaze that went deep inside himself. Perhaps like me, he wondered and tried to come to terms with why it had to be the young and gorgeous Paisley and not his other sometime girlfriend, the thirty-two year old and increasingly decrepit old mare, Arrow.

As I watched him wander the pasture by himself, dozing in their favorite spots, I was reminded of myself, wandering through my mother's house and garden, finding comfort in cherished memories, in certain views that had once held within them her form. I wondered if Torchlight, like I had felt my mother's presence, now felt Paisley still around him, her soft nose touching his shoulder, reassuring him she was gone but not lost. If I squinted my eyes hard enough, I could just about see her at his side.

One of Torchlight's favorite people, equine masseuse Kerry, came to visit the other day. She told me he had given her a heart wrenchingly sad look, and she felt he told her we'd lost someone. But he also gave her the sense, after a big sigh, that life goes on, and so must we.

And so it does, and so we do. And so he has.

Ever since I was little, horses have informed me of joy, love and loss. Riding school horses one never knew how long they'd stay. Usually just long enough for me to fall in love and dream big impossible dreams. Then someone with wealthier parents would buy the pony for themselves, or the issues that sent them to the slaughterhouse from which the school rescued them would resurface and back they'd go. Or maybe the school just needed money and the horse sold to another riding school, paying for two smaller ponies or whatever needed repairing. To a child it barely mattered what the cause, gone is gone, an empty stall soon to fill with a strange body that could not possibly replace the last one, although at least the sale to a private home meant a probably far better life.

But loss is loss, and the only answer to the pain, every time, was immersing myself in more horses. And more often than not, it was the new face that was first rejected as falling short of the last one, that won me over once the first sting of the perceived intrusion wore off. Taking another chance on falling in love with a four legged friend, and losing every time. I never learned and I never stopped falling in love, and they never stopped healing the last hurt, leaving me healthy enough to face the next injury just in time for them to leave me too. Resilience was the sometimes bitter harvest of those brittle days, a resilience and pattern of behavior that keeps me afloat once more.

Walking out to my barn on a brisk October morning, surrounded by barking and playful dogs, I know that for me there is no balm for the wounded soul and aching heart like the company of four legged friends. There is no more effective distraction for the belabored mind than being met by bright eyes and rumbling nickers, an outstretched head nuzzling for affection and maybe a treat, or two, I'm a sucker, and the prospect of being astride any one or all of these cherished creatures.

Putting my foot in the stirrup and settling into the saddle for the first ride of the day, picking up the reins and easing into a walk, my mind finds peace and an alternate universe where there is only this warm back under my body and the pricked ears guiding my gaze. The horse leaves me no allowance to bring along my other life, no room for my other thoughts and no time for feeling anything other than my mount's responses to my presence. There is no palaver with disparate voices in my head. There is only the voice of the horse traveling along my senses, guiding me to our perfect destination for that day.

In this universe there is only one priority and that is how to best enter into a conversation with the horse beneath me, determine and align our most noteworthy efforts for that day, and bring us to a harmonious conclusion upon which we can both rest well until the next ride. And having left grief and torturous thoughts to fend for themselves as I go off for a day of equine companionship and riding, I am more often than not pleasantly surprised to find they did very well for themselves in my absence. The hours of distraction has left my undesirable companions space to reflect upon themselves and come up with less grievous means of delivering their otherwise worthy messages, messages requiring attention for healing to occur at all.

The subtle effects of the equine brand of horsepower reaches far beyond our physical conversation and on into my heart and soul, softens and smoothes the ragged edges of pain, pours oil on troubled waters and builds bridges where oil alone cannot suffice. A horse kiss puts out the corrosive fire of a haunting memory, and his desire to be met by me and held by me lessens the loneliness filling the gap where a loved one used to reside. A good ride reminds me that I am free to rise above my troubles and feel on my face the winds of time that will alleviate all wounds. I am free to heal and to believe in silver linings once more.

And Polly Anna rides again.

In Retrospect, 2019

…Not much has changed. Oh sure, I have moved across the country, divorced and downsized my training business to pursue a career in writing, speaking and life coaching, but I am still that little girl who looks to her four-legged friends when life becomes overwhelming, and to my imagination and built-in optimism for silver linings when the sky seems sure to fall on my head. I live by Hope, and by Golly, I'll die by it, or I'll eat my old helmet.

9 Never Again

January 2009

Another year, and the month of resolutions and a look in the rearview mirror are upon us. I have given up on resolutions, since they have rarely lasted beyond a few days in January for me or most people in my acquaintance.

So no resolutions for me, but to keep on, keeping on. And while keeping on here into the brave new year, I carry last year with me with much still to be gleaned and digested, accepted and, if at all possible, embraced. All at once, old clichés rhyme with age old truths as they help label and define the unspeakable for which I cannot find the words.

The sudden loss of my mother left me with a great many *never again* moments, moments that catch in my throat and force me to realize my world has changed for good, and there is no going back. The understanding has slowly and coldly dawned, that unbeknownst to me, an underground, subtle but powerful spring has fed my garden for years, and now it has abruptly dried up, never to return, and I must carry water for my garden myself if it is to continue to bloom.

In every life there are a myriad of *never agains* both happy and sad. The first loss of a beloved thing or being, the run-over cat or broken toy callously thrown out by the unwitting adult. First broken hearted teenage angst filled *never again*, when life feels all but over. First hangover…first divorce…but also the many little never agains, too personal or inconsequential even to really discuss.

The *never agains* you would bring back if only you knew how. Knowing you'll never again hear your name said just so. The feel of a hand. The eyes that look like that, but only at you. Footsteps on a staircase, hoof beats in the sand, heartbeats in the dark. A certain rumbling nicker, pricked ears silhouetted against the sky. The silky skin of a trustingly lowered eyelid, waiting for a kiss. A mad dash across the pasture for that glorious carrot, or maybe, just to let you know you were long awaited and missed. A muzzle nuzzling your cheek, just so. The best ever canter, the kindest buck, the most exhilarating jump. A sitting trot that felt like riding a cloud. A moment of interspecies communication eons beyond words, soon lost but never, ever forgotten.

All of these are beyond words, they live only fully in our hearts and memories, where with closed eyes we can savor and tarry in their beauty and lingering warmth. They are our legacy and our inheritance, to take with us into the next world, and to leave behind for those who would remember us.

Much has been and continues to be said of the ability of the horse to remember and to process the events of its life, to draw conclusions and compartmentalize these conclusions. I don't have the wherewithal to enter into that discussion again now, let's just say I am firmly in the 'believer' camp. And on that ground, I have wondered lately about the *never agains* in the life of a horse.

They are not really difficult to come by, to imagine. Our horses today are often weaned at an absurdly young age, and the first *never again* may hit them as early as at three months of age. To never again press to your mother's side, or nuzzle her teat for warm milk, or look to her for assurance and guidance seems a cruelly large *never again* to impose on a youngster who in the wild would likely still enjoy such privileges until well into his or her second year.

The enormous life changes fall hard upon each other for years to come. Horses started as young as eighteen months, justified by all manner of human concerns that in no way consider those of a horse, soon leave the youth of a horse behind, not only mentally but often physically. Aches and pains all too soon become the norm. Friends disappear and homes change, careers are predicted and cut short by injury, and all are at the mercy of outside forces of the two legged kind.

The freedom of some measure of space is replaced by confinement in a stall; if truly unfortunate, the horse may soon add *grazing in pasture and running freely with buddies* to the growing list of lost experiences. Resting tail to nose and swishing flies, scratching withers and playing *last horse to the water trough is a rotten egg* all become sepia toned memories of a glorious past, replaced by isolation and loneliness. And yet the horse adapts, accepts and keeps on keeping on. There is much to be learned from our equine friends, from their resilience and hardiness.

As our lives change and are molded by our experiences, as we make decisions based upon past mistakes and future hopes, we can look to the horse with respect and admiration. We may well be at the mercy of forces beyond our control, a force we may choose to consider benign or devilish, but we are still masters to some degree of our choice at the fork in the road.

Horses, on the other hand, are at the mercy of the human race, a race that is nothing if not flawed. Horses can only make choices that affect their inner life, choosing how to respond and how to adapt to our decisions on their behalf, and this they generally do with grace and kindness. Then their choice may have a positive effect on the outer circumstances of their life. But, if that fails, neurotic behavior and a powerful kick may well enter the picture.

Enter Torchlight, who picked neurotic before neurotic was 'in'. Were there a couch for horses he'd have worn the upholstery thin in weekly sessions for years. Yes, I'd foot the bill, of course. I've paid for all his other therapy, haven't I? Yet he remained kind and has never been a threatening horse. No kick here. He simply acted out in hysterics where he could not choose to accept. This, for better or worse, has become a modus operandi within which he often chooses to operate to this day. I have to forgive him and find him interesting instead of giving in to frustration for Torchlight has surely known his share of sad *never agains*. But I like to think his happy list is now longer than his sad list. I remind him of this often, to which he usually responds with a 'And your point is?' kind of look. The tortured, sensitive artist temperament, that's him. 'I suffer, therefore I am.' Maybe I'll have a plaque made for him to hang on his stall. Show him I understand. Make him feel special, for a change.

On his happy list would be that his racing days are long gone and far behind him, and only a few scars remain. A barely noticeable scar from surgery on a bowed tendon (nope, didn't pay for that one). Though no one will ever again 'ear him', (twisting his left ear to distract him from his fear of the starting box), scar tissue and a reflex protective twist of the head when approached unexpectedly remain. Canter work still leaves him a little hot and bothered, still not sure there isn't a race to be run, somewhere. Trailering will never be on the happy list, unless it was that he would never again have to endure a drive in an enclosed space. Is it the memory of the starting gate or just an extreme case of claustrophobia? I'll never know, and I have spent weeks on conditioning him for the ride. To no avail. Perhaps it's just that it's the best suffering he can come up with today, and he is keeping it for himself, blast it. That is my consolation. And he doesn't travel much anymore.

Surely his memories of a sunny California pasture in the shadow of his dam are all but dissipated in the mist of days gone by, but today on his happy list he can write: "never again confined in loneliness to a stall 24/7 to weave myself into oblivion." Nope, he now gets to weave in a pasture, surrounded by friends. Twice a day, reflecting the inner clock that he claims as his own, governed by his personal bio rhythms, (basically at feed time), the equine metronome that is Torchlight kicks off with a savage ferocity sharpened to a cutting edge by the suffering that is defined as waiting for his generously appointed feed bucket.

He prefers the smaller two acre pasture for this expansive expression of his inner turmoil, as the electric fence surrounding the large acre pasture severely limits his artistic interpretation of imagined hunger pains. Since he is never without hay or grass, I allow myself this callous disregard for his existential statement. Lonely he is not either, whatever he may tell you. He has a herd of his own including not just horses but burros and bunnies, dogs and cats, a few well-trained humans and more or less the run of the place.

We are privileged, Torchlight and I and all our four legged friends, and so I write this with humble respect for all those who do not live in such fortunate circumstances as we do. Torchlight and I do know what the other half lives like. We were there for years. But we don't talk about that. Trust me, it's better that way. He'd just need more hours on the couch, and countless pillows would likely meet a sorry end along the way. Let sleeping dogs lie…and all that.

On Torchlight's sad *never again* list would be the loss of his two dearest friends last fall. The young and lovely Paisley succumbed to a disastrous bout of colic, and his old and steadfast girlfriend, the thirty-two year old Arrow aka Mama, finally gave in to a stroke that left her stumbling in tight circles. After five years of courtship and serene friendship, a great many *never agains* must have been added to his list overnight, a night he spent with Arrow's adopted daughter, the burro Tortilla, standing guard over Arrow's still body.

Here we could enter into a discussion as to whether animals feel grief and understand death. All I will say on the matter is that Tortilla ran braying and screaming around the pasture a few minutes after the old mare's passing, kicking at us, the bringers of death in a needle, until exhausted. She stopped a few feet away, then, head hanging, approached her old friend's dead body. We had covered the mare in a tarp to protect her from the creatures of the night, but this sent Tortilla into a new frenzy. Stomping the tarp with her hooves, she tore at the ropes that held the tarp with her teeth.

This continued for minutes on end until we gave in and uncovered her Mama, with the expectation that Tortilla would let no predator or scavenger near her beloved old mare. We were not disappointed. We brought her Torchlight for company and to let him understand what had passed, and he inspected the old mare's body with his usual somberness. Then he and Tortilla posted themselves within a few feet of Arrow and that is where we found them the next morning. Tortilla was resting by Arrow's body as Torchlight stood guard over them both.

Before she passed, old Arrow gave me pause to consider her list of *never agains*. Her owner, though obviously fond of the horse - she had been paying for her retirement for years without complaint - had not been to visit Arrow in about three years.

When I made the call to recommend and ask her permission for euthanasia of the old girl, Arrow's owner burst into tears and immediately left work to come see Arrow one last time. When she arrived, we were waiting in the pasture with the vet at the ready. As she approached us from about a hundred feet away, Arrow, who had been standing quietly, head hanging with half closed eyes as if serenely awaiting her time, suddenly raised her head, and her voice. I heard this old mare nicker and saw her eyes brighten with a fervor I had only ever seen her bestow on her beloved burro.

She began moving in her crablike walk as fast as her geriatric stroke encumbered body would allow her. Horse and human walked toward one another, one sobbing quietly, one fervently nickering, both deeply moved to see her old friend one last time. I had never seen the old mare react to her owner like this before. I could only think that the wise old mare knew her time had come, and that never again would she see her human friend. She would make the most of it, and let the two legged know how much meaning this last meeting held for her.

We buried Arrow where she lay, and to this day it is Torchlight and Tortilla's favorite hangout spot. Tortilla often stands herself right on top of the mound and seems to look deep inside herself. I like to think she is reminiscing and remembering a long list of sweet *never agains.* Her new friend, Bureau of Land Management survivor burro, Salsa Picante (and she is a saucy, snarly little thing, kick you as soon as look at you, but I expect she has her reasons and too long a list of sad *never agains* for a young wild burro like her) seems to respect this gesture, and simply stands close by, but never on, the mound. That is Tortilla's place of remembrance. And that's my story to which I am sticking.

Torchlight has a new friend, too. My new horse Gusto, The Magnificent Majestic, as he humbly requires we call him, he is after all the only real pedigreed warmblood on the place, has brought his own list of *never agains* and he and Torchlight seem to have a great deal in common and much to share. They wander off for hours on end and graze, nose by nose. Though Gusto of course has no racetrack and starting box stories to tell, I know he has plenty of training gone bad stories and I suspect Gusto's happy list includes never again draw reins, tight fists and sharp spurs. At least he seems to begin to understand I really mean it. *Never again.* Won't happen.

I will laugh in the face of his temper tantrums and I will decline his invitation to a battle, I will set boundaries but I will also honor his spirit and desire to please and I will work my lesser self and his gorgeous self into a lather, but I will not crank and spank him. And just lately he appears to be understanding that our *never again* items are one and the same where he is concerned. Fewer and fewer are the days he comes out swinging, *en guarde* and spoiling for a fight; softer are his eyes and brighter his look. More willing and more swiftly come his attempts to meet my requests. We are actually having fun most days. Can I say that?

Hmm, yes, I think I can. Unlike Torchlight, Gusto does not appear to be hung up on existential suffering. He seems to embrace good times and *Happy Never Agains* wholeheartedly.

So this is 2009. A friend told me his wish for 2009 is no more death and no more heartache in my life. I thank him but also know—that's life, it ends for us all one day, no one gets out of here alive, as they say, and in the meantime we all have to endure what happens along the way to that end. Horses know this, too. It is their ultimate strength, this acceptance of life and death and everything in between. But I will embrace that wish along with the sad *never agains* I bring with me from last year, and expand on that wish to include my family of the two and four legged kind, and the world in general just to be politically correct.

But mostly I would wish that 2009 would bring our friends, the horses, freedom from the kind of abuse Torchlight and Gusto can talk about, both the subtle and the blatant, the intentional and the ignorant and the careless. I would wish that when we two legged creatures make decisions on behalf of our four legged companions, we stop and consider which of their Never Again lists we are adding to. And if it must be the sad, which of our personal Never Again lists will this decision end up on. To paraphrase an old saying, surely two sad don't make no one happy…

In Retrospect, 2019

…It's hard to believe a decade has gone by and yet it seems like much longer. Many a n*ever again* has been added to my lists since, and some days the sad list seems much longer than the happy one. But that *is* life, and as Torchlight once told us, life goes on. In the years since my mother's passing, many a difficult choice have been made, including the decision to re-home some of my horses as my situation changed. It was for the best, and they were happy homes, but the list of my sad *never agains* grew exponentially in those days.

It is one of the hardest lessons horses can teach us, that sometimes you are no longer the best possible home, even if you were for so very long till things changed somehow, and now there may be another home, just as good and currently better positioned, to give them the care and attention they need. Over the years I have had to let go of several of my 'heart horses', and while I will always regret having to let them go, and the *never agains* they added to my sad list, I will never regret the wonderful homes they went to.

Sometimes, letting go is paying it forward, and this they have taught me in spades.

# Two Fingers and a Noseband

February 2009

I'm waiting for spring. Looking out my window, dillydallying at my keyboard, waiting for the words to come, I realize those words hold more meaning and reach out in a broader sense than I first thought. I'm not just waiting for the new grass to cast a green sheen over my dully brown pastures, and the leaves to unfurl on black barren branches. I am daydreaming of the tulips and crocus, hyacinths and daffodils pushing through the slowly warming earth of my mother's garden, a garden that lives on in my heart.

And I am daydreaming of a new day for our dressage world, a day where the mere premise of such horrors as Rollkur is met with disdain and instant demise, a day where our sport is devoid of abuse, a world in which dressage fulfills the promise of the therapeutic sport that would be, that could be, *art*.

The Craft of Kings Once More.

If the road to hell is paved with good intentions, the cracks in the pavement must be filled with assumptions. I think it's safe to say that we tend to assume that other people feel more or less as we do, behave as we would, and see the world as we do. And interpret basic concepts as we do. I am at times surprised at my own naiveté. Not to mention embarrassed by the assumptions I have made. Oh, the many, many assumptions that have led to my own personal versions of hell!

One such assumption sat me down and spun my head around the other day. No, I did not require an exorcism, just a wakeup call. It was regarding one of the most basic rules of thumb that was drilled into me since the first day I was allowed to bridle a horse myself. It is so basic, so oft repeated, that I assumed it was more than a rule of thumb. That it was written in the great rule books of competitive dressage itself.

The rule that a noseband, any noseband of any kind, should never be tighter than it could easily allow two fingers to slide under it, thus allowing the horse to chew and swallow his spit. Amongst other, rather important, things…

I have often wondered that the disregard for this rule was so openly flaunted, at barns and at shows. I have watched and winced as trainers, riders and grooms pulled, grunted and wrenched the mouth of a horse achingly shut. I have wondered at the ignorance this misuse and outright abuse of the noseband demonstrated, and that more isn't made of this by the Technical Delegates at shows.

But most of all, I have wondered that a 'crank' noseband, the most efficient way of breaking this edict, has become an acceptable, even in demand, instrument for application on this sensitive and hugely important area of a horse. The name alone has made me cringe from Day One, and I remember having to double check that it was the actual name for it the first time I came across it. I could not believe its purpose could be so blatantly stated, and allowed by our ruling members. I could not believe it was so blithely brought forth in writing and through people's lips, with no thought for what it really meant. Padded noseband and chinstrap notwithstanding, it still uses powerful force to wrench the mouth of the horse shut. Crank and spank takes on new meaning, and finds a new tool.

Being a wordsmith, I wondered how exactly one defined the word crank, and what other words one might have picked to describe this 'invitation to torture noseband' (my definition). When has the word 'crank' ever been associated with anything positive except in its purely mechanical meaning, which would then be a neutral expression describing the job of a machine driven instrument? Which in itself, benign as it is, strikes me as completely out of place in the vicinity of a horse.

Interestingly, I think, there is no other word for 'crank' in my Thesaurus. It simply goes straight to 'cranky' and that's it. I found that mildly amusing. I would likely be 'bad-humored' myself were I a horse in a tightly fitted crank noseband.

My dictionary on the other hand, strikes me as eerily insightful right off the bat. And I quote:

Crank n. *something twisted.*

That seems a wholly wonderful description of the crank noseband to me. I can't help but think it twisted that we would be so immune to the horse's discomfort and ignorant of his bio-mechanical workings, that we would justify tying his mouth painfully shut with a noseband designed to implement a mechanical and exponentially powerful force on an area of his head that dictates the ease of movement through his *entire body*! Sorry, that was a mouthful. But there it is.

Good old Websters goes on to state:

Cranky adj. *Apt to operate poorly.*

Another brilliant, if unwitting, observation by the scholars of, oh, wherever they sit around compiling wonderful dictionaries. Apt to operate poorly. And that is exactly what a horse is apt to do when a noseband of any kind is tighter than two fingers can allow, when the straps cut into his chin and nose and cause his nostrils to flare as every breath is inhibited. And as his temporomandibular joint, also known as the TMJ, is entirely prohibited from functioning as nature intended. Chewing, opening and closing are functions we need above all else if we are to ride a *supple* and *relaxed* horse, two of the most basic requirements of the training pyramid.

The TMJ, the joint where the lower jaw of a horse hinges with his skull, is a fascinating place to study. If you are so inclined, and I assume not everyone else is. (See, I am learning, albeit slowly.) So I studied it and the effects of the noseband in general, asking what I assumed were pertinent questions of informed people like Mary Debono of the *SENSE Method*, my equine masseuse Kerry and my equine vet and chiropractor Dale. Once again, it seems our old masters were onto something when they repeatedly demanded a not too tight noseband.

For starters, it appears that to raise and lower its head comfortably, a horse needs to be able to move his jaw forwards and backwards. If the horse then also has a malocclusion (when the lower and upper sets of teeth do not line up well) he very much needs to be able to open his mouth to do so. Obviously, a tightly fitted noseband precludes this, leading to discomfort or even outright pain.

Carrying a bit induces the production of saliva in the horse's mouth, and to swallow this, he needs to raise his tongue to the roof of his mouth to help send the saliva to the back of his throat. A tight noseband will increase the pressure of the bit on the tongue, making it all but impossible if not outright futile, for the horse to attempt do so. This not only leads to the extravagant displays of foam, saliva whipped to frothy bubbles in the frenzy of a tongue trying to free itself, common in Rollkur horses, but this tension in the tongue leads to tension in the jaw, which carries on to all over body effects that might surprise the uninformed rider.

The base of the horse's tongue is attached to the hyoid bone, a small and fragile bone in the back of their mouth. This bone not only affects the use of the horse's tongue, it has attachments that lead down the front of the horse to the sternum. From the sternum and the lower ribs, powerful muscles attach to the pubic bone in the pelvis. This helps explain the next point. That the sternum is vitally important to the freedom of the head and neck, as well as the back and pelvis.

Suppleness surrounding the sternum is essential to a freely swinging ribcage and the flexing and extending of the back. In other words, freedom of the sternum affects the horse's ability to engage, to extend, to bend and to move laterally. Everything we ask our horses to do under saddle.

It starts, and may end, in the mouth of the horse. For if that mouth is restricted beyond movement by a tight noseband, the tongue tensing in response as the horse desperately tries to swallow his saliva, this tension will travel down the front of the horse to the sternum, in essence setting off a chain reaction of restriction and reduced movement that travels the length of the horse, through all his complicated and interconnected muscles, all the way to his pubic bone and beyond. A too tight noseband literally limits the movement of the horse from the head to the tip of his tail.

Furthermore, restricting and impeding fully and naturally functioning muscles, tendons and ligaments means the unnatural use of joints and redirecting or outright blockage of bio-mechanical patterns. This quite possibly leads to earlier degeneration of the horse's physique due to wear and tear in places never intended for such use in the equine body.

Who knew? The old masters did. And so they decreed again and again, that the noseband should always allow the mouth of the horse room to move. Perhaps it was such an accepted standard and ingrained belief in previous years that they thought it unnecessary to write down in a rule book.

No longer is it so. And the lack of a written rule has allowed it to lapse as a standard and become another little understood and often overlooked relic of horsemanship gone by. In terms of the modern dressage horse, it gives him no protection when the Technical Delegates monitoring a show have no instructions or black on white decrees to back them up. And so with no-one and nothing to inform or monitor their actions, trainers and riders, when faced with a horse expressing discomfort and unhappiness through the mouth, without hesitation turn to a tight noseband.

I am not that very old (unless you ask my ruthless nieces and nephew, then of course, I am a relic myself at the tender age of thirty…something, I am positively ancient) but I actually remember a time without flash nosebands. So much of what happens in the horse world today is accepted as the wisdom of the ages, when in fact a great deal of equipment, feeding and veterinary practice has only been around for a very short time, a few decades. In the big scheme of things, they are largely untested and unproven for the long term. I don't recall ever seeing a flash noseband until the early eighties. You either rode with a caveson or a dropped noseband, and correct fit was paramount and always required the two-finger rule.

But the flash came along and changed all that. It was a fashion statement as much as anything else. It was cute, it looked good, and it framed a horse's long face just so. Far more attractive than the dropped noseband which made a horse's face look even longer. As for function, how many horses actually need a flash? How many need a dropped noseband? Having recovered from my first fashion craze in equine enhancement, and with a little encouragement from Jane Bartle-Wilson who boldly took the flash off a mare I was riding, and by Golly, we survived the experiment, I realized pretty much every horse I rode went just fine if not better without the flash. A correctly fitted caveson or no noseband at all is my standard today.

Some years ago when Torchlight and I first attended a Walter Zettl clinic, we did an excellent job of climbing the rafters and hanging from the chandeliers. Throughout this fine display of extreme equestrian sport and raging equine athleticism coupled with deep seated neurosis, Torchlight's mouth was chomping and chattering loudly, uninhibited by a correctly fitted caveson.

If we impressed, it was by the depth of our inability to perform but the simplest maneuver. It simply was not available. Torchlight was a lightning rod of singed nerves, a two-by-four swinging wildly in hurricane force winds. Oh, the lights were blazing from all four stories but there was nobody home but little old me. And I was on the rooftop trying to fit down the chimney.

It was difficult to hear Herr Zettl's calm voice over Torchlight's clanking and rattling, but none of us gave up, though my embarrassment was keen and sincere and I not only wanted down the chimney but all the way down in the basement and preferably on through a mouse hole where I could curl up and lick my wounds. To his credit, Torchlight kept it together at the end of a frayed string through which I could just barely direct some shape and form and even a few variances in tempo.

Twenty minutes or so into the lesson we managed a walk break on a loose rein (oh yes, I am a gambler and risk taker at heart) while Herr Zettl fielded questions from the audience. One question about made my heart stop. I think I held my breath as I awaited the answer from one of the Masters of our time.

"Shouldn't this horse have a flash on to shut his mouth?"

Knowing I would disagree with an affirmative, I also knew I would have to consider the answer out of respect for his far greater knowledge and experience. To my great relief, the answer was an emphatic "No!" As Herr Zettl went on to explain to the audience, I could breathe again.

His explanation is one of the best and most succinct I have heard. It's simple. If the horse is distressed, emotionally or physically, it will be expressed through his mouth. Force his mouth shut, this distress is not alleviated but bottled up and concentrated, with far reaching consequences. When the horse is relaxed and working comfortably, his mouth will relax and be quiet.

We have a saying in Danish: *'That of which the heart is full, through the mouth will overflow.'* The mouth is the barometer of everything that is happening within the horse, physical or otherwise. Close it down and you lose a most valuable communication tool and seriously restrict access to the horse's body and mind.

Another twenty minutes and Torchlight proved Walter Zettl right for all to see. When Torchlight finally relaxed to within arm's reach of negotiations, his mouth became increasingly quiet and softened as his body became malleable and his mind available. Though we achieved little else that entire clinic, I learned a valuable lesson all over again. Silence the mouth of your horse at your own peril.

Eddo Hoekstra expressed a similar sentiment at a clinic awhile back when we discussed the subject. The mouth of the horse, he said, expresses whatever is happening in the horse's hindquarters. Trouble in the mouth points to trouble in the hindquarters and vice versa. If the mouth can't tell you, some other body part or behavior will, but it may not be as simple to read as the mouth.

In a conversation with then ten time world champion reiner trainer Craig Johnson a few years back, I learned from him a neat concept, the concept of mental collection. It basically means expecting the horse to take responsibility and carry out his end of the deal regardless of external circumstance. Total focus. Something we often don't expect enough of in our dressage horses. At times it seems dressage riders have the least faith in and the least expectation of a horse in terms of his ability to think for himself and figure out it won't eat him. And that he has a job to do.

I like to add another layer to that concept. I like to think not only of mental collection, but mental *throughness* in my horses. That they not only collect themselves mentally, but allow me passage through their mind as physical *throughness* allows the passage of energy and movement through their body. In one word: rideability. This has always been the hardest concept for me to develop with Torchlight. Mental collection turned out to be a much easier ideal to achieve. But mental *throughness* we are still hunting. His deeply rooted mistrust and lack of confidence haunt us to this day, despite his faith in me.

How much harder then, would it be to develop mental *throughness* if the horse is in pain and severe discomfort, not to mention the emotional toll of feeling trapped and possibly acutely claustrophobic, a condition naturally available to the prey animal that is the horse. Then submission is not a willing acquiescence and participation but a bitter surrender, an obedience born of bleak resignation. A high price for an animal we claim to love, to pay for our ambition. A sad end for a discipline meant to uplift and enhance the natural abilities of the horse while preserving and refining his spirit.

I am hoping I am wrong. I am hoping I am a terrible researcher and just missed it and someone will write to me and tell me where to find this rule written down, somewhere we can take it and enforce it. But if that is not the case, then I hope you will raise your voices and put pen to paper, and petition with us, a petition to bring awareness back to the two finger noseband rule and the why of it.

I am not saying never use a flash or a dropped noseband, they have their place. I am simply saying let's use them well, and with understanding.

We need spring and rejuvenation in the land of dressage after years of cold decline, and perhaps with the resignation of the old FEI Dressage Committee and the development of a new, we are about to see that possibility bud and bear fruit. Let's seize the moment and make a constructive suggestion while the door is open.

We need a rule, black on white, a rule that will be a stumbling block to the misuse of all regular nosebands, of crank nosebands and the tack requirements for the abuse we call Rollkur, an abuse that cannot be as easily perpetrated with a properly fitted noseband. If we do this one thing, if we get this one rule written down for all to see, to empower the Technical Delegates and horse owners who, in doubt and unsure of themselves, allow this to be done to their horse, then the consequences could be far reaching and overwhelmingly positive.

Torchlight and I will be the first to sign. Hoof in hand we will stand up and sing "We will overcome." OK, we won't, we'll spare you. But please sign anyway.

In Retrospect, 2019

...I wonder sometimes if we made a dent with this column which introduced a petition by *Horses For LIFE* calling for rules to monitor the use of nosebands at horse shows. But then I look around, and while there is still plenty of evidence of the abuse of nosebands, there is also much movement to make worldwide changes, some of which have already taken effect. Is there hope? Yeah, there's hope.

It was the beginning of *Horses For LIFE* stepping into the fray of international competition and calling for change. By the end of 2009, *Horses For LIFE* would be at the forefront of the battle against Rollkur, and I, a willing participant, found myself sharpening my pen like never before.

11 Educate Yourself!

March 2009

I think I can get away with saying I owe my life to horses without having overstated it too dramatically. For starters, my parents met at a local stable where my mother boarded her horse, Attila. She definitely had 'the bug,' which explains why she was there, but why my dad was there is another story. A bit of a mystery, that I tend to believe has more to do with meeting girls than it does with a deep and undying passion for horses...whatever the reason, it worked out for my brothers and me.

Really it was quite the compliment to my father. Attila was acquired by my mother at the expense of her previous engagement. One day she realized if she was ever to have her own horse, the fiancée would have to go. As a child I found it hard to fathom that she subsequently gave up the very same horse to marry my father and settle down to motherhood. I mean, she had her *very own* horse! And she *sold* it, because of a *boy*! Yuck, yuck, yuck. But I did eventually come to realize that lucky for us, she did, or I wouldn't be out there pursuing my own equestrian dreams or sitting here today tapping away at my keyboard.

Like so many children, horses were my most cherished desire since I can remember having fantasies. It's still a joke in the family. We can't pass a pasture with horses without my brothers mimicking a little girl crying "Oh, look at all the sweet horsies!"

On long drives I kept a white or black horse prancing alongside the car to keep me from boredom. I needed little encouragement for a trip to the stables with my equally horse mad mother, who by then had found a way to return to her first love. My fondest and earliest memories are of rides on an old Icelandic pony, Stjaertni, on a lead line with my mother through the magical golden-green gloom of a Danish forest. Later it was on Sooty through Kenyan coffee plantations alongside my mother on Bhatian or Muishu, both ex-polo ponies. Sooty, a pitch black and typically wicked Shetland pony that unseated me repeatedly and in every configuration known to horse, or rather ponies, since they've famously cornered the market on pitching riders, was introduced to me by my mother as The Black Mare.

As in The Black Mare of the Black Stallion series, a book I had just read and which apparently remained the main topic of scintillating conversation for my eight year old self for days on end. I can still remember the thrill of the promise of a surprise after school, the mystery of the drive to the barn with my mother refusing to divulge anything at all, and the pure wonder and delight when my mother said something like "I give you, the Black Mare!" Out came not a refined smoldering Arabian beauty, prancing on graceful stilts, but a shaggy black pony on stubby legs with a big head hidden beneath copious amounts of filthy, tangled mane. A classic Thelwell pony, with a gleam in her wicked eye, tugging on the rope for the nearest patch of grass. But no matter, my love was alighted and burning brightly. And I could borrow her whenever I wanted. Happiness, thy name is Horse.

Later on, the barn and horses became my refuge from teenage angst, agony and heartbreaks. It is no wonder that so many parents will go to great lengths to keep their teenage child riding and spending time at the barn. It's sanity in a fur coat. Or at the very least, a healthy brand of madness. There is no better alternative to the mall and chatrooms, no better place to forget your sorrows than in the presence of a warmly beating horse heart, in the rhythm of the grooming ritual and the tempo of a trot, the cadence of the canter, the exhilaration of a jump. A horse won't care that your face broke out in pimples (again), that you aren't wearing the latest fashion in jeans (because the money seemed better spent on horse stuff, anyway. At least until you got to school and the ridicule, no matter, back at the barn, you know you were right,) or that you don't have a date on prom night, again.

The horse by its very presence grounds and centers a young and flighty spirit, and gives a fresh perspective from the throne of his back, leaving all cutting remarks and acutely shameful embarrassments in the wake of his jauntily flowing tail. Not to mention awakening lofty goals and burning desires, that distract well from a desire of another kind, a secret and painful crush that dropped your grades from A's to well, less, a lot less. Your horse understands, or at the very least, does not judge, as long as you still love him and bring carrots, it's all the same to him. Not that I'm speaking from personal experience, of course. Of course.

Ahem. So. Moving on.

Horses. Fascination with their mystery, and a need to feel a part of their power and beauty, a sense of freedom and a direct line to something other, something indefinable and larger than ourselves, yet somehow to be found inside ourselves. Isn't that what brings so many of us into their lives? Whether they asked for it or not. And once there, we find them lovable and funny, and soon maybe challenging and frustrating, but we just can't walk away now. There is always that next corner to turn, the one thing to accomplish, a new mystery beckoning.

Where am I going with this? Well, since last month's articles on the use of nosebands, and the steadily growing list of supporters on the petition, I have been doing a great deal of thinking about the responses and the questions they raise. The question for me boils down to motivation. What motivates us to ride, and then to do what we do and defend it unquestioningly?

I can't imagine anyone showing up at a barn and learning to ride because they want to consciously participate in abusing horses. It's love that brings them there, love of horses and everything that they represent. Yet more or less subtle abuse happens all the time, in various degrees of transgression, accompanied by a certainty that the horse is well loved. It's my experience, yes this time absolutely personal and first person, that it's mainly ignorance and blind following of uneducated leadership, and sometimes it's just plain ego gratification, extreme narcissism. It's lack of confidence in ourselves and a need to believe in our chosen mentor. It can be frightening to feel out-of-the-know or to question a trusted leader. Happens to all of us.

It seems to me the important thing is not so much to deny or judge too harshly that this is happening. So easy to do, I'm a wonderful back seat rider if I do say so myself, but to keep educating ourselves, each other and asking questions. And yet, we also have to be willing to make a judgment call that it needs changing and then stand up and ask for change, or if possible, make the change yourself, of course. But first one has to be willing to acknowledge the possibility of another view, another reality.

This requires curiosity and a desire to learn, and a confidence that allows for the shedding of old beliefs. In other words, a confidence rooted in the heart and not the ego. A case in point was a debate on *The Chronicle of the Horse* regarding this petition. It brought a varied set of responses, ranging from support of the petition in any form to ridicule and derisiveness and on to defensiveness.

Ask most people and they would tell you they follow something like a two finger rule on the fitting of their noseband, cavesson and/or flash. Yet use your eyes and - according to the judge who asked our editor to address the issue and another judge and clinician who signed the petition – a very different picture emerges. Some in the debate denied tight nosebands had any ill effect at all. Another group thought it already very well regulated at horse shows. Some thought there was no way to fairly and consistently monitor the fit, what with different horses, different fingers and so on. It could be dangerous to loosen nosebands leaving horses running away left and right. (Which rather leaves a question mark as to the horse and rider's training, does it not?) It was impossible for nosebands to inflict as cruel damage as quoted in our magazine and elsewhere. Horses would never put up with it. Wouldn't they? Considering what else they will put up with, that is just one more thing, isn't it?

But none seemed educated about or interested in the *reasoning*, as in the bio-mechanical reasons that brought us to call for this rule. It was a debate of emotion and anecdotes, opinion and espousing, as debates often are. There was no factual evidence presented what-so-ever. No one seemed to realize there was more to this petition than some do-gooders feeling sorry for horses with their mouth strapped shut. I found that a little depressing. Are we all such a bunch of know it all's that we don't even feel the need to ask *why*? And if it is such a non-issue, what problem is there really with having the rule anyway? Just in case...Ultimately, the petition was blown off as unnecessary. Based purely on a complete lack of information.

Call it naiveté or know-it-all-ness, it could be dangerous. I find myself resenting the complacency in our community that believes and indeed relies on, the status quo. If issues such as this one are blown off by the majority, we not only risk the increase of abuse within our ranks, but a subsequently negative reputation that could bleed over into the public eye and catch the attention of animal welfare organizations like PETA, not exactly known for a measured and balanced approach or agenda.

If we are not seen to actively address the problems within our community ourselves, we could find ourselves hung by a jury of outsiders who care little for the ins and outs of training and equipment, while zealously minding the use of horses for sport at all. Think I am paranoid? Tell that to the outlawed fox hunters of Great Britain.

We can't afford complacency anymore. We are all too accessible for the public eye, stories spread like wildfire on the internet jungle and with the use of video on Youtube, it is easier than ever to provide incendiary proof of abuse to a world-wide, non 'horsey' audience. The movement for protection of farm animals is a worthy, growing and successful one. Not only does it show that the general public do care about animals but that when motivated and given half a chance, will act upon this feeling. It is also worth considering that it would not be a far leap from farm animals to the horse industry...and we may not feel fairly treated by such a movement however fine their intentions.

Hardcore dressage used to involve a small enclave of enthusiasts who mostly learned from traditionalists who knew and understood the benefits of serious training and the pitfalls of shortcuts. You took dressage lessons to learn to ride, and continued with them because the work was fascinating to you, not because it was less scary than jumping or you wanted to ride in a top hat on a super fancy warmblood. Not many of those around back then. That's not to say it didn't happen, but the pool today is much bigger, and with very deep ends. Now it's a huge sport for all kinds of riders with very differing motivations, opening the door to trainers and teachers of varying backgrounds who take the core principles and run them through their own database for their own purposes and spit them out, at times, a very different animal than how it entered.

It's just not enough anymore to simply take our trainer's word for it, especially if we are in doubt as to the righteousness of the application. We all have to ask why and if the answer has no depth, start digging ourselves. Owners have to stand up and take on more responsibility for the welfare of their mounts and their own education, however ignorant and powerless they may feel.

Moreover, owners have a responsibility in how they justify their expectations of their horse and trainer, and whether it is fair, timely and within reason to expect of either. Many trainers feel under immense pressure to perform and more importantly, for the horse to perform as expected. They have bills to pay and a reputation to uphold and improve upon. A lot of principles and good intentions get bent and rules broken under that pressure.

Owners play a much bigger part in the training of their horses than often they realize. It is imperative to the future of dressage as a sport that they begin to question the manner in which their horse is trained, the speed at which the horse is brought along, and the equipment used and how it is applied. If owners don't ask questions, and raise positive and reasonable expectations of knowhow and education, then there is little incentive for trainers inclined to rest on their laurels to further their own education or deepen their understanding of the principles. And I say that as someone who's been there, kind of, and I say kind of only because I never felt accomplished enough to rest too easily.

For a long time, I didn't even realize there were some heavy duty bio-mechanical guidelines for riding a horse. Sure, I understood the basic argument about why a horse needs to use his hind end and why you want to lighten the forehand. In very generic terms, this all made sense to me. I didn't even realize I needed to educate myself further. That came much later, when I found I had a lot of gut feelings and opinions the reasons about which I actually knew nothing at all. People would ask why this was so and I'd be stumped. *It just is* did not satisfy even myself. And it certainly did not satisfy Torchlight! *Because I said so* only ever got me so far with that kid. After he entered my life, there was no more cruising on automatic and getting by on 'feel'. Serious intent and dedicated learning were officially required to pass this course. And like the Energizer bunny, we are *still* going….or rather, *still* learning.

I was lucky to meet a few people that opened my eyes to the wealth of information out there buried in old books and new articles, videos and now DVD's and this very magazine, lucky for us. The hunt was on and I've been hungry ever since, and increasingly ignorant, the great paradox of learning. Oh Lord, it's true, the more you know, the more you realize you don't know.

Still, I get lazy. I love ordering books on Amazon and have great books lying around that keep losing to a good movie or an early night. Hey, at least my 'library' looks really cool and I can appear learned in a pinch. Oh yes, I have that book. (Haven't read it, but I *have* it.) Just look at all those books I have. Don't they look nice piled kind of artistically helter-skelter on my bookshelf? That's for effect, looks like I really go through them a lot. (Can't I learn by osmosis?) Well, I do go through them a lot. I like looking at the pictures of all the pretty horsies. I just don't always read them all the way through.

I'll get there. Not only Torchlight but a new generation of horses make it so. Require it, in fact. If Torchlight taught me to feel to new depths and introduced awareness that I needed to work more on technique, all these wonderful new horses in my barn coupled with frequent clinics with Eddo Hoekstra, are now allowing me to work full out on technique, that which the upper levels require in extreme amounts. But before practice comes knowledge, and that means education. That means delving into the why and wherefores of the teachings we take for granted, seeing which hold water and which do not. It means reading, attending seminars and clinics, watching DVD's (not movies) and doing some independent thinking.

And here I skipped college and thought I got clean away.

In Retrospect, 2019

…It's true, we never stop learning. Life itself is one long journey of learning, and horsemanship is one life school that offers programs for accelerated growth. When it comes to learning, whether in life or around horses, we really don't have a choice, we're gonna learn eventually, hell or high water. We can learn and move on from the lesson, or we can stay stuck in the repetition of the lesson in various forms till we choose to learn and carry on from there. That's life, and that's horses, and there's no use in crying about it.

There is, however, use in crying out about the systematic abuse in our horse world. The possibility of outside influences now beginning to monitor and affect our progress, or lack thereof, on that front is more real than ever. The world of horse racing is under attack and pressure now from a public that never paid attention until they dusted off their hats and mint juleps on Kentucky Derby day. As I write this, the Santa Anita racetrack is besieged by protestors as racehorses continue to break down and die at the track in unprecedented numbers, for reasons not yet ascertained or made public, and the governor of California has just stepped in and shut the race track down until further notice.

People who never cared a whit for horses are asking difficult questions on social media, and various animal rights organizations are beginning to throw their two cents in. Endurance racing has been under intense public scrutiny until governing bodies finally had to step in and sanction countries that were clearly treating their horses — and the competitive spirit — with an abject lack of regard.

More and more studies have gone public proving what the old masters already knew and tried to tell us. That riding our horses rolled up, forcing submission to the point of enslavement and tying them up in all manner of nosebands and gadgets is committing physical and psychological abuse against our beloved horses.

When do we begin to listen?

 Are Classical Dressage Riders From Mars?

July 2009

I am not from Mars, nor am I, though of female physiology, from Venus. I am an earthling who just happens to love real, traditional, down home dressage. *And!* Ready for this? I am not alone!

Have you ever felt like you were either the only sane person in the barn, or conversely, had to question if you were the only or perhaps, the most deluded? Have you ever wondered if your hard bought and closely held philosophies were just flights of fancy and impossible dreams? Have you been ridiculed by others more willing to clip a heel and cut a toe? Well, I don't know about you, but I have a *lot*. So call me Cinderella, that still doesn't make me a Martian.

Many of us who still believe in the core principles of dressage as a discipline with the potential to be an art form with rehabilitating values, operate mostly in a vacuum. We ride alone and we are alone in crowds of the more modern dressage persuasion. We struggle to find trainers and mentors who think like we do, and who not only have talked but walked the path and are willing to show us the way. We resort to books, DVD's and ancient (OK, maybe not ancient, just 80's) grainy videos and travel far and wide for a peek at a drop spilled from the chalice of the Holy Grail.

We interview trainers and get excited, thinking this one really believes as we do and holds the key to the knowledge we seek. Only to find within the first five minutes of the first lesson that talking and doing are two very different realities in this arena and perhaps we leave early, or grit our teeth and stick it out, only to apologize profusely to our horse later.

And when we do find that one horseman or woman who has not only the faith but the knowhow, we will bend over backwards and bankrupt ourselves in our quest to share in their knowledge and experience.

Dressage is a discipline separate from other equestrian pursuits in that it seeks a higher degree of sustained collection than any other curriculum, not to mention varying and intimately connected expressions of that sustained collection. A jumper is collected before the jump only to explode into a soaring arc of extension, perhaps to hit the ground in a flat out run to the next fence before being collected momentarily once more, achieving a moment of supreme engagement as he bascules for the lift off. Certainly a well-trained jumper exhibits high degrees of collection and may be ridden in a balance more off his forehand than not, but he is not asked to sustain this balanced collection as a highly trained dressage horse is.

A racehorse never even sniffs at collection; his whole life is a run on the forehand. A hunter lives his life in a horizontal, and if he's lucky, level balance, and generally western horses are asked to exhibit a low head set and level frame that leaves them heavily front end loaded if mechanically and powerfully engaged. Nowhere else is a horse developed to balance on his hindquarters without cease. To shorten and paraphrase Paul Belasik in his new book, *In Search of Collection*; there's riding, and then there's collection.

As a dressage rider, this focus boils down to a pursuit that by its very nature requires a great deal of formal education to master. Eyes on the ground are crucial to help guide a rider's technical development and know how. *Feel* and talent are helpful, but nothing replaces a good teacher and endless practice under discerning and knowledgeable eyes to develop the skills required for this pursuit of equestrian happiness.

In other words, it's a discipline that can be awfully intimidating and humbling if you don't have access and opportunity to ride good schoolmasters with experienced instructors. And even then it will leave you in the dust again and again, wondering where you went wrong and will you ever get anywhere.

With my gypsyish upbringing and roving lifestyle that has certainly been my experience. I have been blessed with few really great instructors and more 'project' horses than you can shake a stick at. I could lose a few fingers and still count on one hand the well trained schoolmasters I have been privileged to ride. Now, Nuno Oliveira said something like *"Don't ride easy horses, they teach you little, ride difficult horses, they will teach you what it is to ride,"* and I can without pretense say that I have followed, if not exactly on purpose, that instruction to the letter and the 't'. But, and in this I am interpreting Paul Belasik's recommendations for choosing your partner in collection, if you want to ride collection, ride a prospect, not a project. *Now* he tells me.

Lucky for me, now that I am finally getting smarter, I have in the last few years managed to organize some excellent and consistent formal education for myself, but there are days I can't help wishing I had found it a lot sooner, and had a lot more of it. Because riding collection, as elusive as it is, when you accomplish even a moment of it, is such *fun*. And with every such fleeting glimpse, I realize again how very simple it is, if not easy.

It is we humans who complicate matters. If you don't have someone to hold your hand and whip your bottom, that teacher and mentor to help you sort out the mess that is you and your horse…well, it's a *long*, lonely road. Torchlight is an excellent example. Riding him on my own for several years, he had pretty much convinced me I couldn't ride worth a fiddle until my new mentor came along and told me I rode a very tough horse that few would have ridden even that well, if at all. Oh.

Then I returned to training for others, and riding other horses I discovered all the useful stuff Torchlight had taught me, through blood, sweat and a few tears. I also realized all the bad habits I had acquired, and how my seat had changed for the worse as I accommodated a tense and excruciatingly bouncy back whose trot I rarely was able to relax enough to try to sit. Perhaps most of all, I wide-eyed and wonderingly comprehended what fun it was to ride an uncomplicated, non-project horse.

I know the day will come when I will understand and appreciate fully all that Torchlight and all my other projects have and are teaching me, and even now I know I wouldn't want to be or have been without a single one of them, but for now allow me some regrets. Because although riding difficult horses teaches you to be a feeling, inventive rider and trainer, ultimately, if that is all you ride, they can also hold you back from becoming a great one and from acquiring higher levels of skill and technique, especially if you do not have the benefit of constant guidance from a good instructor. It's not that I think only easy horses make it to Grand Prix, far from it, nor do I only want easy horses from this day forward.

But *what* makes them difficult can also be defining in just how far they will let you take them. Is it simply due to physical limitations that they challenge you, or is it a mental state? Is it a tendency to playfulness that leads them to second guess suggestions or is it outright obstinacy? Is it an inborn higher tendency to fear and distrust, or is there a history of abuse, scars that run deep enough to last a lifetime? Ultimately, answering these questions will be part and parcel of achieving higher states of collection.

Because collection demands total trust from the horse to the rider, allowing the rider to guide it through the demanding exertions that develop collection. If this is not possible, as so far it has not been in Torchlight's case, achieving collection would instead require a willingness on the rider's part to completely dominate the horse, in which case much is lost in the process, the spirit of the horse is compromised or even broken, and the result can never compare with that brought about by mutual trust and regard.

So then the rider faces a choice. To listen or to dominate. I have decided to play on our strengths. Torchlight enjoys and thrives on groundwork and together we will learn more about long-lining and in-hand work. Despite all my best efforts, and enormous changes in him over the years, I have not been able to completely gain his trust in the saddle, and we have hit a wall, a place where any increased request for collection takes leave of all relaxation not to mention his senses. At this point I do not know what prevents him from fully trusting even me, his otherwise most trusted partner, and so I can only take my cues from him and follow his breadcrumbs, from the ground.

Perhaps that will lead to a confidence and acceptance on his part that could allow me to experience the collection I know he is capable of, from his back. But if not, we will do what we can, and I am lucky to have other horses that do trust me completely and willingly follow me and alternatingly lead me, as we play on the scales of dressage.

I can't help but wonder how much further on my quest for the higher echelons of dressage I might have been, had the difficult and challenging horses been interspersed with a steady stream of great instructors, good schoolmasters and a clearer focus on where I wanted to go, and how much it takes to get there. There is no doubt in my mind it is easier to create something when you have already experienced it, as schoolmasters allow you to.

Of course, all that said, one day as I ride my wonderful, uncomplicated Grand Prix horse (a girl can dream, can't she), I will look my students meaningfully in the eye and sagely declare that a fun horse is all well and good, but they must ride difficult horses to become good trainers. Just look at me on my perfect pony…

It seems there has always been controversy and confusion accompanying the various perpetrators of dressage that rise to some level of notoriety and fame. The controversy of Rollkur today echoes the outcry and furious debate that enveloped and continues to haunt Baucher and his methods. When we look at an international dressage horse performing, we have to ask ourselves: is it an exhibition of the culmination of mutual trust and regard, a partnership manifested in physical and spirited prowess, or is it simply a display of complete rider domination over a horse reduced to a soulless puppet?

There is always a way to explain, to modify and justify, and good talkers and swift thinkers make heads spin till they nod in agreement, bedazzled and bewildered and on unsure footing. Perhaps because, like me, they lack a fully integrated formal education, it is all too easy for less experienced dressage lovers to second guess a gut reaction to a ride, or even the keenest of observations. When you yourself are still limited in experience, searching to understand, trying to learn in a hard knock school taught mainly by books and your horse, it's hard to argue with someone who seems to have all the facts at their fingertips, however skewered those facts may be.

So it's no wonder that there is such confusion as to what constitutes a correctly developed dressage horse, and it's no wonder that the masses are easily intimidated and impressed by imitations of the real thing, especially when presented with such panache and showmanship as exhibited, for example, by the frontrunners of the Rollkur crowd. It is a wonder however, that our highly educated judges seem to buy into the farce as well.

I grew up with the wonderful fairytales of Hans Christian Andersen, and his stories informed me of the nature of humans at an early age. Even as a child I did not have to look far to see the morals and observations *The Ugly Duckling* or *The Little Mermaid* exemplified.

Other than *The Ugly Duckling*, *The Emperor's New Clothes* was my favorite. It's a sublimely clever story of the tendency of humans to cater to the vanities, not only of themselves, but that of others, in particular if they believe so doing either saves them from appearing ignorant or curries favor with someone they believe to be their superior.

In the story, a vain emperor is known to love fineries and fancy clothes. A clever salesman comes to the emperor empty-handed but makes a great show of presenting the monarch with one nonexistent roll of fabric after another, which he describes in flowery and sumptuous terms. His rhetoric is fervent and convincing, and the vain emperor, unsure of himself and acutely aware of his subservient court awaiting his lead, fails to point out the obvious, that the salesman's hands are empty. Uncertain of how to proceed, the emperor instead nods, oohs and aahs, looking wise and informed, and soon the charade is in full bloom, the clever salesman fertilizing the emperor's vivid imagination with his own devious and fictitious descriptions.

Following the emperor's lead, equally unwilling to appear foolish, the court falls over itself in its rush to admire the imaginary rolls of cloth. The tailors are summoned and to their astonishment, instructed to create beautiful garments for the emperor, out of thin air. They dare not argue with the emperor and the court, nor do they wish to be alone in not seeing the fabrics, so they get to work creating imaginary clothes out of imaginary cloth.

And so it goes, until the emperor decides to have a fine parade to show off his wonderful new clothes, and the citizens ooh and aah, all afraid to blow the whistle, all unsure, thinking perhaps they are mad themselves for not seeing the clothing. Until finally one small child raises his voice and declares the emperor – naked.

Sometimes, when around other horse people, of any discipline, I feel like the tailors and the citizens of this story, puzzled and afraid to speak out, but mostly I feel like the skeptical child amongst believing adults. Either way, the result is the same. I cannot understand that what I see and what they see, is not the same, it seems so obvious to me. But when I find myself the child, I am also bashful, acutely aware of the pitfalls of self-righteousness and the dangers of jumping to conclusions and judging accordingly. I am painfully aware of what I don't know. I have learned, more or less, to look before I leap and to pick my battles with care, that I may survive to win the war.

So either way, I am careful to speak, unless I discover myself amongst others of like mind, then, perhaps, I am too quick to voice my thoughts and opinions. A friend of mine used to say that I was too timid and needed to learn to use my 'outside voice' more. I think perhaps today she would say I took her instruction too much to heart…

Recently, my outside *and* inner voice had a fine time. It was my happy fortune to find myself in a crowd of likeminded dressage enthusiasts, many of which were far more accomplished horsemen and women than myself. Which meant it was that much more enjoyable to sit back and watch and be instructed by people who had done what they talked about, in *the way* they talked about it.

The event was the *Second Annual Classical Symposium* at Kipling Lear Farm near Ft. Worth, Texas. In other words, unfathomably close to my own home. I have grown accustomed to any such desired event or group of likeminded individuals being at least a day's drive or a night's flight away. And here it was, just an hour and a half away.

The symposium was hosted by *The Foundation for Classical Horsemanship* and HHclassicaltraining.com, a foundation and school that have come into being in the past few years thanks to the hard work of head trainer Holly Hansen and a few friends who serve as directors and in advisory capacities, including Stephanie Millham, Paul Belasik and Carol McArdle, all of whom flew in and were present at the symposium. To read their biographies and the list of horse aficionados they themselves have trained with, reads like a who's who list of horsemen par excellence. Nuno Oliveira, Dr. van Schaik, Christopher Bartle, Manolo Mendez…the list goes on.

It was a full day of learning and exhibition, of talking and then demonstrating the talk in action. In a word, paradise for a true believer like me. It was water for my mill, justification for the persecuted, rectification for the ridiculed. In other words, my ego felt much gratified to be amongst people who wholeheartedly agreed with *me*.

But seriously, and more importantly, it was all at once soothing and inspiring. I knew for certain that I and others like me are not alone, only isolated. My fears of personal insanity, fanatical delusion and a Martian heritage were laid to rest and the last nails struck in their coffins as Carol McArdle and Paul Belasik relayed their own stories that in some small ways mirrored my own. In as much as they had experienced solitude in their belief system, insecurity and momentary lapses in their faith, that they had questioned their sanity and perhaps, too, their origins, since Carol herself declared, to my great relief, that we are not from Mars. I guess I can stop looking for antennas on my head now.

We classical horsemen and women may be outsiders in today's dressage arena but I like to think we are the core of future dressage. We keep the dream alive, and we practice what we preach, that one day we and future generations may exemplify that ideal. And if we can't or don't know how to practice it ourselves, we find someone to show us how to or pay someone else to do it for us, not just for our personal pleasure, but for the horse and for their sake. For their future in an increasingly high tech and fast paced world. Because for us it is so much more than a sport. It's a way of life, a philosophy and a belief system.

We live in interesting times. We have public outrage at world class competitions. Division within our governing body, not to mention the international dressage community. World class trainers and veterinarians speaking out and acting upon their beliefs, holding up classical ideals against the pomp and pageantry of abusive practices presented as new and better training methods, while the uncertain and the vain nod agreeably and ooh appropriately.

Could it be the tide is turning, the illusion is saturated and can hold no more naked and vain if convincingly presented emperors? Courageous whistleblowers like Dr. Gerd Heuschmann are giving even the most befuddled citizens of the horse world hard evidence in his book *Tug of War*, and DVD, *If Horses Could Speak*. I cannot imagine reading his book and watching his movie and still being able to believe in the merit and justify the methods he so clearly debunks.

From a slightly different but supportive of the vet's perspective, Philippe Karl's new book *Twisted Truths of Modern Dressage*, offers more clear insights and comparisons in techniques and their fall-out that we can all benefit from perusing. Taking advantage of the teachings and detailed information such publications provide, perhaps we can all let our outer voice channel the inner more often with the ammunition they provide. After all, knowledge is power. Rollkurer's of the world hear my cry!

Power to the Classical People!!!

In Retrospect, 2019

...I have learned that facts are not always the same as truth, and can be easily corrupted and swayed to support just about any supposition, much like statistics. I read with care and conclude with great caution, and stand fast with more confidence than ever before, in part because of my increased experience and results, but also because I have been blessed with the profound mentorship of Stephanie Grant Millham since 2010, and the extraordinary friendships of Carol McArdle and Holly Hansen, all of whom I first met at the symposium mentioned in this column, and all of whom have contributed to my understanding of, and appreciation for, classical principles.

Furthermore, they have all had a profound effect on my life. I moved to North Carolina because Holly did and once I came here to visit and ride in her third Classical Symposium, I knew it must become my home, too. I bought my first Lusitano, my beloved Apollo, from Carol McArdle, rode my first full-on piaffe and passage on Carol's schoolmasters Norman and Preferito, and knew how to develop my first Lusitano because of all Stephanie's guidance on the subject of the Iberian horse and how they differ from all other breeds.

Last but not least, I have long cherished the idea of owning, raising and starting my own Lusitano youngster, in particular one by Holly's fabulous stallion Obtuso, who had me at hello all those years ago when I first met Holly. For a finer soul or a greater gentleman you would have to search far and wide. Thanks to Holly's generous heart and extraordinary love and commitment to her beloved horses, that dream recently came true with the purchase of Otelo, a fine 2018 Obtuso colt who Holly and I will raise and start together, the classical way, in the years to come. Already, he promises to make his father proud, although, as Holly recently informed me, he takes after his father in every way but one. He is very messy in his stall. I can live with that, after all, so was Gusto, and look what a sparkle he left in his wake...

Since I wrote this column, more wonderful horsemen and women have risen to the surface to exemplify soulful horsemanship from within our ranks. From the competitive world, Uta Graf, Ingrid Klimke and Alizée Froment among others, continue to carry the flag. Anja Beran and Dr. Gerd Heuschmann have published in-depth books on what, why and how of Classical Horsemanship. Frederic Pignon and Magali Delgado spearheaded the fabulous *Cavalia* show, which, at least when I saw it on its first tour of the US, exemplified exhibits of true dressage and genuine horsemanship. Their books, *Gallop to Freedom* and *Building A Life Together* are well worth a read.

And last I checked, none of them are Martians, either.

13
To Show or Not to Show... That Is the Question

July 2008

There was a time when I ate, slept, breathed and trained to compete. I was in my late teens and after years of riding school nags, I finally had a competitive horse of my own, to show on a small scene where I got to be a big kahuna. Around that time I remember hearing about an apparently excellent rider and trainer who refused to show, and I wondered why she bothered to train at all? It almost seemed like a weakness to me then. That thought is completely foreign to me now. It seems like surely it belonged to someone else.

Times and people do change. Today I do relate to this trainer I never met, and consider it more of a strength than a weakness to prioritize training for the reward it gives in itself and not (nearly) solely for the possibilities of having the winning ride on the next show day. Less devotion to showing has balanced my idea of training requirements and my agenda, though I guess that could also leave one trying less hard. As always, finding balance is perhaps the biggest challenge of all.

Don't get me wrong, I still enjoy competing. It's just that now I have many different reasons for getting up every morning and working my horses, and the prospect of taking them to a show is only one of them.

I have no problem with people who train to show, I can still relate to them also, to needing that goal, to needing that edge, to satisfying that competitive spirit. It's what drives anyone to excellence, and for some it is the backbone of self-discipline, just knowing that date with a few gallons of Quickbraid and a judge is looming up ahead.

As always, my problem with riders that train primarily to show is what it drives them to *do*, what compromises in training and their horses wellbeing become as natural as breathing to them. I touched on that state of mind once upon a time, and it very nearly did not have a happy ending for my horse, Tempo, and thus, for me. Along the way, he was always on my conscience like a little gentle burr, just scratchy enough to cause me second thoughts, not scratchy enough to make me change course before it was nearly too late.

After a successful season of training and campaigning on less than ideal surfaces, Tempo seemed slightly off in one front leg. A thorough examination revealed he was actually sore on all four legs, and the fact that he had shown as well as he did, without noticeably lessening his gaits until after the show season, was all thanks to his stoic personality, his inherently large heart and the kindness within both. The fact that my vet was also my archenemy in the show ring did not help lessen my chagrin. She left no stone unturned in spreading the word that I had beat her in our championship rides on a horse that was basically unsound, but too kind to show it. Or maybe the judges were biased? My victory seemed much tarnished, and I lost a perfectly good vet to a sore loser.

Despite her efforts to embarrass me, what I remember best was my shame at what I had done to a horse I claimed to love and adore, and what I had not seen happen to him. Photos show that he carried signs of stress around the time of our last competition. He had lost weight and muscle tone, his face looks oddly tired, his eyes have a faraway look. Had I just ignored the signs in my determination to be the best, or really not seen the change that came over him? I'm still not sure. But clearly, being the best came at a price, paid in full by my sweet horse.

In retrospect, pretty much all I had done was train hard without the benefit of good arenas. I trained mostly in a grass field that could be rock hard, but since he never braced or tensed up, I thought nothing of it. I lost my temper at times and was too hard on him, and would go home cringing at myself, berating myself for hours, swearing I would never pull on my horse's mouth again. That is, until the next time my teenage temper took a spill…

The mistakes I made with Tempo haunt me still, and his memory has helped keep me honest over the years, even though my treatment of him left him with no scars, physical or otherwise. My temper tantrums were blessedly few and far between, though they probably escalated in direct proportion to the approaching show date. Tempo was a forgiving fellow and easily recovered from his soreness with a few months off and was back to showing impeccably that fall with his new owner, his sale necessitated by my move to another country.

But can I really blame competition for my mistakes and lack of judgment? No. Human nature would be the basic culprit. I've seen trail riders with no agenda other than lurching down the trail savagely beat their horse in the throes of extreme frustration with whatever it is their horse did or did not do. I've known natural horsemanship enthusiasts to drill a horse to exhaustion as insistently as any competition rider. Human nature is quite simply laced with a need to control and a competitive drive that is at times more prevalent than others, and which is applied according to that individual's personal history, mental makeup and passions.

For some it is about showing dressage, the ultimate cocktail for control freaks with a competitive drive. Jumping and eventing if they have a need for control, finesse, speed *and* reckless driving. Then there's something like oh, western pleasure. Hm, maybe we shouldn't even go there, but let's just say this calls for a special blend of control issues, the need to show, and a penchant and pocket book for bling.

So had you asked me some (rather too many) years ago, I would have told you I wanted to ride in the Olympics. Ask me now and I will mutter unintelligibly and offer a non-committal shrug. It may just be that I am lazier now. I think "show" and I think "bathing, braiding, cleaning tack, polishing boots, early morning calls, trailering, memorizing tests….Do I really need to spend *money* to do that?"

Or could it be that I wonder if the price might not be too high for someone with my particular set of possibly impossible values (and pocketbook or lack thereof), unless an extraordinary set of circumstances were to occur to allow to me to reach for that pinnacle or even the surrounding peaks while remaining true to myself and my horses.

But really it may just be that my competitive drive has been much tempered by passion, rather an odd thing that. Doesn't that usually flow the other way? However, when I consider that the competitive arena today appears to be as much if not more, a political battlefield as a theatre of the arts, I must admit I'd likely be out there putting flowers in their bayonets and singing Imagine, with a little luck only slightly out of tune and inserting 'horses' for 'people'. Altogether now: *"Imagine all the horses…"*

That said, I am happy to think that I will be spending more time in the show ring in the future, because I have a few horses I simply have to take out there. They are just too pretty to keep from the public, you know? But my sights are set somewhat lower for now, like…schooling shows. Yes, a far cry from the international scene, but Rome was not built in one day either, was it? Besides, they are a hell of a lot cheaper than the recognized kind, especially when you are not sure if your horse will blow up or show up.

It's been a long time since I really gave it a try out there in the show world. I have dabbled in it, a little here, a little there. It's always been good for a laugh and now and then even a ribbon. But only now do I really have the horsepower to go at it again, and also have the new and added pleasure of taking students who have the urge. But, yeah, it's been awhile.

After selling Tempo, my life took on a transitory nature, always on the move to somewhere else. It left little room for horses never mind the consistent training necessary for showing. Initially, I pursued the golden dream, and put in some 8 months at a sales barn that very nearly killed my love of riding and showing for good. I walked away knowing that if this is what it takes to make it in this world, I am not cut out for it.

It seemed as much as this place actually tried to give the horses a decent life, the hardcore training dimmed all joy and beat the life out of them, not to mention the staff. At eight months, I had still lasted longer than any other groom they had had, barring the head groom, who largely contributed to the constantly revolving line of grooms. But worst were the young horses already injured, and already losing the battle with a life that left them devoid of spirit. I just couldn't carry on down that road. I felt lost, my dream dispersed like so much confetti from a burst balloon.

For some years I drifted, at a loss without horses, but unwilling and unsure of how to mend a broken dream. When life finally brought me full circle and back to my true love of training, with or without show, I was almost afraid to get back in touch with the competitive edge. It actually hindered a full effort the first few times out, as if I thought that if I tried a little less hard to get it right, if I laughed off mistakes and didn't correct them, I was keeping a safe distance from the honed sliver of steel that was my competitive nerve.

Now that I had found a purity of passion in training for the sake of the horse and not ribbons, it seemed a return to competition might tarnish my resolve. In other words, I didn't trust myself to not blow it again and lose sight of the Holy Grail for all the smoke of pride and glory. And along came Torchlight.

In a way Torchlight helped put the last nail in the grander than life dreams, and I am grateful for it. Because hiding behind my fear of the ambitious self was still the core of those dreams, and they were based on pride and glory, fame and exaltedness. The source of those dreams was the raging ego looking for recognition and signs that worthiness was secured. Well, there was no way Torchlight was here to help me pave *that* road. No matter how many pity parties I threw myself, that would not change.

Instead he forced me to look for alternate routes, along which many lessons, some ad nauseam, have been learnt. Ultimately, by giving up on dreams of his fabulous dressage career, I gave up on my larger than life dreams and got real. And when I got real, I found I could still dream, and the dreams could be as big and tall and grand as I ordered them to be, but at the base was and is always my love for the real thing.

My dreams are now grounded in my love of the horse himself, and in dressage. What real dressage offers and consolidates and creates. A partnership wherein you stumble and you toil and you sweat and hopefully, more times than not, you get to dance and even laugh a lot. And climb a great many mountains that may only matter to you, or may play out in bigger arenas under the gaze of many judges, but still, at the end of the day, the only look that matters is still that of your horse as you approach him.

Because a show ride is still just another training ride, with a little more edge and a few nerves thrown in for good measure. But still, the focus is on what do we learn today. Yeah, you got up indecently early, you used spit and polish and your fingers are sore from braiding, you spent money about which you wonder if it couldn't have been better spent, like, say, on a haircut, but hey, it was nice to get out and test your relationship and ride in another ring and wear that expensive show coat for a change, and that's what hair nets are for.

But there is still the big scene out there, to cause me to ask questions as to how big I really want to dream. Now we are all agog at the latest dressage wonder, the fabulous Moorland Totilas and Edward Gal in the saddle. No wonder, what a gorgeous pair. Have we ever and will we ever see a horse like this again? Was there ever a more elegant and technically superior rider? Admittedly, I have been an admirer of Edward Gal's riding since I first saw him ride Lingh.

But like the grey mare Matinee, I wonder at some signs indicative of gaping holes in Totilas' training, the disjointed and bizarre extended trot for example. It's as if the horse performing up till then is one horse, to be replaced by two for that particular movement. To me, it seems like two different horses come strutting across the arena with only the rider in the middle to keep them still arriving at the corner simultaneously. I wonder at the always slightly left behind left hind leg, the shortened neck with a clenched throat-latch that rarely sees daylight, the low poll and the curb that never seems to ease up. And I wonder how long this incredible horse will last. And this is all before I consider that last I heard, Edward Gal was training with Anky van Grunsven. Rollkur, anyone?

I have no doubt whatsoever that Totilas receives the best of everything and no, I couldn't do what Edward Gal does. The point is, would I want to even if I could? That extended trot reeks of Rollkur, with its disproportionate and overdeveloped foreleg action while the hind leg takes an extended vacation, pun intended.

Somehow, like Anky and others of that ilk, and assuming if one rides with Anky, one rides with Rollkur, Mr.Gal manages to marry the despicable Rollkur with technical brilliance and astounding performances that belie the gaps.

But I have eyes in my head. And they tell me I wouldn't want to have done what it took to get that horse there today, nines and tens notwithstanding. They tell me more than sound dressage training is at play here. More than ever, Totilas demonstrates how hard it can be to separate breeding from training, panache from true form. And truly, I'd still really like to be able to look that good on a horse. Any horse.

Yet I wonder, is that really all dressage is about today? Record scores and go for the gold? And could I fall under its spell again? Nah, even as I write that, I know those days are gone. With Tempo and Torchlight's help I kicked them to the curb and kicked them good. They were swept up and thrown out with yesterday's trash.

Now I know 'they' say classical doesn't show and it doesn't win. But there are enough classical riders out there, at the top of their game and making their way to the tops of the ranks to give me hope. And what is classical but a correctly trained horse who stands the test of time? As I was once told, I am painfully patient, and I have time.

A friend of mine told me about her trainer who is also a judge back in Denmark. She is a staunch believer in what would basically be the German classical ideals and a superb technician with a to die for position. Yet she despises being called classical. It's practically an insult to her.

Because to her it signifies a difference between competition dressage and her dressage that should not exist. When a spectator watching her warm up at a show asked if she was a classical rider, she about spat in her face. "I am a dressage rider," she responded through clenched teeth. Did I mention she is apparently not a very popular judge in her homeland? Because she holds no punches no matter who you are and what you ride, and she does not hold with any political correctness either. A spade is a spade and the horse is trained correctly or it's not, and she will tell you either way. We need more judges like her.

But whoever the judge, I know we need to get out there and demonstrate that yes, classical shows and it succeeds. How else will anyone new to the sport or looking for an alternative know we're here? Classical can't just hide in our back yards anymore. We owe it to horses everywhere to swallow our fears or pride or whatever is holding us back and get out in front, even if it's just a schooling show. And I know now how I will make it work for me.

When I go to show now, I go to have a day out with my horse, a day to test our partnership and our work to date, a day where I hope and intend to excel but will face the judge with my horse and take it as it comes. I will ride down centerline with my competitive edge firmly in hand (if perhaps, not my horse,) side by side with my passion for the purpose of our training, and always with my horse's wellbeing first and foremost in my heart.

Now that's a dream worth dreaming, and one that can take you just about anywhere...

In Retrospect, 2019

...I can still say *Amen* to all of the above. My training business today is limited to a couple of students. As for horses, it's just Apollo and his Welsh pony companion, Braveheart, just outside my front door; and my exquisite young prospect Otelo growing up on Holly Hansen's farm a short drive away. I feel blessed to be able to so enjoy my passion on a more part time basis while I enjoy other pursuits, like writing, speaking and life coaching. I have managed to attract students of like mind, with whom I share a sense of passion and purpose in training, and the fun and challenge of attending local shows, all while putting the horse first.

The horses at the forefront of international dressage ten years ago are mostly gone, all with some story attached about this or that stable, pasture or trailering injury. Make of that what you will. Much has been said and written about their lack of connectivity, soundness and wellbeing, I do not need to reiterate all that. Rollkur has largely been acknowledged as an inhumane and counterproductive training method, only to be replaced by Rollkur Light, also known as LDR (Low, Deep, Round,) basically the same only different, or so they say.

Watch any international warm up ring and you will see Rollkur is alive and well, only not as celebrated. Despite numerous studies pointing to its ill effect on the physical and psychological wellbeing of horses, it still wins. Riders like Ingrid Klimke and Ana Balkenhol who show up in the tradition of their classical fathers, Reiner Klimke and Klaus Balkenhol, are still left under-rewarded for the beauty, correctness and harmony of horsemanship in evidence.

But at least, they are out there, the real horsemen and women who exemplify their love and passion for horses with performances in partnership with their equine partners, putting themselves on the line and in the public eye.

And so am I, and so are my students, albeit on a much smaller scale. But who knows what seeds we may plant on the level of the grassroots scene?

14 Dressage Derailed

November 2009

It's like watching a train-wreck in slow motion. A magnificent horse, struggling in a straightjacket punishingly enforced between his rider's seat and a double bridle leveraged by the rider's back and braced legs, a curb bit engaged to the max. The deep chestnut stallion struggles through a dans macabre, his legs jerking unnaturally through paces that look less like those of a horse and more like a hopping puppet on a string. And then the stunner, the slack tongue dangling from his mouth. And it's blue, a clear sign of hypoxia. Oblivious, the rider pushes the horse on. The horse, his eyes withdrawn and prematurely old with pain, soldiers on. Finally, realization dawns, the rider halts, adjusts the tongue so it is out of sight, stuffed back in the mouth like an old sock in a leaky faucet…and rides on like all is well, nothing out of the ordinary has just occurred. Carry on, folks, nothing to see here, just a little blue tongue, just another day in paradise.

It's like watching a train wreck in slow motion. The FEI makes another reassuring statement, an investigation is underway, the welfare of the horse always comes first. The FEI machine rumbles slowly on, secure in its own entrenched views while one hand washes the other. But past experience has not inspired confidence in the FEI's commitment to standing up for the horse.

Statement after statement, so-called investigations, and subsequent politically correct and bland declarations that are never acted upon or enforced. Our governing body, fully expecting us to continue to place in them our indiscriminating trust, shows blatant disregard for public concern. Oh, they throw us a few crumbs with supposed investigations that lead nowhere, all the while ignoring studies that at the very least should cause grave concern for the welfare of the Rollkured horse, and more appropriately, long ago should have led to action to outlaw Rollkur at all competitions. Still they lumber on in their arrogance, believing we will continue to trust in their sincerity after they have let us all, and most especially the horses, down, time after time.

What awaits us now? Another halfhearted investigation followed by the recurring theme of FEI? Nothing conclusive, but only in the hands of the trained professional? And then - nothing to see here folks, carry on, just a little extreme manhandling of a horse, just another day in paradise.

But the times are changing, the outrage is growing, and the obvious suffering of the handsome stallion may have finally delivered the point break, the straw that broke the camel's back, the last drop. The FEI should know by now, it's not just another day in the life. Enough is enough.

This rider is not the only rider to fall under Rollkur's dark spell, and far from the only rider to employ the technique at extreme lengths of time. Just about everyone knows the stories. At the Olympics in Australia, one world renowned dressage rider continues on and off in Rollkur for three hours in the punishing heat, simply moving from warm up arena to warm up arena to avoid harassment from the stewards. At an international competition in the US, a steward tries to speak up, instructing a rider her Rollkur time is up. She smartly replies she has not traveled this far to be told she can't ride.

The steward is left high and dry by those that should be enforcing their own laws and statements, and is bullied into silence by the very people he or she is meant to inform and police. The trend has been set, match point to the bullies. Rollkur escalates in public use, culminating in this latest public travesty. Once again, a steward is called to investigate. This steward doesn't even try. Shrugs it off. This particular competitor is not the only rider in the warm up ring exhibiting this behavior.

And one is left to wonder. If a rider discovers the tongue of his horse hanging slackly from his mouth, the color of slate, and all he does is nonchalantly stuff the tongue back in his mount's mouth and then carry on as before – is this a common occurrence for him and others? No shock, no concern, from anybody, except this one complainer? Does this happen in training so often that it causes no feeling or empathy in the rider at all? Is this rider and many like him so deadened to the suffering of their mount that a BLUE and limp tongue causes him no second thoughts? At the very least any Regular Joe would dismount and lead the horse off to a safe place for removal of the bridle and a full investigation as to the state of the animal's mouth, wouldn't he?

Ah, but there's the rub. Hello! What was I thinking? This was no Regular Joe who wouldn't know better! This was a trained professional, a top sporter, as the Dutch like to call it, and Rollkur in all its depravity is justifiable in the hands of a trained professional and top sporter. Because this makes them smarter and better and implies they have such high goals the rest of us just can't understand how right they are to do what they do, it's just so beyond us, and they so above us, they have left us behind in the dust of our own ignorance. So he would know whether or not a limp and blue tongue is cause for concern, unlike us mere mortals who just see the signs of a horse well beyond pain and deep into torture.

I'm sorry, I'm being sarcastic. I get sarcastic when I'm angry, and I admit, I am angry. I am incredulous at the naïveté and arrogance exhibited by the heads of our ruling body who think we will continue to accept their indolence and complacency in the face of such obvious abuse.

So, here comes the defense to the rescue. "Why attack poor so-and-so when he is clearly only one of many perpetrating this form of riding, and when he has to do it if he wants to win, he said so himself, he *has* to?" To which I say why not poor so-and-so? He clearly places winning ahead of the welfare of his horse and was the worst on the day caught on camera. Too bad. If he doesn't want to come under attack for riding like a monster, don't ride like one. He claims to only ride this way for short periods of time. Not only is there ample evidence to the contrary not only in his case, but in the case of any Rollkur rider, but he is missing the point entirely. We don't want to see a horse ridden in Rollkur, at all, for any length of time, period.

Here's my other favorite. "But the horse just got his tongue stuck between the bits, didn't he?" As someone who once rode a horse through an entire test in a double bridle with the horse's tongue caught between the bits (while I put on my show coat he played with the bits, then the bell rang and I rushed to the ring, not realizing something was utterly wrong till I headed down centerline. Being young and stupid I rode the entire test with no contact and only fully understood upon leaving the arena what had happened.) I can tell you that a horse accustomed to having his mouth handled with respect will tell you in no uncertain terms that he is in *pain* and you better not take even the slightest contact.

Which leads me to this point. A tongue does not go blue just from being over or between the bits. It goes blue when blood supply is cut off. This means extreme pressure. And whether the blue tongue was caused by the extreme pressure of a severely and constantly fully leveraged curb bit or from being caught between the two bits, is neither here nor there in the final analysis. Either tells us the horse is abused. If he could carry on as he did with a tongue in a vice between two bits, this horse is accustomed to severe pain and subjugated beyond a personal willpower, stripped of any ability to defend himself, so far gone he does not even try.

If the tongue went blue from bit pressure alone, clearly the forces applied to this horse's mouth are so far beyond what could be considered normal, humane or necessary; it can only be called - abusive.

Let's see. What else? Oh, right. The rider in question now tells us the tongue clearly was not blue. So we are all colorblind as well as ignorant. This view is supported by people signing a petition to support said rider, Rollkur and Intelligent Horsemanship - I'll get to that in a minute - who outright state that they saw no evidence of abuse. Did they watch the same video I did? Perhaps someone could kindly define 'abuse' for me, so that I may understand how continuing to ride, never mind apply extreme pressure to a tongue already blue from lack of circulation does not in any way constitute abuse. Oh right, but the tongue wasn't blue. It just wasn't a healthy pink? I am at a loss.

So, the petition for Rollkur and Intelligent Horsemanship…let me count the ways. No, I better not, I'm overwhelmed with sarcasm. The saving grace is that at the time of writing, this petition has less than eighty signatures, at least half of which are anti Rollkur supporters leaving a statement. But let me say this. 'Intelligent' implies giving something thought, applying lessons learnt with empathy and making a wise decision based on experience and facts.

Uh-oh. Facts. According to the FEI and our Pro-Rollkur friends, we just don't have enough FACTS to support our claim it is abusive. Never mind the 2008 statement by the FEI Veterinary Commission which, according to *Epona TV* stated that:

"The FEI condemns hyperflexion in any equestrian sport as an example of mental abuse."

That was conveniently stricken from the minutes and apparently never made it past the initial press release.

Never mind all those studies showing the effect of Rollkur on the horse's breathing, saliva production, overstraining of anchoring ligaments of the skull leading to tissue and bone growths in the very area being flexed deeply, causing pain and subsequent head tossing and lameness (leading to draw reins and so on.) Not to mention damage to the fragile hyoid bone and surrounding apparatus, essential to swallowing and breathing, causing among other things, excessive drooling. Never mind anyone who knows even a little about horses and their eyesight thus know they can't possibly see where they are going - in itself a stressful situation for a claustrophobic flight animal.

Then there's the stress and strain and ultimate injury through bastardization of bio-mechanical functions as they are short-circuited and redrawn in man's desired and unholy image. Dr. Heuschmann provides us with a whole book, a whole DVD devoted to the study of just what Rollkur does to the musco-skeletal regions of the horse, but none of this holds the interest of the FEI and our Rollkur friends, so much for facts. Who needs them? Not the FEI, not the people in charge. They just need spectators, and revenue.

No, we are all just hysterical anti-Rollkur and anti-Intelligent Horsemanship crazies. Witness the words of David Hunt, president of the International Dressage Trainers Club who recently was quoted in *Dressage Today* dismissing the Rollkur debate as *annoying*, and blithely claiming that the dressage horses of today are happier than those of yesterday. How on earth does he compare the horsemanship of our past great riders to our top and most controversial riders today and make such a claim, and why bother? There have always been good and bad riders, happy and unhappy dressage horses.

But compare the joyful victory lap of Reiner Klimke in 1984 as he and Ahlerich skipped the lights fantastic in perfect harmony with an endless, effortless, one handed single tempi change series all the while waving at the crowd, to today, where horses that have just won the World Cup can't handle a medal ceremony and bolt with rider screaming and sawing on her double bridle? Who needs the runner up to give her horse a lead-in into the arena?

The horses of the past stood well enough for ribbons and trophies, and finished with proud and sometimes playful victory laps, but today? Today our so-called top riders want to *walk* the victory lap, or worse, attend the medal ceremony *on foot*. Are you serious? It's embarrassing to the dressage community as a whole. This, according to the FEI, because they must consider the safety of the horses. Isn't that sweet? Supposedly the best trained horses with riders espousing their wonderful relationship with these said horses, and they can't handle an awards ceremony or a victory lap. It's unsafe…

But mention the dangers of Rollkur and the FEI has nothing to say but glib and politically correct sweet nothings. Are the inmates in fact running the asylum? As for these top sporters and their partnership with their horse, apparently it only goes as far as the curb can hold them, and when there is no trust, only coercion, even that control can run out.

So how does someone like David Hunt define and identify happy horses… unless he believes subjugation and daily pain tops a horse's wish list, I am not sure where he is looking. Perhaps he is confusing the equine version of the North Korean military march with a joyfully expressive horse. (Totilas must make Kim Jong-Il very proud.) Well, he doesn't have to look far for that.

Never has the trend to enforce extreme and unnatural flexion like Rollkur flourished so far and wide as it does today. Yet the condemning testimony against Rollkur of vets and trainers of international stature, David Hunt's very own peers, show that the Rollkur debate is far from a mere trifle, far more than an annoyance, and surely any debate within our community that addresses the wellbeing of our horses should be welcomed. Especially when there is not only mounting evidence against the practice, but when two eyes (heck, even one squinty eye would do,) a little bio-mechanical knowledge and sheer common sense can tell you there is something seriously wrong with the practice of Rollkur.

But perhaps I err on the side of my soft and mushy woman's heart after all. Because, silly me, it isn't really about the horse anymore, never mind dressage, is it? It's about money and prestige, about success and ratings and numbers.

At the recent Global Dressage Forum in the Netherlands, the FEI's statement that they were to look into the Watermill Scandic case, and that the welfare of the horse remains front and center in their concerns, was reiterated by FEI's Executive Sports Director David Holmes, in the first five minutes of the forum. However, the last five minutes of the forum were perhaps more to the point, and certainly more telling.

As the story goes as reported by *Eurodressage.com* and other news outlets, Moderator Richard Davison asked Arthur Kottas what he thought of Totilas. Totilas being the latest wonder horse to hit the scene in best Rollkur fashion. A magazine at the forum shows Totilas and rider Edward Gal in what can most kindly be described as a bizarre distortion of, allegedly, an extended trot.

Mr. Kottas was brutal in his honesty and is reported to have said everything from "I can't tell what gait it is…" to "He reminds me of a Tennessee Walking Horse…" At which point Ton de Ridder, a highly regarded and international dressage trainer and coach who was on the panel, instructed them all that Totilas should not be discussed at the Forum saying : "…he's a crowd pleaser. He fills the stands and we should be grateful for that." This was not challenged by anyone but a lonely German journalist who pointed out that this was just a touch hypocritical. They had been so proud of their forum, how every subject was open to discussion. Every subject but the latest, most crowd pleasing, most abject example of Rollkur at work.

So there it is. It's about filling stands and coffers. And as for the FEI acting on this? What are the chances? They have not had a good track record so far. As Epona TV questions:

"Why has the FEI chosen to ignore the recommendation from its own veterinary commission that the FEI should not support the practice? And why has the FEI chosen to shut down the welfare sub-committee, without replacing it with another body to safeguard the welfare of horses?"

Why indeed and what will it take? Will three petitions that between them total almost 18,000 signatures count? Will they pay attention to the sudden appearance of several anti Rollkur Facebook groups already totaling some 3000 members? How about the website DressageDisgrace.com, devoted to fighting Rollkur swiftly gaining attention and members? Or the letter to Princess Haya, President of the FEI, from the Chairman of the British Horse Society, in classic understated British form emphasizing the need for a proper investigation into "...a competition horse contorted in a way it never appears to choose for itself when in its natural state". All of these and more signal a time fast approaching where Rollkur becomes a mainstream issue, to the degradation of not just the dressage community, but ultimately, the entire equestrian community in the public eye.

Does the FEI realize that apart from anything else, their inertia and lack of commitment to the horse's wellbeing puts us all at risk? If we do not address and take seriously accusations of cruelty within our community ourselves, these issues will become the new cause of animal rights organizations who may well be indiscriminating and cut us all across one board and then where will we be? Ask the outlawed fox hunters of Great Britain just how powerful such a movement can be over time, however absurd the notion may seem to begin with.

As for David Hunt's assertion that dressage horses today are looking 'so much happier and more comfortable,' we are back to another debate - defining the happy horse/athlete. Growing up with traditional dressage values, it was clear that wringing tails and impure gaits due to tension and constriction and a horse so overpowered and simultaneously unbalanced—physically and mentally—as to require a constant full engagement of the curb, neither indicated a well-trained athlete or a happy horse, and in-depth retraining was indicated. Statements such as David Hunt's ought be held up as a great big question mark as to where we are going in the future, and will our sport survive such leadership?

Because if he, President of the International Dressage Trainers Club, can look in the face of a Rollkur horse, with its jerky gaits, over-salivating mouth and glaringly blank, hollow eyes, and call it happy, we are in serious trouble indeed.

What almost frightens me the most is the assumptions made now about dressage. That dressage *is* Rollkur. It is now about 'shapeshifting' and 'modern dressage,' and classical or traditional dressage, based on real horses and honest values grounded in the wellbeing and natural bio-mechanics of the horse is just a frumpy old lady poking around in her backyard on her fat pony. Real training, real dressage is not what the masses want to see, and the paying masses are who the FEI want to hear. After all, they clap far louder than a horse can express his pain and their money weighs far heavier in FEI's pockets than the fate of these horses on their conscience.

It worries me that people no longer recognize that Rollkur is a torturous technique that is happening *to* dressage and to horse sports across the board, but that they simply identify it *with* dressage. It is heartbreaking, it is all the more tragic when glorified by a sport and discipline which holds at its core the uplifting of the horse by improving and strengthening his natural abilities and spirit.

Because the practice of Rollkur does nothing of the sort, and in effect, dismantles the natural bio-mechanics and defenses of the horse, leaving him vulnerable and open to a reinterpretation of his abilities that renders him a grotesque if flashy puppet.

Who are these people who feel justified, indeed elevated and superior by engaging in this practice? Are they monsters? I wanted to know, and so I began surfing the web and looking at faces, to see what hid under the tall hats and over the shiny boots. What I found left me feeling oddly sad and hollow, drained of anger. They all look like such nice and friendly people. I wanted to see horns and warts, pointy teeth and scaly tails. What I found was tall and handsome, blond and pretty, blue eyed and charming. White teeth glinting in full smiles that were inviting and warm. Could these all be good people who were just misguided beyond suspension of my disbelief?

So what is this? A Dressage version of Dr. Jekyll and Mr. Hyde? I just can't fit the pieces together. These cruel riders and their tortured horses don't match these smiling and friendly faces, with their sincere and believable declarations of love for their equine partners. I guess they just love to win, more.

And who are the people in power, who are the people who kowtow to the power mongers of Rollkur, allowing them to ruin a beloved sport, a sport that once represented the pinnacle of equestrian endeavors? It's people like David Holmes, FEI Executive Director of Sports, who made the following statement last week, contradicting his opening statement at the Global Dressage Forum one week before:

"It is ironic that we will presumably conclude that (the rider) hasn't done anything wrong," Holmes said, *"...The horse put the tongue out which became blue at one point, but that has happened to myself with one horse and he fixed it as soon as he noticed it."*

This is supposed to make me feel better? This is supposed to convince me the FEI is on the job and putting the horse's welfare at the fore? Who are these people? Do they hear themselves talking? Well, at least he's not color blind.

But our Sports Director blithely and apparently without remorse confesses to having caused such pain in a horse himself, hardly making him a qualified judge of equine welfare - then he goes on to make a joke of the previous weeks statement by FEI that an *objective* investigation will take place. He *presumes* they will find the rider has done nothing wrong? Then I will *presume* all 'objectivity' will fall in favor of Rollkur, it is smoke and mirrors, its grandeur and its empty promise, its bullies and despots, and the horse will once again be left to fend for itself, thrown under the bus by the FEI gravy train.

It simply highlights again, that what the FEI and the Rollkur crowd continue to fail to understand, something so simple, so simple that even we non top sporters can understand it, is that it's not about classical versus modern. It's not about top sport versus the rest of us.

It's about Rollkur. That Rollkur is not training, never has been, never will be, not in any shape or form, or for any length of time. It is not training, it's abuse. And we don't need a bunch of studies to prove it; we just need eyes in our head and a heart in our chest. But for those who need scientific evidence, it's out there, too, should they be willing to look. But that's the problem so far—they may or may not look, but either way, they are not willing to *see*.

The FEI now faces a huge dilemma. Do the right thing and by doing so imply they have been wrong so far, and face the wrath of the Rollkur crowd, a considerable and powerful bunch. Let it slide once more and surely even they realize, the tide has turned, and it will not be in their favor. Enough with the nonsense, anyone with a heart can see there is no excuse for Rollkur good enough.

And Paul Belasik tells us why in his latest book, *A Search For Collection*:

"The reason why you can't pull a horse's head down to his knees and hold it there is not only because the current science approves or disapproves. The reason why you can't pull a horse's head down to his knees and hold it there day after day, hour after hour, is the same reason why you can't pull a man's head down to his knees and hold it there. The reason is that it is demeaning to the dignity of the horse or man. It is an ethical, philosophical problem, as well as a scientific one. Even in the handling of prisoners of war there are conventions of dignity. When you act this way toward a horse with this unprovoked, irrational and unrelenting constant aggression, you demean everything: the horse, nature, yourself, the art and the observer."

Indeed, the FEI demeans us all by continuing to defend Rollkur, its perpetrators, and ridicules us by expecting us to believe their fallow statements and absurd concoctions, about length of time, professional application, and the happiness of horses. The time has passed for talk; the time is now for action. Rollkur is not training, it is abuse. And FEI? Enough *is* Enough.

In Retrospect, 2019

...That was a mouthful! Reading it now, I am surprised at my own candor and tone, for it is very unusual for me to go there; and amazed it went to print, but Nadja was nothing if not bold. But that blue tongue was the last straw for so many of us who had been waiting for and looking to the FEI to take charge and do the right thing, for the horse.

Sadly, I have long since lost any hope that the FEI has the best interest of horses at heart. The recent endurance horse debacle highlights once again that the FEI has the best interest of the FEI at heart, and horses will pay until it is in the express, financial and political interest of the FEI to pay attention.

The ensuing battle of wills between the FEI, Rollkur defenders and anti-Rollkur activists like Dr. Gerd Heuschmann and French classicalist, Philippe Karl, was much like watching a bad soap opera that started with a bang and lots of drama, but ended in a fizzle that went nowhere much.

I continued to chronicle the unfolding absurdities in my columns, "Rebel of Love," "Smoke and Mirrors," "Life After Kittelgate," and "Dressage Debacle Debunked" which I have chosen not to include because they are much like "Dressage Derailed." Same stuff, different day... Since then, I have decided to leave that world to its machinations and focus on what I can do at the level of the grassroots. We did our level best back then to bring the issue of Rollkur to the forefront of the equestrian mind, and planted some seeds that I like to think are slowly beginning to bear fruit.

Time will tell.

15 Gusto's Journey

March 2010

"So. What now?" said I.

"Hmm…" said Torchlight, thoughtfully munching a smattering of alfalfa, carefully extracted from his four-way mixed hay.

"What do I write about?" asked I, with a touch less patience.

"Hmmm….." said Torchlight, sorting his hay carefully into piles of descending favoritism. Alfalfa first, then Timothy, next Orchard and last Brome. He stood and considered his handiwork with pricked ears, then reached out for a bite of alfalfa and mixed it with a touch of timothy. His eyes closed as he savored the flavor combination.

"Oh for Pete's sake, man, help me out here!" I exclaimed. " I cannot do another piece on Rollkur or whatever we're calling it today, I don't care if our two revered leaders are name-calling and cat fighting, maybe we're imploding as a movement and the top brass are out to lunch, I am just sick of it all, so *what* do I write about? And don't you dare say *hmmm*!"

"Well…" said Torchlight and looked at me slyly from the corner of his eye. "If you had a treat it might just jolt my imagination, trigger an inspiration. If you catch my drift." And then he winked, slowly, but most decidedly, very deliberately.

I pinned him with narrowed eyes but Torchlight knows me well and cares not a whit for slitted eyes. Instead he nuzzled my pocket and waited with a raised eyebrow, confident of imminent success. Sure enough, as if of its own volition, my hand reached into my pocket and handed him his drug of choice, miniature alfalfa cubes with berries. A sure hit, every time.

"Aaaah." said Torchlight. "I feel inspiration seeping into my veins now, it will reach my brain momentarily and I will comprehend. But," said he with innocence stamped on his forehead, "another one of those little thingies might speed the epiphany."

Clenching my jaw and smiling tightly, I handed him another.

"Oh yes," said he. "Oh yes. I understand now."

"What?" I demanded. "What do you understand?"

"You might ask the Oracle" said Torchlight.

"*The Oracle? What* Oracle?" I all but yelled, patience threadbare and tattered.

"The Oracle of Lower Siberia, of course." Torchlight's shrug and raised eyebrows conveyed a slight exasperation that I was unfamiliar with said Oracle. Not to mention loud.

"The Oracle." I repeated stupidly.

"Mm-hmmm. The Oracle. How's your Latin?" asked Torchlight.

"My...what?" said I.

"Your Latin. You know, root of languages like Spanish, French...."

"I know what Latin is," I interrupted, rather rudely. "I don't speak it, though."

"The Oracle does, it's maybe all it speaks, other than horse. Could be a problem, then, a bit of a language barrier there." said Torchlight slowly. "How about Pig Latin, know any Pig Latin?"

I could not believe I was having this conversation. "You want me to speak *pig* Latin with a *horse* that speaks *Latin*?!"

"Actually, he is an Oracle that happens to be incarnated as a horse." Torchlight corrected me. "But you have a point there. He may not be too impressed with Pig Latin. He might even find it offensive. Kick you out on your booty."

"That's a relief," said I lamely, "Because I don't speak Pig Latin either."

Torchlight took a big mouthful of alfalfa, as if to fortify himself. Then he spoke through the corner of his mouth, keeping his head low and eyes deliberately on what would presumably be his next order of hay: "What about Aramaic, know any Aramaic?"

"A-ra-ma-ic?" I was momentarily speechless.

Torchlight took the opportunity to "professorize" some more. "Yes, Aramaic," said he, looking down at me along his, well, long nose. "It's an ancient..."

"I know! An ancient biblical language, thank you very much, Professor T." I took a deep breath. This conversation was not going as I had hoped. Ever my muse, until lately I could always count on Torchlight for inspiration. Now he just seemed intent upon running me around in circles. Could this be revenge for a few too many twenty meter circles of my own back in our heyday? All right, thought I, payback's a bitch, but let's play. Let's play along till I sneak it out of you, you dastardly muse of mine.

"So. This Horse Oracle of yours speaks Aramaic, too?"

In way of answer, Torchlight said, "Do you?"

"NO!" I sputtered, losing sight of my game plan. "I do *not* speak Aramaic and what good is an oracle if all it speaks is two basically extinct languages? If you ask me, that Oracle of yours sounds like a pretty pretentious little wanna be, wanna be, well, Oracle! If he's so smart, why doesn't he speak English, or French or, or German for Pete's sake, whatever, but some modern language anyone can understand!? Huh?"

"Now, now," snickered Torchlight, "Hold your horses." He snorted as he almost got hay stuck in his throat at his own pun.

"For one thing," here Torchlight had to pause to collect himself, so amused was he at his own comedic prowess. "For one thing, he lives in Lower Siberia. I don't know if he speaks Aramaic, but it might be more useful if he was to learn to speak Russian!"

I had lost the game, and I knew it. Furthermore, so did every other horse in the barn not to mention those snarky little donkeys in the front pasture, Tortilla, Salsa and Taco. Donkeys I called my friends. Horses I called my friends. And they were all laughing at me. I might as well have been thrown by one of them and be sitting in a puddle of mud, wearing a horse apple for a hat. The chorus of equine amusement was bad enough, but the burro's braying just added insult to injury. Or was it injury to insult? My ears hurt almost worse than my pride.

"Fine," I muttered, trying to gather my last shreds of dignity. "Fine. Abandon me in my hour of need. Fine muse you turned out to be. See if I'll keep you stocked up on miniature alfalfa cubes with berries." Admittedly, and I am not proud of this, 'berries' came out rather, well, let's just say I was kind of sneering.

Torchlight followed me to his stall door and hung his head out after my, about to be, vanishing back. "Oh come on, be a sport, come back. I'll tell you another story."

Pausing, but not yet turning - after all, I didn't want to appear too desperate - I said, with a touch of sarcasm, "Does it involve another Oracle?"

Torchlight choked his snort on a mouthful of scrumptious Wyoming orchard grass. "Well, that depends."

Oh no, thought I, oh no, I am so not going down that road again. But what choice did I have? I was stuck and I knew it. Worse, Torchlight knew it. "OK." said I. "I'll bite. On what does this depend?"

He tugged at the back of my shirt, leaving a healthy green stain. "Come on, turn around and I'll tell you."

I turned and looked into his soft brown eyes, pursed my lips and told him with my best steely eyed baby blues that I was not in the mood for any more of his pranks. But Torchlight was relentless.

"It depends on who you ask," he said softly and really, I must admit, quite sweetly. He rubbed his nose on my shirt front, then laid his head across my left shoulder for a snuggle, his favorite cuddle stance.

"And who, pray tell, should I ask?" I let him talk me into stroking his face, my left arm draped over his head. Which got heavier and heavier on my shoulder. I steadied myself with my right hand on his shoulder.

"Hmmmm?" he mumbled, lost in cuddle land.

Only a little - and of this I was proud - testily, I repeated my question. "Whoooo should I aaaask?"

"Oh. Gusto, of course."

I stepped back slowly releasing his head but holding his nose in my hands and looked him steadily in the eye, waiting for the punchline.

"Because...Gusto is an Oracle?" I asked suspiciously. Gusto was many spectacular things, but an Oracle?

Torchlight twisted his head slightly in my hands the better to rub the side of his nose in the palm of my hand.

"Well, *he* thinks he is!" The barn erupted in raucous neighing again. Game on, thought I, and stomped to Gusto's stall.

"So, are you or aren't you an Oracle?" I asked Gusto unceremoniously.

"Do you speak Aramaic?" asked Gusto.

Oh my aching head. I sighed. I was definitely going in circles. "No, I do not speak Aramaic, Latin or pig Latin. Nor do I speak French, German or Finnish, never mind Croatian. I do, however, speak Danish and a smattering of Swahili. Jambo sana, Toto. Does. This. Help?"

Torchlight chimed in again. "Hey, how do you say alfalfa cubes with berries in Swahili?"

One dirty look from me and he was bobbing his head, trying to catch a juicy straw hanging and perilously close to falling out of his mouth, eyes innocently on the ceiling, counting birds nests.

"Gusto, come on, what is all this Oracle business and Aramaic and whatnot. What's the story?"

Gusto pulled himself up in the way only he can, somehow majestic, wild and infinitely gentle all at once. "Well, if you must know…"

"I must," said I.

"*I* am the story." He said it simply, and watched me, waiting.

I was sitting in Gusto's stall on a bucket, notebook in hand, waiting expectantly, "So?"

Gusto eyed me thoughtfully. "Remember the first time you sat there like that?" he asked.

"Yes," I smiled at the memory. "You had been here three days and I was sitting here chatting with you, and you lay down at my feet and I got down on the ground with you, and then you put your head in my lap, so I sat with you for twenty minutes and stroked your face while you closed your eyes and just breathed. It was the sweetest, most profoundly moving thing."

Gusto nodded, his amber eyes liquid and glowing in remembrance. "I was reliving my life," he said quietly. "I was feeling every moment I can recall, every step that finally led me to you. I needed to go there one last time before I began to let it go. From the time I was just a little princeling, punk foal in Germany, till the moment you stepped into the stall at my old home. Somehow I always knew I was destined for something special, but I also knew it would be a hard road before I would find that one person who would see me become what I really am. But it's what I had to go through to get to you." He eyed me with a wicked little gleam in his eye, but softened the blow with an affectionate nudge. "Otherwise, you could never have afforded me."

"I can't argue with that," said I. And truly, with his breeding and class, I could only ever have dreamed of it. Had he not been found to be practically unrideable beyond a certain point, labelled a rank rearer, I would never have been sitting here on a bucket calling this horse my own. Only the love and generosity of Gusto's owner, and the sage advice of my mentor, Eddo Hoekstra, made it so.

When Beth offered me this horse, I had already heard about him, both from her but also a few friends who had seen him at his worst along the line. I called and emailed these witnesses and all but one told me to stay away. This horse was done, rank, dangerous. One friend who had seen his last wreck however, said, "It wasn't his fault. If you don't take him and give him a chance, I will if she'll let me." Both she and Beth gave me a detailed account of the accident that subsequently led Gusto to me.

Beth had a young rider working with Gusto and she was doing quite well, although he would still exhibit some issues in certain areas, like freezing at the mounting block. But once he was moving, with a little help initially from a person on the ground leading him, he was working as well as could be expected.

They decided to take him to a clinic for the weekend. The schedule did not allow for much preparation, but still, the first day went well enough. However, on the second day, it was decided that he needed lunging to address what was determined to be a slow hind leg. This proceeded to in-hand work, with the focus on half steps. The clinician warned that this might not be pretty, and indeed, it became a nightmare for all involved.

Trapped in short and tight side reins with a whacking whip at his hind legs, Gusto reared up, tangled his left front leg in the side reins and fell over. Somehow, thrashing and unapproachable, he scrambled back up with his leg still caught in the rein and repeated this pattern twice before the bridle and side reins broke. He was close to being tangled under a fence, but narrowly avoided this second trap.

As Beth watched in horror, the clinician assured her that this was actually a good thing, as he would now learn that rearing could get him hurt. But as Gusto reared in panic, fell, rose and fell again, struggling in his pain, claustrophobia and rage, Beth's decision was made. She had never and would never stop believing in this horse, but she knew she had to seek help in a different place, from a different angle. She had been to my Eddo Hoekstra clinics, she had seen me ride and how Eddo teaches. Not long after came her first email making me an offer I could hardly refuse. Or could I?

I emailed Eddo, confused and uncertain. I had just given away a horse and was happily reduced in horse expenses. I really didn't want another horse. But this horse was calling me. Despite what everyone said, he was calling me, day and night. But I really did not want another project horse now. Especially one that reared. I asked Eddo for advice. He gave it, plain and simple. "You can't not look at him, with that breeding and at that price, or rather lack thereof. Forget everything else, and just go look in his eyes."

One look in Gusto's eyes and my world changed forever.

"My sire is a king amongst horses, you know. So was my grandfather. And I embody their bearing and caliber. I am the culmination of the long life of a man who bred for championship horses." Gusto said it simply, without pretense. "My father, Weltmeyer is his name, is known to be sensitive and intelligent, proud and in command of himself, and I take after him, physically, too, or so I have been told. Sometimes, that means we are labeled difficult. But really, we are just not about to be bullied and forced and though we are more than willing to work, and work hard, it must be fair. I don't mind a little burn in my muscles, I am proud of my abilities and happy to flex them, but I see no reason to tolerate pain. I cannot tolerate unfairness. I will not be taken advantage of. I was born to be of willing service, but not a slave. But you already know that," he said and blew in my hair. He was quiet.

"This destiny you speak of," I hesitated, not sure whether to interrupt his solemn silence, especially not with a question that could be taken for a jest. But his very presence, laser like focus and keen intelligence had always impressed upon me that here was a horse unlike any other I ever met. And after all, earlier I was discussing ancient languages with a horse. Anything was possible. "I am not joking now, but really, ARE you an Oracle?"

I was rewarded with a little snicker.

"Now that does depend," was all he said. Here we go again, I thought, sorry I asked.

"On?"

"On how well you listen and whether you receive the message."

Oh, not a snide answer after all. "On how well I listen." I repeated slowly, tasting the words, letting their impact settle in.

"Yes, we horses, our messages have always been intended for the seekers, for those who listen deeply. If you listen deeply and sincerely enough, just about any horse can be an Oracle."

We sat in silence once more, listening to the wind easing in and around the barn, to the birds chattering quietly in the trees outside. A cat meowed somewhere in the barn and I felt more than heard the steady, deep breathing of horses all around me, as if we were all in a warm, pulsing cocoon of Gusto's making, woven by the power of his presence, the threads of his tale.

It slowly dawned on me, this wasn't just Gusto's story, this was the story of horses all through the ages, all around the globe. They had always been messengers to those who would seek. Numinous messengers of that which lies beyond intellectual understanding. And all the horses were listening in, like the tribe sitting closely around the campfire, hanging on every familiar word as their storyteller spun once again his tale from their past, present and future.

"I was a handsome foal." Gusto broke the silence. A derisive snort was heard from Torchlight's direction. Gusto studiously and with dignity ignored him. "Or so my mother told me. But then, she too was beautiful, and from a very distinguished line herself. Not a day went by she didn't tell me I was bred to be a champion. I had heard of horses disappearing to other countries, never to be heard from again, and worried about such a journey in my future, away from all I held dear. I asked her if she thought I too would disappear into an unknown world. She snorted and said, "They will never let you go. Babies like you are kept in the home country, my dear. So don't you worry. Go nap in that patch of soft grass and sun and I will stand here and guard your dreams." So I stopped worrying. I dreamed I would always be with my friends and family, my brothers and sister who ran with me then."

Here Gusto fell silent once more, but by now I was not about to interrupt his story. Torchlight had no such reservations.

"I had that dream, too," he said, albeit in a voice so low I hardly heard him. Mumblings around the barn went up like a whispered Greek chorus. Apparently, this was a common enough dream amongst foals.

The barn fell silent once more. Somewhere, a horse breathed a deep and heavy sigh, almost a moan. Gusto stirred himself once more.

"But when I was three, that all changed. The breeder died, and his family sold us all, willy-nilly, to the highest bidder. I'll never know where they all went, though sometimes they visit me in dreams. I think some have gone on into the Great Meadow by now, where all horses go when they leave this place, though it seems awfully young for them to have moved on. A few times I have thought I would be there soon myself. A few times it seemed preferable to what I had to live through here. But then my family and friends would come to me, and stand close by me, share their warmth and their breath the way we can only do in dreams, and I would know, it was not time yet, and I must not give up the fight. I still had purpose."

Gusto took a deep breath and swung his head to look me right in the eye. "They told me I would find you. That I would know you when I saw you. And that I should follow you, no matter where you went."

"And you did!" I laughed, remembering. When Beth brought me Gusto, I turned him out in a large round pen with a run connected. I walked slowly around the pen and into and out of the run, hoping to build a connection with this new and mysterious horse before I asked him to follow me on a lead rope. Beth had already warned me he could rear and perhaps even come at me pawing, just leading him around the barn. Gusto immediately exceeded all my expectations. His eyes never left me, and he followed me closely, wherever I went. It was the beginning of a beautiful friendship, as they say.

"You were forewarned, too." Gusto said with certainty.

"How did you know?" I asked, surprised. "I never told you, I didn't want to impose any expectations on you or me." I added, realizing how true that was. I had been forewarned, I had felt the pull of a life-changing event, but I was afraid to believe in my own senses.

"They told me. In my dreams. They said they were showing you the way, too, that you also would know when you saw me. They implored you to take leave of all your senses but the sixth one and take a chance on me."

That explained the calling I had felt, as early as six months before Beth even offered him to me. Beth came for an Eddo Hoekstra clinic and told me of this lovely horse she had, and of all the tragedy in errors she and he had endured together. I felt a pull but ignored it, seeing no way forward. Beth's trainer imported Gusto at three with Beth in mind, lucking into a horse of exceptional breeding, intelligence, temperament and talent due to the breeder's circumstances.

Feeling inexperienced and unequal to the talent of her prize horse, Beth, as so many owners with a talented horse, entrusted him in the care of trainer after trainer. And like so many horses loved by owners who do not trust themselves or their instincts but instead put their faith in trainers, who may or may not have the correct skill-set for their horse, Gusto's career soon took a turn for the worse, into rearing, bucking and bolting, and finally refusing to go forward at all. It is easy to judge and condemn trainers that cause such exquisite horses to become rank rebels, but in truth, when I ride Gusto, I see how tempting it is to mine for the gold buried deep in his DNA, when the nuggets are strewn so close to the surface.

"Oh," I said, realization dawning. "I understand better now, my mind fought all the logistics, but my heart kept urging me on. And then there was the thing with the book."

"The book?" Finally! It was Gusto's turn to ask a question. I felt almost smug.

"A few weeks before Beth contacted me about giving you to me, I was suddenly and unrelentingly compelled to buy a Walter Farley book. I thought I just wanted to reconnect with the beloved books of my childhood. I went online to buy a Black Stallion book, but somehow what arrived in the mail was Walter Farley's *The Island Stallion*."

Gusto's ears perked up. "Any mares in it?" he asked with sudden and intense interest. Ever the ladies' man, as I found out on one trip where his paddock was adjacent to the mares pasture. This turned out to be the source of unending and passionate attraction for my chestnut gelding. He appeared to be unaware of this one little difference between himself and other male horses, and I was not going to be the one to break it to him.

"Yes, Gusto, there are mares in it. But what's more, it's about a young boy who forms a deep and extraordinary bond with a chestnut stallion." I waited for the point of this to sink in.

Gusto considered this piece of information. "Oh, kind of like you and me?" he said brightly.

"I like to think so." I let my finger run down the middle of his forehead and rest in the soft spot between his nostrils. I tickled him and he nudged my forehead.

"Me too," he said and we let it hang in the still air for a long, contented moment.

"You know," said Gusto. "I was pretty excited really, about traveling, taking the first step on this journey of my life, flying overseas and all that. I liked my new person, she was funny and I could tell she really wanted to do the right thing. I felt pretty spiffy, like I was a real horse now. I thought I'd go out and make my mark on the world; show them what I was made of, what could be done with the raw materials of where I came from. And at first, it was OK, it was all fine. I missed home, my family, but I was young and strong and I had a person who adored me. Nothing was too good for me. When she rode me, I felt capable, I could do what she asked of me, and I was happy to try. I knew I made her feel wonderful up there. But then the trainer convinced her she was ruining me, that she should turn me over to the trainer for a year, as she was too inexperienced to do me justice. Justice? I was three years old, maybe four, how much did or should a trainer expect of me by then?"

Gusto gazed into a distant past, and heaved a big breath. He hung his head and pawed gently at the shavings.

"Well, I soon found out. And I would not call what happened next justice. Misguided, painful, frustrating, yes, but not justice. You have a word for it, I think, in your world." Gusto nudged me.

"Oh," said I. "I see. I think we have several words for it actually. They keep coming up with a new one when the last one doesn't cover it up anymore. So that did happen to you?"

I had had my suspicions, because although his x-rays are miraculously clean, what we did find in soft tissue damage was extensive. Starting with a severe imbalance in the muscling of his back, an imbalance that when recognized by Beth had helped prompt his move from a trainer for the first time. He was only four or five years old, and already, his physiology had changed, his right hip had noticeably dropped a few inches and remains dropped today, an imbalance we have addressed through therapeutic shoeing and I continue to address through gymnastic training. He could not move in a straight line but would crab along, hanging to the left, and he still finds it difficult to maintain a left-lead canter on a straight line.

Accompanying this dropped hip was a bulging, spasming muscle in the loin area that has now released, but a slight difference can still be seen if one looks closely. Imagine, I received him as an eleven-year-old, and these injuries were still in evidence. Only Beth had attempted to alleviate these injuries over the years, with rest and therapy, but whenever he returned to training, so did these issues.

My equine massage therapist, Kerry Gowin, found severe scar tissue in abdominal fascia, poll connective tissues, as well as the uneven and completely incorrect back muscling, and he exhibited an extreme tendency to curl up and break at C-3 and C-4, along with TMJ imbalance. Gusto held himself rather than carried himself. He had never wanted to talk about his past before, though. He was just happy to put it behind him, though he always spoke tenderly of his owner.

"She only did what she thought was best for me. And she always bailed me out. She'd fly to wherever I was to check on me. She never stopped believing in me or looking beneath the surface of my behavior or the trainer's stories."

But his body he could not hide. It told its own story. As talented and magnificent as he was, I initially had a hard time defining what always left me feeling oddly imbalanced when I looked at him. And it wasn't just the awe that hit me every time I remembered he was mine, or rather, I was his. This horse, so many other trainers' problem horse and/or reject, was and is the most profoundly moving horse I have ever had the privilege of being around, never mind riding.

Funnily enough, as he began to improve, and his body changed, I could see more clearly what I had not been able to label before as it faded away into a new and increasingly balanced physique that allowed for the flow of energy from tail to poll. When Gusto arrived, all energy and movement stopped at his lower back, and reappeared in the front end. In response to this lack of flow in his back muscles, his hindquarters swung jauntily from side to side at the walk and trot. As supple and mobile as he is, part of this swaying - his Marilyn Monroe walk as Beth calls it - is naturally his, but it is becoming less pronounced as he relearns to allow locomotion through his back, where it is absorbed and redirected as impulsion.

Nonetheless, each session begins with his hind leg moving more up and down than forward as he lets go of his back all over again. Once released, he swims over the earth in powerful strokes.

His beautifully arched neck that appeared with statuesque immobility out of an overly muscled shoulder now swings at the walk and enters the withers and back unimpeded by excessive shoulder flesh. His back which appeared rounded but somewhat low, has become a supple line from withers to sacrum, and movement now undulates freely over his loins and large back muscles. He is more or less free of scar tissue and his back has re-muscled in correct patterns. His neck 'pops' every time we stretch it with treats. But it's taken me 18 months of slow and persistent work and the support of a team of therapists and therapeutic shoeing to make it so. Not to mention Gusto's willing heart, still soft and open even after all he has been through. He is the oyster and the pearl, and you can't just take one and leave the other.

"Ach," said Gusto and turned in disgust. I watched him as he walked the length of his run. I was about to rise and follow when he turned and marched right up to me, nose to nose. Cross eyed, I tried to return his gaze. I tried to remember where it is horses can and cannot see.

As if reading my mind, Gusto said quietly "You know where horses see the best?"

My eyes hurt, not generally used to being cross eyed for this long. But I did not want to break the tender connection of our noses. For one thing, it was kind of sweet, for another, maybe it was a horse thing and I could be committing some major horse etiquette faux pas. My nose, and my eyes, stayed put.

"Er, is it something to do with monocular peripheral mysticism or something like that?" I asked, somewhat nervously, sensing a change in Gusto's demeanor. I felt like I was on trial or at the least in an exam. Too bad it was not a multiple choice question, I could have made an educated guess.

"Try ventricular." Gusto winked and broke the connection. He took a step back and watched me closely. Gratefully, my eyeballs uncrossed without incident and I rubbed them while I considered the clue.

"Erm, ven-tri-cu-lar," as if I was in a spelling bee and would spell it for him next. "...like in...the heart?" I asked, and was rewarded by a slow nod. "Oh! Oh! I get it!" I raised my hand like a schoolgirl. Gusto waited expectantly, ears pricked, head cocked, flicking his tail at a fly. "The heart! You look into people's hearts!"

"Bingo!" called Torchlight and the call went up around the barn. "Bingo!" called Triton in his sweet young tenor, not really understanding but excited to be part of the fun. "Bingo!" drummed Banner in his deep baritone. Echoes rang from horses up and down the barn aisle. "Brrrriiinnngo-oh-oh-oh oooHH!" brayed the burros in perfect unison. I covered my ears.

"Silence!" trumpeted Gusto. The barn wound down in a murmur of chuckles and fell into a reverend quiet once more. Gusto dropped his head till his eyes were only just a little above mine, though far enough away I, mercifully, could avoid going cross eyed. He looked at me intently.

"The hearts of humans, yes. We horses came to give service but the Great One knew this could be a bitter and difficult task in the company of the two-legged. So he gave us the power of insight. To instinctively know what moves in the hearts of the people in whose care we find ourselves, that we may know their pain, their despair, their anger and their fear, and have some understanding when they channel this darkness into our mistreatment. Through understanding comes compassion, and with compassion comes the strength to endure. We are messengers, yes, but only by moving in your midst and subjecting ourselves to your darker selves may we shine our light and deliver our message. And this requires strength, trust and understanding, empathy. Only by witnessing the truth that lives in your hearts can we hope to have the faith and strength to fulfill this task."

I was stunned. I never quite thought of it that way before. "But…" I stuttered slightly, "that is a huge sacrifice! Why would you subject yourselves to such a thing?"

Gusto wagged his head side to side as he considered this.

"There is no real, lasting sacrifice in the service of the Great One," Gusto said. "And perhaps you forget, that if we can look into the hearts of man and see all the darkness that moves within, then we can also see all the potential for good and kindness, the light of compassion, the seed of change that lives in you all, waiting for the day you find the courage to bring it to life. This, too, gives us strength. And we can mirror either. Therein lays our choice and our message."

Gusto tilted his head as if listening to a voice inside himself. Then he continued, his expression darkening, somehow seeping sadness.

"It also, however, causes some horses to allow themselves to be used far harder and far more cruelly than I think even the Great One had ever anticipated. These horses are gifted with such compassion, such insight; they feel the pain of the perpetrator far more deeply than their own. And they carry on despite the cost to themselves. They are called stupid by some, but really they are simply kind beyond human comprehension. I could not, but then I did not feel that it was my purpose to do so. I knew mine was a different path. Many cannot. They fall by the wayside, as so much wasted potential, they are accused of being problematic, rank, having a bad attitude, or their bodies break down. We can only hope that one day their loss will add up to the dawn of a new understanding in the hearts of the people whose hands they passed through."

"Others bear it, but without real understanding, only a resigned submission, weaned too young to have received the full education of their mother's wisdom, or born to mothers who never learnt themselves and have no wisdom to offer, only tales of horror and caution. They have been bullied into submission so young their hearts stop growing long before their bodies, before they have grown to the place where they can truly allow for or undertake this service or the strength of our purpose. They are in a place of perpetual arrested development."

"When they look into your hearts they see only that which frightens them, and it does not awaken compassion, only fear, and so they hide, they hide behind what kindness they can muster, that which comes naturally to all horses. But they can only hide for so long, then their hearts can no longer hold their fear and pain, their heart cracks and they explode. These are the horses, about which they say, oh, but he was so calm, so kind, and then one day he just went crazy over nothing, exploded out of nowhere. But really, it was their hearts that stopped growing and could hold no more pain and no more fear."

"Like Moose," I said quietly, thinking of Gusto's neighbor.

"Yes, like Moose."

"Like me," said Moose sadly from next door. Moose, who had adored his kind owner and held all his fear and frustration from a terrible past on a tight leash till he came to me and I unwittingly opened the door to all his pent-up suffering with my questions and suggestions.

"Moose," I said tentatively, "if you ever, you know, want to talk…or…" I stopped, unsure of how to proceed.

"No, not yet," said Moose quietly. "Let's just keep doing what we're doing, it's helping. But I am not ready to go there, yet, maybe one day." I left it at that.

We sat there, Gusto's nose to my forehead, and I contemplated the enormity of what Gusto had told me. Why? Why would they keep allowing us such privilege? Why, if things had become worse than even their Great One had allowed for, would they keep going? I looked at Gusto and he saw the question written all over my face.

"Because all this is far greater than any of us, and yet it depends upon each and every one of us. Because our Great One is your Creator, and the Universe is home to us all. If we leave one, we are all left behind. You can't have the pearl without the flesh, and you can't have the flesh without the shell, there is no shell without the sand and the sea, whether you like it or think you need it or not. It's not always pretty, it's not always fun, but a deal is a deal, and we will persevere until we have completed this service. It's bigger than all of us. We are drops in the ocean."

I scratched my head. I really needed to change the subject. This lesson in Universal Love stuff from a horse was making my head hurt worse than an FEI statement.

"Uhm, not to change the subject or anything?" I felt my way carefully. "But, what happened next?"

Gusto tossed his head and rolled his eyes. "What didn't happen next? Someone told my owner she really needed to get me out of that first barn, because they saw how I was bound up in a straight jacket, and then she noticed the changes in my back. So she did. She always tried to do the right thing. But she knew I was special, and she wanted so much to see me reach my full potential."

"I went from trainer to trainer, I got better, I got worse, we'd start out fine and then if I gave them an inch they'd take a foot, if I protested they'd ace me, I went to Florida, I came back, I went back to Florida, I came back. I'd give it a try each time, try to give each trainer the benefit of the doubt, knowing my owner loved me dearly and was really trying to give me a chance. But each time they'd say one thing and do another, or they'd say it outright and she'd say no and they'd do it anyway. They'd feel what I could become with time and demand it today, before I had anything but raw talent to carry it off. It would hurt and I'd get scared and mad, I couldn't figure out how to do what they wanted me to when the pain was so bad. I'd try to tell them but they didn't understand so next thing I knew, I was deemed a bad boy and drugged or beaten."

"They trussed me up like a turkey and rode me like an ox. Often, they'd only ride when my owner wasn't around. Or they wouldn't ride me at all. If she showed up they'd drug me to ride me. So finally, I just would have to say 'no' on my own. If they wouldn't listen to my owner, they'd have to listen to me. And one day, she said 'enough.' She always gave me another chance, though, you know? She'd bring me home after another disaster, and I'd come off the trailer wound tight as a yo-yo and rearing just in case someone was going to take a swing at me. She'd love on me, get me all checked out, take care of me, turn me out and let me be a horse. I was lucky, and I knew it. I knew a lot of horses along the way who weren't so lucky. Some of them I still see in my dreams."

"Well, in the end, you and I were both lucky." I said, wanting to draw him away from such sad thoughts.

"Hmm, yes we were." Gusto rested his forehead on my chest and I stroked his ears. "When I had that wreck in the side-reins, I saw it in her face. She just said, 'enough,' it's time to let him go, one way or another. Then I knew it was close, I knew it wouldn't be long. And then you stepped into my stall."

"And then I stepped into your stall."

"And here we are," we both said. And we laughed.

I gazed at Torchlight as he chewed contentedly, eyeing me back with a gleam in his eye.

"Thank you." I said and smiled; a peace offering after all my earlier grumblings. "For sending me to the, err, 'Oracle,' I mean."

"Did you learn anything?" he asked, that gleam still in his eye.

"Oh I hope so. It wasn't for lack of Gusto's trying, at least."

"Yeah, but did you learn anything?" he repeated patiently.

"Well, I learned you are all Oracles." I said, trying a little light hearted banter.

"I meant did you learn any Latin or Aramaic?" Torchlight ducked my swatting hand as if he thought it would actually connect. Old habits die hard.

"Oh, sorry, forgot." I apologized.

"It's OK. I knew you were kidding." He scuffed my arm.

"So you know who Gusto is now, don't you?"

I frowned. Where was this going now? It had been a long day and I was really not up to anymore guessing games.

"Come on, Tom, give me a break. My brain is just smoking as it is."

"I'll make it easy on you," he said. "Who am I?"

"Well," I said, still wondering if this was a trick question. "You're, well, you're…Torchlight?"

"That's right" said Torchlight. "And if I'm Torchlight, then?"

"Then…?" said I, still lost in my inner wafting fog.

Torchlight took a step back and drew himself up to his considerable height in an easy stretch. He released in a pleasurable shudder and turned back to his hay. As he walked away he tossed it off over his shoulder.

"Then Gusto, my dear, is the Torch Bearer."

I smiled in beatific bliss.

In Retrospect, 2019

…That was one of the most fun columns for me to write. It started out as a joke I wanted to play on Nadja, after all the drama and ill feelings of the columns following Dressage Derailed, all the furious updates and re-hashing of the then current events, columns no longer relevant today and so not included in this anthology.

We had recently discussed, with not a little wild giggling, the latest antics of a certain Russian horseman who claimed to be conversing with his prophetic horse in Latin, or something to that effect.

I sent Nadja the first few pages, solemnly declaring this the beginning of my next column, expecting a horrified email in return. Instead, the joke was on me when she insisted I carry on. So now I had to come up with something, and the idea was a Black Beauty kind of story with the horses telling their own stories.

Nadja and our readers so loved the concept that Nadja asked me to carry on in this fashion, but at that time, I began to struggle with inspiration for the column, having rather a lot on my own plate. I wrote a few more columns in my usual style, before our focus shifted entirely to my great adventure in Kenya on horseback. But more about that later.

Gusto, who I still miss every single day, stayed with me till his passing in 2017, at which time I wrote the following…

Some Things Are Not For The Taming…

When most people told me to stay away from the horse I came to call Gusto, my then teacher Eddo Hoekstra told me to look in his eyes. What I saw was not the flickering rage, broken spirit or dead soul I had expected. Instead, I felt my presence acknowledged and met full force by a keen and friendly curiosity, tempered only by the promise of defiance. In the years to come I would learn to appreciate his fierce warrior spirit and utter dedication to the integrity of his own dignity, though it came at a heavy price, the tale told all too clearly in his broken body.

I learned to joke that his motto must be "I have an opinion about that." I found that behind all his wild majesty and naughty shenanigans, his constant need to challenge the status quo, beat the molten heart of an extraordinary character just waiting to be acknowledged for his magnificence, and his pride in the same. When I fully understood and embraced this, his world was my oyster. He gave me all of himself to the last drop, trusting I would never demand too much, or try to keep him for myself.

Gusto was never a horse to be taken for granted; his compliance was always a gift and never a promise.

Gusto was a horse who demanded I meet him in a place of equality, and more often than not, it meant I had to step up. He demanded to feel respect and be respected or it was game over. We never reached the heights for which he was made, but over the nine years we had together, he learned that I would love and nurture him no matter what. That I had his back. That with the help of Stephanie Grant Millham and Classical Horsemanship, I could and would help him heal inside and out, and most of all, that he could trust me, that I would never demand his service in the face of pain, cruelty or unfair demands.

Gusto knew full well what had been taken from him, but together, we experienced flashes of the magnificence to which he was born, fleeting moments of a glorious feel of shared power and lithe balance. We glimpsed a future we would never have but at least, we dreamed a little dream together.

In our last few years together, I felt the full effect of my devotion and dedication returned in his throaty nicker of welcome and the warmth of his gaze upon me, the beam of golden affection enveloping me as I entered the barn. I knew the truth of his heart when he presented his forehead each day for a kiss in what became a ritual greeting, or tenderly wrapped his head and neck around me or one of the girls who helped care for him. I felt his friendship when I wept in his stall and he carefully took the muck fork from me and pressed his head against my arm, asking me to stop and stay with the pain of my breaking heart, to lean on him while it broke.

When his time came, he laid his head in my lap and comforted me as only a horse can, and in that moment I knew that while he belonged only to himself, he had given me all he had to give, in all ways. Our time had come to part, for a horse like him is never one to keep, and never in the face of loss of dignity. A horse like Gusto is always his own, first and foremost, with a destiny of his own and a pride and poise that will not be subjugated. He will break before he will bend in the face of injustice. If Gusto taught me nothing else, he taught me that some things are not for the taming, only for the loving, just as they are.

16 Pretty is as Pretty Does

September 2010

I cannot remember a time when the love of horses did not sing to me its seductive siren song, coursing through my veins like a drug. I do not remember choosing horses, or a moment of realization that I loved them, or my first ride or the first time I let my hands run over a silken hide. As far back as I can remember they were always a part of me, of my life, my dreams and my memories. It seems a choice made in the womb or long before, or not a choice at all. It simply is. It is an irredeemable part of me.

I cannot remember a time when my eyes did not obsessively seek the shape of the horse amongst the cows, sheep and goats that passed before my sight on long road trips. The appearance of a horse never failed to delight me, no matter how shaggy, how old, how bigheaded or weak it appeared. It was a horse, and it had blessed me with its very existence, however fleeting a moment it was. And I was blessed with a mother who shared in and enabled this passion.

I fell in love with every horse I met, and this persistent, recurring infatuation carried me through the ups and downs of the lowly riding school rider who falls in love with every new horse only to see it lost to lameness or a wealthier child.

Further down the road, the same tendency to fall in love regardless of physical merit led to a reputation for handling difficult horses, and bringing out the best in them. And this reputation led me to Torchlight. This time it was more than infatuation. This time, it was love at first sight. It was of no matter that he belonged to someone else, it did not matter he was an off-the-track Thoroughbred recovering from a bowed tendon and tended towards extreme hysterics. Something in him spoke to me and it was a powerful, undeniable call. He challenged me on every level as a horsewoman, a trainer, a rider and even as the devoted owner that I became. Torchlight was my trial by fire, and I am still not sure I passed.

Torchlight inspired this (relatively) regular column, and our story has been told in past issues of *Horses for LIFE*, but even semiretired as he is now, he continues to inspire and demand from me the best of everything I can be. Torchlight taught me that sometimes love alone is not enough, but love informed…now that can move mountains.

I still fall in love with every horse I meet, but now I see more than just a beloved form. Now my eyes seek and consider conformation, hoof angles, shape of head and set of neck, the line and size of shoulders, hips, hocks and stifles, the proportion and balance of forehand to hind end, the length of back and the size of jowl. My mind considers previous training, handling and injuries, sifting and sorting till I have an overall picture of where this horse has been and where I think he needs to go - and how and why. It is this 'How and Why' that has become my guiding light, the question mark at the end of every session. What did we do, and why? And what did it do for the horse?

"I told her pretty is as pretty does."

A trainer I worked for said that to me once, right after telling me that another trainer, this one an Olympic silver medalist and decade long member of the German team, had commented to her that I was a very pretty rider.

This of course popped the balloon of my pleasure at such a fine compliment before I had even finished inflating it, not to mention hurt and infuriated me, but it has stayed with me over the years and, oddly enough, helped me stay the course. This trainer would the one day praise me for my inborn feel, for allowing myself to wait and not allowing technique to overpower the horse; the next, flay me for relying too much on feel and too little on technique.

It was the first time I began to consider what is more important: feel or technique? Combined with her cutting remark, it was a powerful cocktail that still heats my blood. And though at the time it was said with a sarcastic smirk, and stung like a bee just as it was meant to, she inadvertently threw me a bone that I have chewed relentlessly ever since.

Is it just pretty or is it also meaningful? Is this 'pretty' an empty vessel?

Today it has become a major bone of contention in our global dressage community. All these pretty, pretty riders, in their pretty, pretty matching coats and top hats, on their pretty, pretty horses…these self-proclaimed "top sporters." What are they actually doing? Is it just pretty to the eye but at best, does nothing for the creature submitting itself to the ride, at worst is it the unimaginable, call it 'pretty abuse'? Or is it empowering, moving and pleasurable, physically and on every other level, for the horse, the rider, the observer?

These riders that succeed at the highest levels of competition, are they doing their bit to further not only their mount's life and wellbeing, but also the many worthwhile causes of horses worldwide, or are they simply bitting the horse to enslave him to their pleasure and gratification, the lining of their pretty shad belly pockets? Is it all business, promoting this stallion, that mare, their offspring, this sponsor's product, this rider's name, or is there still room allowed to consider the horse as an individual, for his own particular and alternative worth, a worth not measured in sperm count and dollar signs?

The techniques widely employed today, are they about the horse first and foremost - developing him in a harmonious and mutually beneficial manner - or solely about controlling a pretty product intended to sell other, pretty, products?

What does this 'pretty' *do* for the one part of this equation without which none of this would exist?

The much heralded World Equestrian Games are here. I know a few people who are going, and they have been asking me what to look for. It is rare today to see anything to which one can point to and say: "There, that is what it should look like." So instead I give them some general guidelines, rules of thumb.

First of all, I ask them to mentally remove the rider from the equation, in other words, imagine the horse moving through the program all on his own. Often a pretty rider masks all the turmoil below him or her. Now ask yourself, would a horse willingly use his body in this manner if all on his own? It is a fair question, considering everything we do in dressage is supposed to be built on a horse's natural tendencies, a moment of play and proud exhibition in the pasture, for example. We, as riders and trainers are supposed to be asking for and training towards the horse being able to extend these moments almost indefinitely at our request.

So, is the horse comfortable, are his muscles soft yet powerfully engaged? Are his *eyes* soft, his jaw flexible? His tail relaxed and rhythmically swinging all the way from the top of the tailbone, in fact an extension of the spine and as such, an indicator of the state of tension or lack thereof in that spine.

Does he look proud, joyful to be there?

Next, I ask my friends to look only at the front legs and forehand for a little while. Notice everything, how they draw the leg forward, how they swing the shoulder and articulate the joints. Do they look as if they are swimming across the earth, undulating like a seal in the waves through the neck and shoulders? Or do they look like a puppet on a string, the neck short and restricted, the front legs jerking up and down spasmodically? Look for skin folds at the base of the neck, a telltale sign the neck has been retracted. Does the neck look smoothly muscled, one long broad sheet, the arterial groove clearly defined and undercarriage of neck flaccid and relaxed, or does he bulge in one place and hollow in another, often with a bulge right behind the ears and jowl indicating an erroneous head set, not self-carriage?

Now, take time to watch just the hind-end. Do the hind legs consistently stay in front of and go just up to, or barely beyond the plumb line from tail through hock to ground? Do they reach equally, or does one get left behind, flailing out behind the tail every stride as Totilas has demonstrated in the past? Does the horse's back right behind the saddle demonstrate a tendency to bow up, flexing and undulating, or does it stay permanently sagged, leaving the rider sitting in a sling, crossways on a hammock, only held back by appearing to run the saddle into the neck of the horse? Is the rider carried in the trough of a wave, or proudly surging along on the crest?

Now put the front end and the hind end back together, still leaving the rider out, and see if you still think that front end belongs to that hind end. Or is the only thing holding them together….the rider?

Now, let's get really nit-picky. Is the poll, determined as between and right behind the ears, at the very most a few inches behind ears, consistently the highest point, and do his ears point up not tending towards a horizontal flapping? Or does the neck rise to its highest point around the middle of the neck, only to sag like a fishing pole carrying a heavy fish, muscles bulging right behind the ears?

You want to feel like he is pushing through his poll and the flat of his forehead, that his neck, although beautifully arched, is as long as it can get, supported fully by a broad base and extending to an elegant narrowing behind the ears, telescoping from base to poll, allowing for space between every vertebrae, flexibility of poll and jaw, and space for the parotid gland, blood flow and breathing. And yes, does his nose tend more ahead or behind the vertical, does the horse demonstrate an open throat latch or is his head squeezed into his neck, like a turtle peeking out of his shell?

Look at his jowl line. Is there space and a tendency to hollowness in the groove between jowl and neck, or does it consistently, unrelentingly bulge, a sure sign of a horse in a forced and rigid position, not a horse carrying freely from base of neck, allowing for rhythmical undulation all the way through the poll, which would push his nose forwards at the walk and canter, and allow the neck to lengthen while remaining poll high in extensions. Are the hollows above his eyes free of fluid or bulging with the pressure of a forced and held in headset?

When he bends, does he again bulge in the jawline, or can he reach into the bend all through his spine, including all the way through the poll, again allowing the throat latch to open and close as his balance and coordination allows.

Recently some pictures of Totilas were presented on a website, accompanied by the assertion that he today is the world's greatest 'gaited warmblood'. And indeed the pictures, freeze frames taken from video, support that conclusion. Not only does he exhibit seriously impaired gaits, looking at these pictures I added this list of questions to my previous checklist. Ask yourself: is the horse in an uphill balance, balanced on an engaged pelvis, or just leaning back?

Does he lean into turns or stay upright? His withers should be like a shark's fin in the water, always vertical to the horizontal plane even when turning, or pirouetting. Is he moving into the direction of travel, resting dynamically within his center of gravity or leaning back, out of and away from it, simultaneously forced there and saved only by the extreme forward nature of the manner in which he is ridden, continuously one step ahead of disaster?

These freeze frames show us without a doubt that claims of impure gaits winning and excelling in today's dressage arenas are all too true. Yet these serious faults can be hard to spot amongst the exorbitant and jaw dropping performances of today's incredible equine athletes. Watching for purity of gaits can be tricky — just ask the judges who have been rewarding tremendously questionable gaits in the past few decades, and continue to do so even though technology now highlights these extreme faults.

Clearly, it is easier to discern the faults when allowed to watch in slow motion or even still photos, frame by frame. But what is still true and possible to discern by the naked eye, is that we want to see the angle of the forearm match the cannon bone of the opposing hind leg, easily discerned at the walk and trot. The walk should still be four beat, the trot two beat and the canter three beat.

IF it's still to be called dressage, we need to answer the questions mentioned above with certainty. Yes, they are poll high, exhibit an open throat latch, are powerfully flexing through core and their backs and working from their haunches. Yes, the rider rides a surging mountain, not a soggy valley. Yes, they exhibit a true walk, trot and canter. Anything else is simply a caricature. By FEI's very own standards it, is not dressage.

We are told that judges cannot tell a hyper-flexed horse from a classically trained horse as they do not watch the warm up. Every single observation that I ask for above separates the hyper-flexion trained horse from the classically developed one, even when they are no longer held in a straitjacket. It really is not that hard to tell the difference. In the end, their posture and their gaits tell you the truth.

Why does it matter? You may well ask. I could get very technical now. I could address in depth the issue of Diagonal Advanced Placement or DAP, where the hind leg lands before its diagonal foreleg counterpart, and even leaves the ground before the front leg, introducing the 'ground tension' talked about by riders today as the horse has to push off ever harder resulting in a spectacular show trot, not to mention interrupting the natural rhythm and gait of the trot. But most importantly, let me point out that it is telltale of a tight and unnaturally contracted back, a 'statically arched but no longer swinging back' as Stephanie Millham calls it in a recent, succinct article on the subject. Furthermore, this unnatural loading of the foreleg places it under enormous stress, leading to injury. Simply put, the horse is uncomfortable and likely to be injured by the exercise. Surely, that is not our aim, no matter how spectacular the results?

I could spend a few days on the two-beat canter or the four-beat canter, (not to be confused with the school canter of classical schools), all exhibited by today's top dressage horses, clearly viewed in the above mentioned freeze frames, in movement perhaps most easily detected in the canter pirouette where the 'bunny hop'—cantering on both hind-legs instead of one, has become prevalent and an easily discernible fault.

But let's just say this: The 'statically arched back', preventing the correct movement and transmission of energy through the large back muscles, leaves the horse with an unnaturally still, high back, which can fool the eye, leaving you thinking the horse is working over his back, when in fact he is bracing in his back and core muscles - and a hollow lumbar region, his weight very much on his forehand. When asked to come back up, in lieu of shifting his weight and balance to the now blocked hind end, the horse is left no choice but to continue to lean on his forehand. The back under the saddle and forehand drop as the head and neck come up, the rider settles into his hammock and drives harder and harder to keep the show afloat. The canter loses impulsion, and ultimately, its natural rhythm. Once again, he is at risk of severe discomfort and ultimately, injury.

Every point, every observation I have mentioned above are of bio-mechanical importance. They are not just a philosophical or esthetic consideration. They are literally at the core of the overall consideration of the welfare of the horse, a consideration we owe him if we are to claim to put his welfare first, as everyone does.

Simply put, a consistently low poll, shortened neck and following closed throat-latch lead to lack of lateral flexion, difficulty breathing and swallowing, impeded blood flow, degeneration of the occipital joint and connective tissue and vertebrae, not to mention blocks important bio-mechanical functions that allow for the transfer of weight, engagement of core muscles, refinement of balance and lowering of haunches.

The braced back impedes the transmission of energy from the hind-legs, the correct, dynamic use of the core and haunches, leading to soft tissue injuries and calcification of the spine, often exhibited by soreness in the sacroiliac and lumbar regions. The impure gaits in turn lead to ever more loss of balance and rhythm, leading to leg injuries to mention just one possibility.

And I won't even touch on the mental and emotional stress it would place on any being to be asked to perform at extreme levels in such an unnatural manner. I will offer one phrase for your consideration. When you watch a horse, ask yourself this. Could it be he is performing in a state of 'learned helplessness'? It is no more unbelievable than the abused wife who stays with and even defends her brutal husband, the hostage who comes to the rescue of her kidnapper. Horses are, ultimately, often too kind for their own good.

As dressage riders and horse lovers we live in unprecedented times. We have watched as our sport evolved to the point where every rule and guideline is broken, and still it wins. It's like a swimmer being awarded the gold medal for drowning in the most spectacular manner.

These rules and guidelines were not grabbed out of thin air. They have been tested and bent and broken before, over centuries of the human ego searching to reinvent the wheel, faster, bigger, better.

All we see today is the wheel reinterpreted yet again, dressed in the emperor's clothes and exhibited on a different, larger stage, yes, but not reinvented, as much as some would like to think so. And reinterpreting a subject does not guarantee the subject will be the better for it, only different from what was before. It's just more circus under a bigger top.

Still, the wheel turns and in the past horsemen seem to always end up coming back to the horse with renewed humility, recognizing that these natural laws of the equine species, these guidelines of accumulated experience are as sound and in the best interest of the horse and human as they ever were. I am hopeful we are seeing the wheel turn once again, and that soon we will see a return to allowing a horse to be a horse, and while helping him be the best he can be, we no longer accept the outright brutalization of the natural laws that govern him as they should us.

Perhaps we will see a turn of the wheel bringing us closer to the heart of the horse once again with this year's World Equestrian Games. I am happy to know there are people there who will do their bit to support the horses and riders trying to get it right. Who will see beyond the pretty, sparkly bling and look through to the heart of the matter, and recognize when 'pretty' is also harmonious, a partnership forged with and between the natural laws and abilities of two sentient beings, willingly, kindly and with respect from both parties. And when it's not.

People who won't just say: "Oooooh, but it's so pretty!" but also "What does this pretty *do*?" Not for the rider, not for the sponsor, not for the owner, not for the audience. Not for future generations of super horses and for a sport gone wild.

What does this pretty do, not *to* the horse, but what does this pretty do, *for* the horse?

In Retrospect, 2019

...I can pretty much (pun intended) just say, yeah, what she said. The exercise described here is still one of my favorite exercises to put people through, because it is so interesting to watch the change in their face and eyes when they begin to break it all down, and suddenly they begin to see the jarring disharmony of what they thought to be a magnificent performance. Try it sometime; you'll see what I mean. It's a real eye opener. Just one warning... once you have seen it, it can't be unseen, and your eyes will never lie to you quite the same again.

In the decade since, plenty has been said about form and function by other, far more accomplished equestrians than me, not only in the dressage world but in the world of jumpers. George Morris and Jimmy Wofford, among others, have spoken out, decrying a lack of education and functional form now haunting jumper riders across the board. I have had my own run-ins with these differences, and found them most confusing as a Dane encountering American ideas, in particular the differentiation between show jumpers and hunter jumpers, for I had always thought jumping to be a straightforward tangent to dressage.

I am by no means a skilled jumper, though I love showjumping and riding cross-country. My studies have always centered on dressage, while dabbling in jumping whenever possible, which has not been nearly enough so far. But when I have ventured out for jumping lessons, I have found myself often at a loss as to the requirements of my position, a position that has always come naturally to me, for which I believe I can thank my upbringing in a culture of traditional, cavalry-based, horsemanship.

Growing up in Denmark, we were required to do all the usual stuff—all manner of seat building exercises, ride and jump without stirrups and reins, gallop cross country and over natural jumps on hacks. One minute we'd be riding dressage, the next required to shorten our stirrups a few holes and go jump that thing over there. There were no special saddles unless you could afford it, and no huge differentiation made between one or the other, the jumping position was a natural outgrowth of the dressage seat. The release was automatic as the horse required in the moment, and your feel and balance informed you.

Imagine my surprise in my first jumping lessons in the United States with a trusted friend, some twenty years ago, to be instructed in sticking out my bum (also known as the duck rump, and hugely uncomfortable,) turning my toes out and focusing on a crest release while criticized mercilessly for all the natural form I had previously been rewarded for. Being unconfident in my own education and ability, I listened too closely, and it took a year of suffering and one show for me to finally understand what was happening, and discard all the nonsense with which my head had been filled.

Going into the warm-up ring for the first jumping show on a horse I trusted and enjoyed immensely, I was filled with uncertainty and anxiety, fed by a confusion regarding my form versus function. Once I had trusted my body to do what it needed to do over fences; now, all my instincts had been muted by the enforcement of a position I could not make sense of. I felt stiff and off balance. Had I really lost touch so completely with what once came naturally to me? Did I really suck as badly as my friend told me?

Walking on a loose rein, I watched as other riders seemed to float by effortlessly in two point positions, gracefully popping over the warm-up jumps. One rider in particular caught my eye, and as she cantered by in perfect poise and bopping harmony with her horse, she unwittingly handed me a priceless gift. As I watched her, it was as if I was hit with a wave of information loaded energy in her wake, my senses flooded with what *that* felt like. My body remembered and I picked up the reins, discarded all the lessons of the past year, and rode like the girl I was. A girl who grew up immersed in the traditional view that form must follow function, and was taught accordingly that harmony was in the balance between horse and rider, not the subjective eye of a judge.

As I rode into the ring, I was still nervous, but I was ready. I had two clean rounds and a hell of a good time. As I rode, my friend watched while chatting to a judge who remarked what a great leg and position that rider had, that with that position the rider ought to be showing equitation. My friend proudly claimed me as one of her own and gleefully told me the story in great detail later.

I never told her I had just thrown all her dictates to the wind and ridden as my horse, body and previous training dictated. I also never told her I had to go home and look up 'equitation classes.' I just quietly thanked all my old teachers who taught me a classical horsemanship that ultimately is always pretty, always tries to do what's right for the horse, and will never go out of style. Even on the African Savannah, but that is a story for a little later.

# 17   The Year of the Clinic

January 2011

Whoosh…there went that year. And with the passing of 2010 went the first decade of a new millennium as we enter the second ten years of the next thousand. It's a little more exciting, a grander vista, when I think of it that way…Where will dressage be a thousand years from now? Well, that I do not know, just fantasizing about that is a whole article in itself, but for now, I will stick to where I have been these past years. The better part of this last decade I have spent here at our farm, starting over and tying up loose ends, building and rebuilding, learning and relearning, discovering and remembering, branching out and filling in the blanks. In other words, what an interesting decade it's been for yours truly, and no year more so than the past one.

2010 was the year of the clinic, a cornucopia of the learning I have sought after all my life. In past years I have attended anywhere from two to ten clinics yearly so it is not that clinics are new to me. Living in a rural area, clinics are often the only mode of receiving the kind of instruction I seek.

So since 2005, blessed as I am with a decent facility, I have been actively hosting clinics myself in order to learn as I seek. But in 2010 I experienced the 'perfect storm' of clinics. I continued with my long standing Eddo Hoekstra series, exploring a playful and technically challenging version of the classical German system where, as Eddo's mentor, Walter Zettl puts it, you ride like a baby in front and a gorilla behind.

Then, as an ardent student of all things dressage, I also lucked into and welcomed the possibility of hosting both a trainer well versed in the French ideology, Carol McArdle, as well as a long time student of Nuno Oliveira's, Stephanie Grant Millham. And as if that were not enough, I had the privilege of bringing several horses to a Manolo Mendez clinic hosted by my friend Holly Hansen, who also provided me with the opportunity to ride in a trainer's seminar to be taught by Anja Beran. Disappointingly, this seminar was cancelled at the last minute due to illness. Another time, I hope.

And right there, at the end of the year, I tucked in a visit to the Parelli center in Florida where Linda Parelli invited me to attend and provide feedback on one of her latest concepts in exploring horsemanship, the Game of Contact.

I have come away from this year with a deep and profound respect for each of these teachers, a sincere appreciation of their individual journeys and a little awed at their commitment to the horse and to teaching according to their beliefs.

It was also a year of being pulled and swayed in all directions, sometimes frustrating, other times enlightening, often confusing—but always interesting! The pendulum swung in every direction, and sometimes I was not sure which way was up, but as so often is the case, the ultimate answer often lay in *it depends* and *in moderation*. Most of all, I learned to trust and depend upon my own feel and the feedback of my horses.

Attending clinics is often an exercise in self-restraint, especially with a new teacher. It is tempting to launch into your life history, your mount's past and present challenges, where you've been and where you want to go, what you think you've accomplished so far (just so they know you're not a complete idiot although your horse is about to make you look it) when most clinicians really just want a minute to evaluate you and your horse for themselves. They will see in an instant what they find lacking and needing attention, and they don't really need or want to know why. They bring their own set of preferences and priorities, and they far from always match those of your last instructors.

At one clinic in the past decade, with none of the above mentioned people, I was chastised for not wearing gloves, as they "were invaluable in the feel of the rider's hands, helping to feel and separate sensations from the horse's mouth and body." I didn't quite find that to be true. At home, I seldom rode with gloves unless it was cold, although I did use them for groundwork, but ever the dutiful, self-doubting student, after that I would sometimes smack myself (though, truth be told, not very hard) and force myself to wear gloves, although I personally felt it inhibited my feel.

Then in my recent clinic with Manolo Mendez, I dutifully wore my gloves, only to be reprimanded for wearing gloves as "…you cannot feel the horse well enough when wearing gloves"! All I could do was smile, say Thank You, (inwardly feeling rewarded for my own personal opinion) pull off my gloves and carry on. What would he care that another teacher, just as sternly, had told me the exact opposite? That I rarely wore gloves at home but allowed myself to be swayed and carry on appearances because of someone else's opinion? Why should I? Lesson learned, and this time, I was only too happy to be corrected. Another reminder that ultimately what counts is what my horse and my own feel tells me.

Not everyone supports and appreciates riding with teachers from different systems. I don't have a problem with that. If you grew up well-rounded in a system that really works for you and every horse you have come across, you are singularly blessed. I never had access to one instructor or any one horse for long enough to become devoted to one system. I did, however, ride a lot of completely dissimilar horses. So now, exploring where the different theories come from isn't just interesting, it's necessary. It's a way of mapping where I have been and finding out it has a name.

It's not unknown, slightly questionable territory after all; it's a relief to find someone else already discovered and named it. It's a way of validating my own little discoveries, made in the quiet of my own backyard. No, I have not been blessed with constant access to great teachers over the years. On the contrary, I have been largely self-taught with the exception of a glorious year here and there with some wonderful instructors, and lately, access to regular clinics.

But mostly, until these past few years, I have learned by trial and error and from some very, very challenging horses. Horses that by the simple virtue of not playing by the books taught me to ride from the heart, not the mind. To ride not from what I knew, but from what I might find. Who had me looking over my shoulder because if anyone saw what I just did they might think me nuts. Not cruel or abusive, just nuts. (But lo and behold, the horse just changed. I guess he does know what he's doing after all.) And now, by learning from all angles, I can begin to understand why I do what I do, what it is that the horses have shown me over the past many years.

Perhaps because I am so largely self-taught, I also have a deep need for a more grounded, official education. To name what so far has been nameless. To understand the lines in the sand, the hieroglyphics on walls in hallowed halls. A diploma might be nice. Something to point to and say: "See! I'm official!"

I want to understand why one teacher might not want me to do this, when another teacher says absolutely do that and why yesterday my horse said, "Do this" but today he says "What the heck?" Only if I truly experience and understand the similarities and differences can I apply any of them intelligently, and can I discard one or the other. I want to be what Nuno Oliveira called a *thinking rider*. Speaking of Nuno Oliveira, I recently read a quote attributed to him. He purportedly stated that:

"Equitation is not an exact science. It is important to feel and not have a system in the mind."

So far, so good. But not everyone appreciates a *thinking rider*.

One of my past clinicians had little but derision for anyone who rode or believed differently than he. There was only one way: his way. He ridiculed me for my searching, my books, my videos, my earnest questioning of techniques and ideas and philosophies. Although I had the utmost respect and regard for his abilities, both as a rider and trainer and indeed, a teacher, I finally was offended enough to remind him that not everyone had the privileged upbringing of his past, growing up in the presence and riding under the watchful eyes of classical masters for years on end.

He was somewhat astounded at this outburst. Taking advantage of his stunned silence, I carried on. Some of us have been digging in the trenches, looking for nuggets for a very long time, I told him. Not a whole lot of classical masters to be found in the wilderness of Africa or the hills of Texas. For some of us, books and videos are the only sources of information for long periods of time, and our horses are our only teachers. And some of us actually want to learn for ourselves, not just be told this is how it is.

Because not only is every horse different, but so is every rider. How it feels to me may be different than how it feels to you. For one, we are built differently, which in subtle ways will affect how our nervous systems interpret information. And every time a rider gets on a different horse, he will be changed in some form or another as well. I am not the same rider on every horse in my barn. I cannot ride our little Lusitano the same way I ride my gigantic draft cross. Nor can I expect my rehabilitated warmblood to respond as does my TB who has spent almost his entire life, well treated and trustingly at my side, yet almost crippled by a pasture injury.

Never mind horse to horse; I could never ride Torchlight the same from day to day! He is mercury, ever rippling and changing and challenging me to catch him if I can. There are general guidelines and requirements to be sure, a common goal, but a static and permanent, train by numbers type of training? Not in my life.

Apart from breed and temperament, a horse's conformation presents its own challenge for the rider and imposes its own little changes in the rider. When I settle my six foot frame and corresponding legs onto a 15 HH, short backed Lusitano or a 14.3 HH Morgan, I cannot rely on the exact same set of skills or take for granted my balance and coordination as on a horse better suited to my size—like my 17 HH draft cross or a 16.2 HH well-built Hanoverian. I must change and adapt to the new situation in which I find myself.

Similarly, the horse is challenged to carry and understand this particular rider's weight distribution and relative balance and skillset. His reactions will change distinctly from rider to rider. Unlike a shorter, short-waisted person, on any horse

I have to work overtime to lower my center of gravity, and my sheer length and height on either side of that center means I have enormous power, my body itself becoming a lever, my seat the fulcrum upon which I can leverage the horse. It sounds so clever, and on a large horse it stands me in good stead.

But in reality, it is very hard for me to perform this with finesse and suppleness on a smaller horse. I have to fine tune and make adjustments constantly that I am not called upon when on a bigger horse that takes up my leg and balances my long neck and back with his own. Once again, I cannot rely solely on one set of skills or position. Apart from anything else, I have to shorten my stirrups on a smaller horse or my legs dangle in the wind……that alone can have a profound effect on my feel and interpretation of the situation at hand.

All this just to say – I am wary of claims that only one way works. So I have to explore them all. And this past year, I got my wish.

When I have received instruction over the years it has mostly been in what I would consider the classical German vein, the kind of dressage taught by Walter Zettl and Eddo Hoekstra. There is no grabbing the horse's mouth and holding on for dear life here, as the Germanic tradition is now widely, and unfortunately, not unjustly, accused of. There is an emphasis on the rider very gently, lightly, giving the contact, a mere lifting to, and not beyond, the corners of the horse's mouth, a contact the horse takes and embellishes only as he is released into a swinging, lifting back and rising withers.

Then, and only then, the horse defines how much contact he needs to perform as requested in this new and refined balance, a weight in your hands that draws your back as much as it does his, that connects you to his back through your seat, a holding of ethereal hands to ensure balance that varies and eventually diminishes in need of support as the strength and ability of the horse to balance within his self-carriage increases. It is a concept I am well at home with, comfy like an old pair of sweatpants.

But what of the French, who swear by the lifting of the forehand to directly load the hind end? *Tout de suite!* Who laughs at the German trained horse, still hanging off his shoulders years later? What of the lifting rein and seat and core, one rein or both together, that appear to charm a resistant horse so much swifter than a low, restricting contact, largely represented by the Germanic style of riding of today?

The German trainer will tell you it leads to a low, braced back and dropped withers, a false headset and disengaged hindquarter. I have seen this. The French will argue it leads to true balance and collection, forgoing the compromise of any extended periods of training that leaves the horse loading the forehand. This, too, I have seen.

A student like myself will tell you I have seen the best and worst of both and think the truth is in the middle, and the horse at hand will determine the method. In this, I have happily found myself supported not just by my horses, but by the teachings of Nuno Oliveira, through his books and my sessions with Stephanie Grant Millham. Stephanie will frequently reference her teacher and it is often a message of moderation.

Although Nuno was widely referred to as a Baucherist, Stephanie often points out that Nuno, when asked, would say: "A little Baucher goes a long way." She also points out that he rode each horse according to that horse's individual requirements, not that of a particular system. One thing is crystal clear when you ride with Stephanie. You are riding first, foremost and always for and from the release of the horse's top line, through what Stephanie calls the 'remedial stretch and bend'. You proceed always and absolutely from this center of balance and relaxation, suppleness and willing submission, and should you lose it, you return to this beginning and reestablish this connection again and again.

It is home, a safe haven, the base of tranquility to both you and your horse. It is the fountain from which springs true dressage, the art of dressage. This, as Stephanie would say, is the hard part. The advanced work is easy as long as you have this foundation. And stay true to it.

When one reads Nuno's own writings, it is easy to see the influence of the master on one of his most devoted students. On the subject of 'A supple, correctly worked horse' he writes:

'So many times riders attribute bad character to horses having a habit of rebellion, when often it is caused by starting certain work without sufficient preparation....

The good rider is not he who, seeing resistances and serious difficulties appear in a new exercise, tries to conquer them at any price, sometimes using violence and brutality, but rather he who, on seeing the resistance rise up, knows how to return to the beginning, to the preparatory exercises, until he has obtained the flexibility and relaxation necessary to start the exercise he is trying to teach...'

I had never encountered the concept of lifting or stroking the reins until I rode with Jane McLoud, who had more effect on my early search than I probably knew at the time. Fiercely devoted to the horse's well-being and correct training,

Jane will allow no low hands grabbing or hanging on the mouth of the horse, no 'sponging' or seesawing, no auxiliary aids.

But unlike many Germanic trainers, even the 'light' ones, Jane did teach the lifting rein. But it was not directly about shifting weight, but rather the following of the horse's mouth, the following rein. Simply put, following wherever the horse went, to show him a light and steady contact that merely followed but never imposed, thus imbuing the horse with trust and curiosity in the hand and ultimately, in contact.

What I found though, was that often the contact that resulted from this was lighter because the horse was free to lift from his withers and *drape* rather than *drop* his neck from the base into the contact, as one often sees with the blocking, low hand.

What set her teachings apart from what one often sees in French taught riders, was that there was a strong emphasis on always and immediately returning the hand to a neutral position as the horse responded. That as the horse relaxed and drew the contact, or even *thought* about it, the rider either adjusted to encourage the horse or if, even better, the horse actively sought it himself, allowed the horse to draw the hands back to neutral. Neutral is that supple place the Germans prefer, where a straight line from elbow to bit allows for the flexing of the elbow, the loosely hanging hinge action of the shoulder and for lightness in the connection.

Jane also taught me the palms up stroking of the reins, (not to be confused with combing the reins) a seldom taught method and yet one of the most useful techniques for teaching contact that I have come across. When I asked where that came from it was Liz Searle, Jane's mentor, who answered: "Oh, it's an old method from the south of France."

It was the first time that I really began to awaken to the fact that there were different schools of thought where dressage was concerned, schools that sprung from different countries and traditions. Until then, I think I thought every decent dressage rider rode as I had been taught, 'light German' and when I saw a heavy-handed rider I simply thought they were misguided and ignorant.

Now I learned there were completely different schools of thought on how to get what ultimately, surely, had to be similar results. Yet Jane and Liz did not teach from the French school. They taught me from the same place as Walter Zettl teaches, the same place from which my original teachers at the riding school in Denmark taught. Liz had learned from the Swedish Baron Hans von Blixen-Finecke, whose emphasis on horse and rider biomechanics was legendary, and thanks to Jane's generosity, I had the privilege of riding in monthly clinics with

Liz on a variety of horses for the better part of two years. Between that and daily lessons with Jane, my education took a steep uphill turn for the better.

The Baron, too, taught in an old Germanic tradition that did not compromise a calm, light and giving hand. That perhaps incorporated modified French teachings without ever giving away the origins. Liz and Jane just happened to openly incorporate methods from other places that they found worked, too. In a subtle, indirect fashion, they taught me to not limit myself to one approach. As long as it does not involve gimmicks, auxiliary aids or harshness, I am interested.

That has become a main tenet of my search. I revel in riding in one school of thought only to switch to another, and in between finding the middle ground where my horse says, "Yes, that's it!" I find myself confused and exasperated, disturbed and frustrated only to wake up and have the big A-ha light shining in my face. Yes, I can ride with contact and swinging back and still experience lightness. Yes, I can ask a horse to directly shift his weight to his hindquarters and ride forward on a more uphill, still swinging, 'drawing through his poll' horse. But I have my caveats now, informed by my horses. I can't shift the weight through a braced and/or chiropractically challenged back and I can't experience lightness on a horse hanging off his shoulders. Are you impressed? Wait! Don't answer that.

As I have experimented throughout the year, I have found my horses and I questioning and searching within all our lessons, some of which were diametrically opposed, all of which had merit, often from minute to minute and in one big muddily mess! Little by little I have made sense of it, weaving my way through all these different approaches and traditions. I find none of them are all wrong and none of them are all right. It all depends upon the timing and the skill with which it is performed. But most of all, it depends upon the horse.

Our Lusitano, Tazo, will not - and likely never will - draw my hand in the fashion my warmblood prefers, with absolute conviction. However, since his neck is set on somewhat lower and flatter than most of his breed, and due to the compression of past training, just picking him up, shifting his weight and riding on does not work either but soon leads to an even shorter neck and tighter back. He needs a subtle blend of both, where he is allowed to find his own balance. There is an excruciatingly narrow window within which he lets go and begins to swing while embracing his inborn balance and gifts for collection while using his neck well.

My warmblood, though unusually gifted for collection, will not connect as well and relax his back with the direct shifting of weight as the Lusitano, although he happily shifts his weight as long as I have first released his back fully. And I mean *fully*. But I have to feel very closely and sometimes make a little compromise in front to back balance in order to safeguard his back's full release and hind-leg engagement. But then it can be a useful exercise for this 'stretch monster.'

My Thoroughbred with scar tissue and chiropractic issues will tolerate no direct shift whatsoever and can only handle being ridden in the light Germanic fashion, calmly forward to a light and following hand with countless transitions and lateral work to supple and engage. Then he works beautifully and comes up into self-carriage with no protest.

My draft cross, though as many drafts and draft crosses given to hanging off his shoulders, can tolerate very little direct shifting due to chiropractic issues from having been laid down for surgery, and will get just as heavy from any such attempt as he will if not suppled and ridden well enough in the light Germanic way. He is another exercise in a careful compromise in philosophies leading to the best result. Like the Lusitano, the window for the perfect balance of neck to back and hind leg is excruciatingly slim. I apply a little of each and he ends up giving me the moon…

Should I try to ride any of these horses purely from one narrow understanding of a single philosophy? I would get a very varied set of results, and far from all good. I would fail far more than I would succeed. But there is the catch. I find few really good trainers do it all one way though they claim to represent purely one side. When I listen to and watch my teachers or other really good trainers in action, they are all capable of these apparent compromises. They don't all call it that, but to my outsider's eye I see the similarities more than I see the differences. I see horsemanship, and perhaps, when it comes down to it, the heart of good training has no name other than that - horsemanship.

As I have understood, therein lay Nuno Oliveira's genius. He adjusted to the horse. He studied different philosophies; he discussed, debated and adjusted again. And he rode a wide variety of horses.

When you ride with Carol McArdle, you'd better be up early, wide-eyed and awake and show up fully caffeinated. With a razor sharp intellect, photographic memory and an encyclopedic knowledge of all things horse, her lessons are rich with historical and anecdotal evidence, peppered with stories of her international career as an event rider and her eventual metamorphosis, through a chance encounter with British phenom Christopher Bartle, into a devoted, passionate student of dressage and a Grand Prix rider and trainer.

With Carol, as with Stephanie, I get to momentarily quench my thirst for knowledge, for debate, for a deeper understanding of where the different teachings come from, how they came about, why, what kind of horse and culture helped shape the method, where do they converge, separate, run parallel or diametrically oppose.

After years of exposure to the different schools of thought all over Europe and in America, riding with Eventing greats such as Bert de Nemethy, Jack Le Goff and Jimmy Wofford, Carol discovered a deep love of dressage through her time spent in the barn of Christopher Bartle. Finding herself resonating with the teachings of the French school, these are the principles and techniques she teaches, explains and presents with incredible clarity and excellence of communication. Having had the privilege of taking lessons not only at home on my horses but also on several of her schoolmasters, I know first-hand that Carol exemplifies the best of what her varied background and the French school has to offer.

Her horses were an absolute joy to ride, and there were no hollow backs or fake headsets to be found. There was lightness, there was impulsion, a demand for technical excellence and there was a great deal of fun and redefined learning to be had. I admit to some whooping and outright giggling as I followed her guidance and put her horses through their paces to the best of my abilities. It was humbling as I realized my limitations, and outright exalting to view the road ahead. And through it all, Carol guided me with a passion and confidence, not to mention a great deal of Black Irish humor. In other words, it doesn't hurt that she is wicked funny. Though while we're at it, don't expect too many jokes as you ride. Carol is an intense and devoted teacher, and her focus is absolute from the moment your lesson commences until it's over…so yours better be, too.

And yet, one of my favorite things about Carol is her willingness to listen, to receive your feedback, to discuss and allow you to question her teachings according to what you feel your horse is telling you. There is no ego, no 'my way or the highway.' There is her truth, and then there is you and your horse's response and interpretation of that truth, and she is not just willing, but outright curious to hear it.

When I think about it, that is my favorite thing about all my teachers. That they are willing to sit down and talk to me, to discuss, listen, answer questions, and follow my ramblings as I try to put it into terms that make sense to me. The first teacher since Jane McLoud I had to fully and happily indulge this need in me was Eddo Hoekstra.

One of the perks of hosting clinics is the extra time you get to spend with your clinicians, over breakfast, lunch and dinner, and often, with Eddo, a late night dialogue over a cup of tea, sifting through the day's lessons, the challenges and breakthroughs, the inherent learning of a day well spent in the company of horses.

Eddo's lessons are demanding and challenging, ceaselessly changing and shifting as you seek a better balance and coordination with your horse. There is no rest for the wicked! Or your brain. Eddo has an endless supply of exercises, and often if you are not sure what he is asking, you just look at him. He will be performing along-side you most of the time. I must say, he has an excellent passage and wonderful lateral work! Fun aside, he really does demonstrate for you what he is seeking, and isn't shy about bringing in poles and cavalettis to enrich the lesson, laying them out in various geometrical patterns to supply focal points around which he tailors the lesson.

One of the first things that struck me about Eddo was that rather than focusing on a certain outline, he focuses on skill-building in you and your horse, in the firm faith that this will lead to powerful improvement in balance and skills and thus the horse and rider's self-carriage. His motto is that of his past well-loved teacher, Jan Kluijtmans, *"You can do more than you think."* In Jan, Eddo found a true teacher early on in his career, a teacher whose teachings and philosophy he could not find in any other until he met Walter Zettl. I often hear Eddo echo these words of encouragement in his lessons, encouraging and supporting his students through moments of self-doubt and lapses in confidence. And sure enough, more often than not, students, and their horses, find out they can do more than they ever thought.

Another favorite line of Eddo's that struck a chord in me and immediately endeared him to me is that, *"There is no 'I' in TEAM and you and your horse are, or should be, a team, right?"* As with my other teachers, when Eddo teaches, the horse is always paramount, and the intention behind an exercise is always benign, always with the horse in mind. From Eddo, I first began to understand how a rider and the exercises influence the balance of his horse, for better or worse, and that this balance will affect and inform all other choices made by the horse.

Since then I have concluded that the training pyramid so loved by the masses is missing one very important element that apparently is taken for granted by those in-the-know. The word 'balance', next to each and every step on the scale. After all, without balance, none of those steps may be performed well. Yet, it is often this simple component that is missing while other culprits are blamed.

It was also Eddo who finally broke down a wall for me, a wall between me and higher learning about who can try on more demanding exercises, and when. The answer being anybody, and sooner than you think, as long as you approach them with care, an eye for balance and an acceptance that you may not get there with perfect poise right away! It was also through Eddo that I developed a better understanding of how these exercises were meant to improve the suppleness and wellbeing of a horse, rather than just being a means to showcase his apparent level of training. When that piece of knowing fell into place for me, a whole new vista of understanding and learning opened up for me. I also for the first time really understood the chasm opening up between 'classical' equestrians, and trainers and riders who train mostly to compete.

True for all these clinicians is a love of the very art of training a horse well. They have all been there and done that in the competitive world, even if they no longer actively participate on that scene. And it is not that they shy away from competition but rather that they no longer hear that particular siren's song. Perhaps it lost its charm, struck a sour note. Perhaps, like me, they are perfectly willing to show again, should the right horse and situation arise. But show at any cost, on a horse that does not enjoy the spectacle? Somehow that is just not the point anymore.

When you watch Manolo Mendez handle a horse in his extraordinary, very personal execution of a mix of groundwork and physical therapy, you know you are watching a master at work. I also wondered if what he does could really be taught, or is it a case of one man's genius, a touch, ability, a feel coupled with such vast experience that it cannot be explained let alone copied well. I had the opportunity to ponder all of this, this past spring when I handed over two of my horses for Manolo to evaluate through his in-hand work. I had brought both of my rehabs, Gusto and Moose, of similar backgrounds but with very different outlooks, and having heard of Manolo's unique version of groundwork, I was looking forward to turning them over and watch the work unfold.

What happened next was an in depth peeling away of the layers hiding the essence of each of these horses, hidden under years of abuse and mishandling. The most interesting of these was without a doubt Gusto who suffered years of Rollkur type training, but fought back vehemently until labeled unrideable. When I reread the passage quoted from Nuno Oliveira earlier in this article, I thought of Gusto. He and his story are the epitome of the essence of that piece.

As Manolo applied his knowledge and know how, Gusto became more and more involved with his own process. He reached and stretched and flexed his muscles as Manolo applied everything from in-hand exercises to acupressure to techniques gleaned from an extensive field of therapeutic approaches. Manolo identified all his tight spots, his imbalances and irregularities, and by the end of the second day, I met a new Gusto, the horse he might once have been, with a new freedom and elasticity in his stride. Watching Manolo work Gusto helped me see what I had been missing, simply because I did not even know it was available.

Gusto had already come a long way from the rearing rebel that flounced into my life two years earlier. Now I got to have a glimpse of the past and future, all rolled into one. What I had thought non-existent or perhaps lost, was only hidden. I came away with a great deal of food for thought, and freshly in love with my own horse.

Looking back, I realize it was like watching a masterful art conservator apply his tools and techniques to a grimy painting and, moment by moment, reveal the lovely original beneath the tarnish.

It's a collaborative effort, and every one of my teachers can claim a piece of this pie! Sometimes because they saw something so different, sometimes just because they said the same thing, only differently. But all because they are generous, passionate and completely devoted to the horse, and to passing on their teachings and the wisdom of their own teachers. For now, my mind and my own riding and in-hand and line work are all bubbling around in one big melting pot as I experiment, learn, make mistakes and sometimes, just happen to make a big difference in somebody's life.

Come to think of it, the same could be said of my last big learning experience of 2010: Linda Parelli's presentation in Florida of her new concept, The Contact Game. A new concept that covers and reintroduces some very old ground. Through her studies with Walter Zettl over the past five years, Linda has gained a whole new depth of understanding of dressage and the principles that guide it. I have known Linda for some six years now, and it has been fascinating to observe her on her journey and how she brings her own keen intelligence to the subject matter at hand.

A controversial persona, what many people do not know or care to give Linda credit for, is the one thing that endears her to me the most. She is an earnest and passionate seeker in her own right. And though we don't always agree, she never ceases to impress me with her ability to observe, analyze and verbalize. Not one to be bound for long by conventional thinking, she is able to cut through the fog and reinterpret, most succinctly, that which many of us fail to define entirely, or at best need an hour to express.

So when she invited me to Florida to attend her first presentation on the concept, I did not hesitate to accept. Simply put, with the Contact Game, Linda brings together in one concept all her observations and dissertations on how a horse comes around to taking contact and connecting from back to front. What made it all the more fascinating was that as I sat there for several days and listened and observed as Linda worked with a wide range of students and horses, levels of ability and experience, I realized that this course was the perfect book end to my year of clinics.

It wasn't because Linda presented a new array of techniques; on the contrary, these were all familiar to me. It was that she turned the spotlight on to them from a different angle, brought them all together in one setting, under one heading. I saw shades of the French school, of the Germanic, of pure biomechanics teachings, of the subtle blend that I learned from Jane and Liz and that I now get to explore further with Stephanie, Carol and Eddo. It was, simply put, just the straightforward ways of any well rounded horseman.

It wasn't anything new under the sun, it was that horsemanship that cannot be pigeonholed, that cannot be claimed by any one country, discipline, philosophy or person. It was horsemanship that has been taught for centuries by long gone masters, exposed by yet another inquiring mind. And it was, in retrospect, an ironic setting for me to receive confirmation for some of my own hard earned lessons in dressage, here at a most unconventional, non-dressage, dressage clinic.

It also, by virtue of its setting, told me once again, that there IS only one way, and that is the way of the horse. The individual horse. All of these philosophies are right, and all of them are wrong, and whether blended together or separate, they are all capable of moments of blissful perfection or dreadful destruction.

The more I have ridden different horses, different breeds, and gained knowledge of the culture and demands that produced them, the more I have begun to see why there are different traditions, different schools. And I just can't entirely discount one or any of them. Because just when I do, a horse shows up that says, *"Hey! Gimme some of that. For today, at least."*

In Retrospect, 2019

...That was my last *Riding by Torchlight* column for *Horses For LIFE*, and the longest! It was a pretty good bang to go out with, now that I think about it, a full circle of sorts, from the early days of searching to a new sense of the width and breadth of Dressage. I had found my place in the equestrian world by returning to my roots, with an education now, more firmly than ever, grounded in Classical Horsemanship.

By then, the magazine was becoming so huge, each issue taking so long to assemble and publish, that it was becoming more of a quarterly than a monthly. It was becoming harder to find my place and voice in all that brilliant information. But more than that, I lost focus as I began to suffer from the effects of a burn out that had been a long time coming. Soon after, I would decide to take a break from the daily training of horses other than my own and those of a few close friends, a decision that was neatly followed by the opportunity to go on a horseback riding safari in Kenya with Offbeat Safaris.

I was to write an article about the safari experience for *Horses For LIFE,* under the *Riding By Torchlight* banner, but the article somehow grew into a book, my memoir *Each Wind That Blows,* and only the first chapter ever made it into the magazine. It wasn't long after that, that Nadja and I parted ways. After an eight year working relationship that had sprung from a mutual love of horses, it sadly ended in a mess of brilliant, but perhaps overly ambitious, ideas gone bad. Perhaps just as well as within a few months of our unhappy farewells, the magazine itself vanished off the face of the internet.

It was the end of a truly insightful, eclectic and visionary magazine, and it was with sadness and regret that I discovered its disappearance, and the unfortunate effects on worldwide subscribers left hanging. While feeling only gratitude and pride to have been a part of it at all, I can well imagine the frustration of paying for something not received.

As for Torchlight himself, he did not enjoy collection for more than a few strides at a time for reasons we never discovered, though in all likelihood his racing days left him with compromised vertebrae that could not allow for the demands of collection itself. Nor did he enjoy semi-retirement. With my changing lifestyle, I often found myself no longer able to give him the kind of focused attention he craved.

Ultimately, he and Curly, my permanently injured Thoroughbred, went to the loving home of a talented and sensitive young trainer in the making, Sarah, where they are loved, adored and Torchlight ridden gently to this day. She has since added my ex-husband's Lusitano, Tazo, to the herd, making her one of my favorite horse people to check in on.

Banner, my beloved draft cross, was a victim of my divorce. Left with three 'heart horses', Gusto, Banner and Apollo, I was faced with the excruciating *Sophie's Choice* of equestrians…who do I keep? I knew I could not continue to provide properly for all three. Gusto, even at twenty, remained a professional's horse, as did Apollo. Only Banner, still rocking on at nineteen, could be re-homed in relative safety.

It was with utter heartbreak that I watched the trailer go down the road that day, as Banner left North Carolina for his new home in Kentucky, just some four hours away. But Cassie had proven herself a worthy recipient of my gentle giant's aging body but still powerful heart, under which spell she had fallen immediately. Cassie gave Banner a wonderful home for the next eighteen months, gifting me with photos, videos and even a painting courtesy of his enormous feet dipped in paint that eased my sorrow at his absence.

Then one day he simply began to lose interest in food and surroundings, and within a few days, he lay down and died with his head in Cassie's lap, causes unknown. He lies buried under an enormous tree in a mountain meadow in Kentucky, but he will always live proudly in my heart, and in Cassie's, for he was a 'heart horse' to us both.

As for my Magnificent Gusto, I had lost him some six months earlier to a freak founder that presented as something completely different, or grew from something completely different into a founder. With all his vim and pizzazz, his pride and warrior-like energy, I could not imagine putting him through years of the challenges and restrictions that come with rehabilitating a foundered horse.

With his previous owner, Beth's, blessing, we gave him a healthy dose of painkiller and walked him the short distance from the rental barn through the woods to my little farm, where he was laid down in the field where I would bury him, on a south facing slope overlooking the pond. His final hour was spent milling around the pastures with Apollo, checking out the home I had thought would soon be his. Now, I get to stand on my deck and look out to where he lies buried in the soil of my new home state, where Apollo and little Braveheart, the Welsh Pony companion, nibble on the spring grass, and remind me of all the times in Texas when I stood on an east facing deck overlooking the fields, admiring my herd of horses, chief among them a certain exquisite Thoroughbred I called Torchlight.

Bonus Materials

Before there was *Riding by Torchlight*, there was a smattering of stories published by *Horses For LIFE*, a kind of parallel finding of voice and footing between myself and the magazine.

In our earliest conversations, Nadja and I discussed my past history with horses, as well as what was coming up for me, chief among them, the East Meets West Clinic taught by Walter Zettl, that was my brain child and my chief concern in the spring of 2005. Nadja requested I write about the clinic after the fact, but in the meantime, that I provide her with some stories from my past experiences.

Here are the best of all those efforts, some of which still leave me scratching my head in wonder. I've also snuck in one little story that never found the right issue and so never made it to print, but I thought worthy of including here.

Equine Hoof in Mouth Syndrome

An extremely rare but serious occurrence

Published sometime in 2005

Equine Hoof in Mouth Syndrome – or EHMS – is indeed so rare an occurrence that I had never heard of it till it happened to a horse in my care. When it happened, I was entirely unprepared as was his trainer (my employer) and we lost precious moments to panic and bewilderment. In the interest of helping people who may experience this unlikely and bizarre event in the future, I decided to tell Quincy's story to a broader audience than my usual barn regulars.

Now, before you rush off to call the vet for an explanation, or switch to your search engine to Google EHMS, let me warn you. Your vet has never heard of it, you will not find it even on the vastness of the World Wide Web. So rare is this syndrome, so unusual, that Google or Yahoo as you may with all your microchips and megabytes in hand, you will not find mention of it. There is no research and no evidence, only the stories of we few privileged and oft times unbelieved witnesses, who wish we had had the presence of mind to photograph this horrific wonder to prove our outlandish story.

Quincy was a handsome 16+ HH 'dirty' Palomino Quarter Horse gelding, a lovely mover and an opinionated fellow, who regularly challenged his owner's abilities and tried his trainer's patience to the ends of its admirably far-flung limits. Nonetheless, he was adored and well loved, and his voice was heard far, wide and ceaselessly upon his owner's arrival. That is, until his not always well earned pound of carrots had arrived in his bucket. In other words, Quincy was a loud and spoiled brat. He was also talented, obviously very intelligent, manipulative and could be highly entertaining. One couldn't help but like him. (As long as you didn't have to ride him, like me.)

One early Tuesday afternoon, I had fed lunch which was then followed by my lesson on the horse chosen by my trainer to be my victim that day. It happened to be Willie, a beautiful black-bay Thoroughbred who lived around the corner from Quincy. It was summer, and summer doors were on a few select stalls. Of course, Quincy being Quincy, Quincy was one of those chosen few. So when I rounded the corner and passed by his stall, I could see through the bars of the closed door into the shadowy interior. That is, had I looked over my shoulder as I headed on past him.

I did not, and would not have, had it not been for his sudden, piercing neighing. I kept on walking, thinking how spoilt he was, and did he really think he deserved a second helping of lunch? Then he screamed again, and this time the desperate edge to his voice sliced through my Post Lesson Exhaustion Induced Dullness of Mind. (This is another syndrome that I may discuss in the future, PLEIDMS.)

I paused and he neighed again, and there was no mistaking the tone. Nonetheless, as I turned I opened my mouth to gently remind him he had already had lunch, when through the bars on his summer door I saw a sight my brain refused to compute, and for several seconds tried to explain away with several implausible explanations, although none were as implausible as the actual truth. My mouth remained open but no sound came out.

Was his right rear hoof stuck behind his ear, caught on the halter? No, wait, impossible, we never put a horse away with a halter on, and I had put him away myself only a few hours before.

Was his hoof somehow stuck behind his ear itself? Impossible, it would simply slide off. But, but, but?

I reached the door and opened it slowly, somewhat illogically thinking I mustn't startle him in this awkward position as well as trying to give myself time to understand what I was seeing. Once the door was open and there were no bars to impede my vision, I was able to fully take stock of the bizarre and dangerous position Quincy had somehow placed himself in.

Quincy's right hind foot, shoe and all, was stuck in his mouth.

How long he had been this way is anybody's guess, but he was quivering and wet with sweat, and his eyes rolled painfully up to my face from his contorted position, his breath pumping rapidly through flared nostrils. For a few seconds I stood spellbound with disbelief, then I touched his neck and said, stupidly, "Don't move, Quincy, I'll be right back." His eyes told the story. Where was he going to go?

I ran from his stall, yelling for my trainer, Jane. Irritably, she emerged from her office where she had been embarking upon a nap. "What?" She snapped.

Panicked, I simply yelled "It's Quincy; he's got his foot stuck in his mouth!"

"He's *what*?" she demanded. I repeated myself and she threw her hands up in the air with a violent shrug and shake of the head.

To her credit, Jane did not panic, but likely assumed I was suffering from momentary insanity, always a distinct possibility, and approached Quincy's stall with annoyed confidence. However, upon a brief inspection of the situation, she lost her composure as surely as I had lost mine, and we babbled in harmony about farriers and vets. "Stay with him, I'll go look for a farrier. I'll call a vet. I'll look for a farrier. I'll look for a vet. Stay." She commanded.

I stayed and entered his stall again, stood by his side, my heart pumping, adrenalin pulsing through my veins as I once again looked him over, trying to think, to be clever, to find a solution to this awful dilemma. In his eyes was a weary panic, exhaustion from his contorted three legged position apparent in his shaking body. I examined his hoof and mouth, made note of how, impossibly, the foot had twisted in his mouth so that the two ends of the shoe were stuck under his upper and lower front teeth, and tried to imagine what a vet or farrier could possibly do for him now. If we sedated him, he'd fall down. If we tried to keep him up much longer with some faint and absurd idea of the farrier removing the shoe, he would surely fall down from sheer exhaustion himself. In both cases, if he fell down he'd break both jaw and leg or hip and pelvis.

All the while I tried to maintain a calm and soothing chatter about help being on the way, just hang in there. But as I finally took in the reality of the situation, I realized there was no time to wait, no time to spare, no more hanging in there. Quincy was about to give up, and then all I could do was keep him company till the vet arrived with a merciful shot of euthanasia.

As if sensing my realization, Quincy suddenly performed a remarkable feat. On his three legs, his body stretched and twisted beyond the realms of a desperately precarious balance, he hobbled and wobbled a half circle around me. He now had me sandwiched between his half-moon shaped figure and the hard, cold wall. If he went down, I'd go down with him, and *under* him. I got the message. It was now or never.

For the first time in my life, I experienced that flash of sensory communication between myself and another non-human, sentient being. With no verbal dialogue possible between us, I looked in his pained eyes and heard not only the plea for release, but a brave commitment to helping me help him in any way, at whatever cost, however painful. I agreed, my heart in my mouth. "Okay, Quincy," I whispered, "here we go."

I placed my right hand on his poll, and my left under the fetlock. One last look in his eyes, we both knew what must be done, and our timing was blessed perfection. Knowing I was about to cause him severe pain, I apologized, then pushed his head and foot towards each other, and as I pushed, I felt him determinedly stretch an impossible extra inch through his neck. I let go with my right hand and was alert enough to wonder briefly that he was able to maintain the extra excruciating stretch as I grabbed the fetlock and pastern between both hands and twisted the leg, allowing the shoe to pop free of his teeth. All the while I prayed to any and all gods that this might work.

It worked. I was almost as unbelieving of our success as I was of the 'accident' itself. Quincy stood trembling, head hung low, breathing rapidly, right hind-leg hanging limply. I gave him a quick hug and ran to relieve Jane's anxiety. Then I returned to his stall to await the vet. I was confident we were not simply awaiting the mercy shot now.

The vet soon arrived and found Quincy with severely stressed and overextended if not torn tendons and muscles. Within a few days, Quincy developed a sizable collection of fluid on the inside of his thigh that required piercing and draining for several months. All in all, his recovery took over three months, but he did recover in full, and returned to his old shenanigans. We shared a special little bond from that day on, of the kind you don't really demonstrate - just a knowing look as you pass each other by, a little pat on the neck, a quick nuzzle on my shoulder. Quincy's owner was wonderfully grateful and appreciative. I didn't feel I deserved it. Quincy had told me what to do. I was just following orders.

The story ran like wildfire through the little horse community, and was met with equal amounts of disbelief and wonder. I had my fifteen minutes of fame, though it felt circumspect. Quincy was the real hero. But the disbelief I could understand. It's still met that way. In all likelihood, you are feeling those very things right now.

But a true story it is. I don't have the pictures to prove it, except the ones in my head that no one else will ever see. But for me, it is more than a great story, and pictures in my head. It was the first time that I so crystal clearly felt direct sensory communication with an animal, a sense of will, choice and expression thereof. It's unfortunate it took a serious emergency to provide me with that experience, but I like to think Quincy's suffering was not in vain, for since then the sheer belief that it was possible has provided me with more opportunities of less urgent nature and ample more evidence.

A few years later I was in need of letters of recommendation for a new work visa. Quincy's owner Connie kindly and readily agreed. I have always wondered what the immigration agent thought when he read the following:

"Susannah had occasion to actually save the life of my horse when he had a freak accident. It was her prompt attention and skilled response to the situation that literally saved his life. The vet said the horse would not have survived had she not been able to remove his hoof from his mouth."

Now you know all there is to know about EHMS – and next time you hear about Equine Hoof in Mouth Syndrome, you can nod wisely and say: "Yes, I have heard of it. Pretty rare, that."

In Retrospect, 2019

…Quincy is still in that same stall, still in Jane's care, both still trucking along, these twenty odd years later. They don't make them like they used to.

On a fun side note: on July 28, 2019, Connie, an accomplished actress, read this very story from the stage of Theatre West in Los Angeles, during the production of *It Happened In LA*. A fun feather in my cap, even if I didn't get to go watch, but I heard the crowds went wild.

Dressage Cross Training and Other Mad Hat Ideas

Published sometime in the fall of 2005

"You want to…*what?*"

That was a common response upon sharing my and professional reiner Craig Johnson's plans for the 'Walter Zettl East Meets West Clinic' in September 2005. Raised eyebrows, dropped jaws or rolling eyeballs and shaking heads. That, or a blank stare. "Why? Whatever for?" was another. The outcry on several internet dressage forums reached a fever pitch upon receiving news that not only were we teaching dressage to reiners, but also to Pat and Linda Parelli.

A few years back, I gave Linda Parelli a Walter Zettl tape. I thought it remarkable and a mark of their commitment to their personal journey of horsemanship that since then, the Parelli's have made every effort to experience and learn from Herr Zettl for themselves. Craig and I felt they had something very unique to add to the clinic itself.

But not everyone saw it that way. Some declared that they simply couldn't see 'wasting their money on a dressage clinic shared with reiners and Natural Horsemanship aficionados. What could they possibly learn from watching dressage taught to non-dressage riders?' Admittedly, it was mainly a few talkers and a great many spectators, but fascinating nonetheless.

Showjumping guru Jimmy Williams had this painted on his trailers: "It's what you learn *after* you think you know everything that matters…." For me, that statement defines the intentions of this clinic.

From all fronts the reactions were mixed. Some immediately resonated with the concept and were intrigued. Others declared it an event long overdue, calling it innovative, genius and inspired. It was found to be absurd, pointless, a waste of Herr Zettl's time….or just a non-issue, what's the big fuss and what's the point?

I found it fascinating that people at the top of their individual game, like Walter Zettl and Craig Johnson, immediately found merit and purpose in the concept. No strangers to cross training, the format appealed to both. But some outspoken individuals whose levels of competence, due to their internet anonymity, can only be guessed at, appeared threatened and appalled at the very idea.

Someone once suggested to me that the most educated and confident in their knowledge will always be open minded to new ideas and applications, or novel concepts, whereas those in the middle will feel threatened and those on the bottom simply follow those in the middle. I often wondered if that wasn't exactly the tendency we were seeing at work here.

Have we drifted so far from the roots and philosophy of traditional dressage? Didn't dressage develop as a beneficial, pragmatic system to improve upon and develop any horse, for any purpose?

There was a time not so long ago when, upon declaring myself a dressage rider and later, trainer, I was met with an expression of respect and comments on the beauty and artistry of the discipline. Now, I find myself greeted with suspicion, often feeling a need to explain what *kind* of dressage enthusiast I am. It is no longer enough to say dressage, now one must define exactly what one does, or more importantly, what one *doesn't* do. I find myself wanting to say that I am not one of THOSE dressage people. I don't use gadgets, gimmicks, Rollkur. I do not confine my rides to the arena. I do cross train, jump and trail ride my *dressage* horses.

I used to say, as a means of classifying myself as one of the *good* dressage people, that I am a Classical Dressage enthusiast. That is, until a highly regarded clinician smiled benignly at me and asked *which* Classical School in particular I might be referring to. Hmm. Initially, I wanted to say the French, riding in lightness and all that, right? And of course, I have been known to hero worship Nuno Oliveira.

But then the Spanish Riding School and their Austro-Hungarian lightness was certainly always upheld as the ideal where I came from...

And, wait, I also grew up on Reiner Klimke and all he represents and cannot decry the German School. Much of what I employ I learnt in that tradition. I once read, that upon asked what he did with a horse that wouldn't piaffe, Reiner Klimke responded "I put him on a train to Nuno Oliveira." That story has stayed with me, reminding me that no matter how accomplished you are, there is always more to be learnt, and others to learn from across boundaries and philosophies, with humility.

Since then I have searched beyond either Oliveira or Klimke. I have read countless books on the subject of dressage and horsemanship in general, and though I am not at all sure which tradition *they* all came out of, all did have in common the focus on dressage for the common good of the horse. The basic concept of dressage as a means to prepare the horse for any kind of ridden activity, as in the European tradition; primarily hunting/cross country, jumping, trail riding. What I have always taken away from those studies has been the knowledge that dressage is for the sake of the horse, as opposed to dressage for the sake of dressage. The gymnastic development of the horse for improved comfort, athleticism and longevity.

Now why wouldn't that apply to say...a reining horse?

One could easily rephrase the old saying about the rose...*a horse by any other name is still a horse.* Be it a particular breed bred for one discipline or another is really meaningless when it comes to true dressage. The basic biomechanics remain the same regardless of conformation and temperament. It still has four legs, a back, one neck and one tail, all connected to one another in more or less the same manner. The horse still has to carry its rider on its back. In order to do this, he employs the same basic means to do so, the same muscle groups and mechanics. These may be used in a gymnastic, beneficial manner, or not. These may still be positively strengthened, reinforced and protected by dressage training regardless of what sport the horse is ultimately employed in.

Why *wouldn't* a reining horse benefit from this? Why wouldn't *any* horse benefit from true dressage? And why wouldn't we all benefit from exploring this avenue?

With all the accusations, controversy, confusion and argument surrounding the *sport* of dressage today, what is becoming of the *art* of dressage? The *purposeful* and *pragmatic* dressage?

I have been accused of refusing to go along with the times. Times change, rules change, and the horses bred today are not the supposedly dreary horses of yesterday. But...they are still horses, aren't they? And were the horses of yesterday really so deficient? Or simply different? We now have horses with magnificent gaits and impressive extensions but they appear unable to collect. Look at pictures of yesteryear and you will see honest collections *and* extensions. A rare sight today as 'leg movers' blind us to the beauty of real 'back movers'. It begs the question: is the importance of breeding taking over from the emphasis on training? No matter how well bred, a horse still needs to be trained to collect and extend over his back and will benefit from true dressage training. But I am getting off topic.

Or am I? The competition world today appears to have become our most extreme and eye popping divergence from the principles and ideals of traditional, or true, dressage. The debate rages around the world. In the meantime, by all accounts, some of our top international riders are intent upon turning the dressage arena into a fashion show à la Paris catwalks. Spectators already turn away from the warmup rings in disgust, never mind staying for the competition. Will a fashion conscious dress code make the difference?

At the end of the day, the question must be: how do we bring back real dressage? Dressage that is about the training of the horse, not the color of our coat and does it match our horse? Does it flow well with that extravagant toe flick?

There will no doubt be many attempts and many suggestions.

In the meantime....down here at the grassroots, although I could not and would not reasonably expect everyone else to enjoy the opportunities in cross training, I *would* argue that here is a wonderful opportunity. It is precisely in applying dressage to non-dressage horses and riders that we may rediscover how beneficial and multifaceted dressage can be. It is in the application of time proven principles to unusual subjects that we reach the core of real dressage. To develop any horse and rider to be the best and most beautiful their abilities will allow. Making the ordinary horse, extraordinary. In riding our designated dressage horses we learn plenty about how to develop a lovely dressage horse, and that is all good and right as it should be. But, in a sense, we come to take it for granted. We expect a certain result from certain exercises, and eventually we get it.

When testing these same basics on horses and riders trained for other purposes, we learn more, we become more thoughtful trainers and riders. We have to stay even closer to the ideals of practical dressage, we learn more about *why* we do the things we otherwise just …do. How may dressage help not only this jumper and eventer, but this reining horse, cutting horse, roping horse, and their riders, improve in their specialty? Initially, we may not always know how, but we may rest assured, *it will*.

We learn that dressage is everything, and far, far more, than we ever thought it could be. That this one discipline may improve *any* other, whilst returning to, and learning more of, itself.

So what's in it for the western rider? Well, plenty, not least of which is that they have a wealth of knowledge and experience to share with us also. Dressage will undoubtedly learn from exposure to the principles and ideals of western riding.

Western riding as a sport is as yet relatively grounded in an awareness of practical applications. Dressage has spent some 2500-4000 years developing, defining and redefining, plummeting and reaching new pinnacles, going from necessary and practical to abusive to art and back again.

Reborn as a competitive sport in the early twentieth century, teetering between art, grim determination and ego gratification. Western riding, on the other hand, developed out of the vaquero tradition (with roots that go back to bull fighting, and thus, traditional dressage) in the past 200 years and as equestrian sport in the past half century or so. It still remains close to its ranch roots.

Developed out of showing off your ranch horse, the disciplines center on ranch chores. A comfortable, obedient yet explosively powerful horse for the long rides and cattle drives, a cow savvy horse that let your hands be free to handle the rope for herd work. A dependable, responsive partner that would get you out of a bind and hang in there on the endless, hard days. In western training there are no terms other than the ordinary, and almost everything still has an everyday, directly understandable application. Even so, there is many a western rider whose skills have reached the level of artistry.

Still, a western rider's explanation of what he asks of the horse remains within the pragmatic domain. This often illuminates the refined and at times elusive, principles of dressage, bringing them back to earth and their original intent, gaining depth and perspective in the process as they are seen in a new light.

Early on in my training experience, I learnt that different people often have very different expectations of their horses, and not just in terms of training. And they more or less get what they expect. Expectations help define our equine experience. Whether our expectations are reasonable or not define the manner in which our expectations play out in reality. But generally speaking, if we reasonably expect our horses to perform in a certain manner, odds are, they will. For better or worse. This can be a bitter pill to swallow; it may even require some soul searching and self-examination, if one is so inclined. And a regrouping in terms of training. But it is inevitable that we have expectations one way or another. They may as well be for the best.

Western riders have certain expectations of their horses that we could well learn from. Expectations of versatility, obedience, and the ability to focus and maintain in spite of external intrusion. The ability to accept responsibility and perform accordingly. What Craig Johnson calls "mental collection." With the ever present end goal of a slack rein, the westerners immediately take up the challenge of creating a horse waiting for the next command, responding to a word, or seat and leg aid with no direct bit to hand contact, other than the inevitable contact the weight of the rein affords.

Perhaps by accepting from the beginning that such a horse is possible, sooner rather than later and not only in French Equitation or the hands of Nuno Oliveira, dressage riders may the sooner trust in a waiting horse, lighter contact, and clearer seat communication. Rather than a glorified end goal, it is a very real, very present opportunity every time we ride. I am not suggesting every dressage rider let go and ride with the wind. We would not reach the gymnastic and collected gaits without the aid of reins, but perhaps they could be attained sooner and much improved through a consistently softer rein, with the expectation that with proper preparation, our horse remains in hand.

What we consider proper preparation changes as our expectations evolve.

In the hands of an accomplished western rider, even the most spirited and energetic horse learns to wait, without losing any of the radiance that defines it. It learns to stand on a loose rein, while remaining at attention. And the very expectation that this is possible is what helps mold the reality. I have heard it said that our dressage horses are just so spirited and powerful you can't expect them to stand still for the halt and salute that initiates a ridden dressage test. No, if you never expect them to, then I can't see why they should, either. Yet a reining horse will walk in on a loose rein, creeping into the arena, halt and remain motionless, only to explode in powerful gallops, rollbacks and sliding stops. After which he walks out quietly on a loose rein. And all this while the audience hoots and hollers, whistles and claps.

Cutting horses, some of which these days are so much influenced by thoroughbred blood as to look purebred, are taught to take responsibility for the cow in front of them. They keep that cow from returning to the herd at all cost. On a loose rein, while the audience rewards every drop and turn and victory with thunderous applause, hooting and hollering. Not distracted by the noise, or acting like a racehorse on Derby day. He was never expected to.

Certainly, I am speaking generally. I am speaking of trends. There are exceptions to every and all rules. There are good and bad riders and trainers in every discipline. So much more reason to explore. To expect more from our horses, each other, and our selves.

What western riders offer in practical application and higher expectations of the horse's mind, the dressage world may complement with refined aids and techniques as well as a deeper understanding of collection and improved balance.

The word collection gets flung around when often the reality is mechanical engagement without gymnastic benefit or improved hind-end orientated balance. A reining horse becomes more comfortable as his gaits level out in smooth strides. Although basically gymnastically involved with top line stretched from tail to poll, the nature of his balance remains almost entirely front end loaded, and the ability of the powerful hindquarters to perform is inhibited. Much like a tractor trying to push forward with the front end loader on the ground, tremendous energy and strain goes into pushing the forehand along. A mere indication of dressage type balance with deeper gymnastic engagement of stifle, not just hocks, would lighten front end and could well mean improved spins, more powerful slides, and in the long run, a sounder horse and useful longevity.

The cutting horse performs in the ultimate forehand to hind end balance. Crouching in front of the cow like a playful dog, then heaving his and the rider's weight left and right in unbelievable bounds to trap the cow in front of him, tap dancing his front feet while heavily anchored in deeply bent hocks. Surely no one can watch these phenomenal athletes at work and be left untouched, in anything short of awe of their capabilities.

How may dressage help these wonders of the equine world? As an alternative to the traditional warm up of loping, I would speculate that a solid basic dressage foundation and warmup pre-competition would not only minimize warm up time, but mean less strain on his back and hocks, as well as a calm, organized mind, with energy not so much depleted as reorganized, ready to be channeled in appropriate directions.

For any western discipline, the addition of a solid gymnastic foundation goes a long way towards preventing injury and long term wear and tear. Working on true gymnastic collection and hind end balance in between more conventional western riding and showing, would mean stronger, better balanced horses with longer, healthier lives.

For the English contingent, cross training is every bit as beneficial. In adding western principles to my day to day training, I am finding my horses more pliable, responsible and fun to be around. I expect more from them outside of the traditional schooling and receive more. Adding the expectation that my horse should be able to perform on a loose rein, from gallop to halt to rein-back, in self carriage and balance, has added timing and responsiveness to my dressage ride, while increasing our commitment to remain on a soft contact throughout. My horse takes more responsibility for staying round and engaged. Adding gentle rollback exercises, a very playful movement for horse and rider, has increased awareness and accessibility to his hindquarters. And relaxing my body position to a western frame allows me to reconnect with a more natural balance before reaffirming the positive tension inherent in the dressage position.

So much for training horses. How about the riders? The dressage tradition has not only defined and refined the exercises and techniques for training horses over the centuries, it has done the same for riders. The cavalry employed a multitude of seat and balance improving exercises which have been passed down for generations. New studies in rider biomechanics affirm the intention behind these exercises, as well as providing new and more specific means to achieving the harmony and balance we strive for.

From dressage we may not only learn about the deeper physically related issues of the horse, but how to prevent their negative manifestation. We learn why gymnastics and the collecting balance are so worthy of our attention, and desirable in our horses, offering them health and soundness, as well as longevity free from injury. With a true dressage foundation comes a built in knowledge and focus on horse and rider biomechanics. With exercises developed just for suppling, others for collecting, and yet others to do both, there is much to be learned from the building blocks developed over millennia of exploring with the horse.

Where the western tradition focuses on the horse as a tool, and why and how to get certain results for certain tasks, the tradition of dressage focuses on improving the horse for his own sake, and for our mutual enjoyment. The successful marriage of the two could culminate in a horse capable of great artistry, power and passion, yet gentle enough for a child to handle.

In the western tradition, the saddle provides an interesting opportunity. Although far from infallible, as an important tool for the working cowboy, it provides support to help keep the rider in the saddle under even the most difficult circumstances. Simultaneously, it encourages and allows the rider to relax into a natural balance with the horse, thereby reducing the likeliness of a spill, as well as allowing the rider the relaxation to soon feel the results of the application of weight aids. This balance may sometimes be more difficult to achieve in an English saddle, where a natural fear of loss of balance and falling may be more immediate. Perhaps this is why in the English tradition we have had to come up with all these exercises to train the seat! But anyone who has watched a horse at any kind of cow work or in the throes of a spin, can be in no doubt that the rider requires exceptional balance and in depth harmony with his mount to succeed in remaining topside. These riders are truly on their balancing point and possess a refinement and feel unique to their tradition.

In the English tradition ad hoc, where the saddle offers little to no security, the rider's seat and balance are immediately imperative to his survival. In dressage in particular, with the focus being on refinement itself, position becomes more than a question of sitting safe and pretty. Like any accomplished western rider, a dressage rider's position becomes a fine tuned instrument in itself, a powerful and intimate connection with the horse, capable of great harm and great artistry. To avoid the first and seek the second, riders and trainers throughout the centuries have been on an endless search for ways to perfect their communion with the horse.

The search goes on, but in the meantime, we have plenty to share, regardless of horse and saddle used. One tradition complements and furthers the other. Just look at Oliveira and Klimke, and the mystery of the piaffe…

In Retrospect, 2019

…I still believe in the beneficial effects of cross training, and sharing concepts and ideas between disciplines. But like Nuno Oliveira said of Baucher, a little goes a long way. I have since found that one must be ever vigilant in the spicing of dressage with cross discipline techniques and ideas.

True dressage is already there, in a way perfect, having already explored all the avenues for physical, psychological, even spiritual harmony with the horse. It exemplifies a discipline of body, mind and soul, that seeks to enhance and preserve, not only the body, but the mind and spirit of the horse. As such, the submission we speak of is in fact *acceptance*, a harmonious and mutual agreement between us and the horse that this is a pleasant, systematic, if at times challenging, endeavor we are engaged in.

In particular in the case of western (and by extension Natural Horsemanship which finds its roots in western) and dressage, it gradually dawned on me that where in the world of dressage a good partnership is defined by this willing acceptance based upon preparation and understanding, in the world of western it is more generally defined by an outright submissive horse, and the expectations and techniques inherent in the traditions differ greatly for that reason.

The techniques employed from the get go demonstrate this difference. While dressage has gone through its own eras of horrific abuse of the horse, in the Classical Horsemanship of the past century, we not only wait till the horse is a minimum of three years of age, we spend many months preparing the horse for the ridden work. We develop him physically and mentally for the task from the ground, allowing him to become accustomed to a posture, balance and alignment that will allow him to carry a rider with relative ease, even from the beginning. The transition from ground work to ridden work is done gradually, over time, with a constant focus on relaxation and the development of suppleness, strength, balance and confidence. The young horse is taught manners in an integrative fashion that start from the moment he is haltered for the first time, manners and cues that generally translate well to life under saddle as each are brought together over time. The handlers strive to set the horse up for success at every turn, to build trust and a sense of pride in accomplishment. The mantra 'less is more' is a standard.

While some western traditions, in particular on the West Coast, grew out of the vaquero tradition, western horsemanship traditions in general are based entirely upon life on the ranch and range. There was rarely time for niceties. They were often dealing with outright wild horses. The horse needed to go to work and make himself useful sooner rather than later. He had to be dependable and unquestioning of his rider's authority. Horses were started swiftly and sometimes, brutally, and techniques were developed primarily based upon how to achieve *submission* in a hurry.

In both traditions, much depends upon the handler himself, the level of feel and tact he brings to the equation, and there are good and bad horsemen and women in both fields. But overall, I have found the difference in technique, expectations and ensuing results to lie in the fine line between submission and acceptance, and clearly prefer the latter for myself.

I also, over my many years in Texas, witnessed all too often a brutality in achieving the Western idea of lightness of contact and level of submission that I could not ever endorse, and I understand there has been some outcry lately about the level of abuse in western riding as well. When cowboys would heckle me for riding on contact, I could only wonder what they thought they were doing as they did what they did on their way to riding on a looped rein.

So yes, while I still feel the tradition of dressage, the grandfather of equestrianism really, has much to offer other disciplines by way of its comprehension of horse and rider biomechanics and equine balance, I have come away from these many years of exploration finding that mostly what other disciplines offer dressage, is a reflection of all it has already comprehended and defined over the millennia. And that these reflections are not always all they are cracked up to be.

And so, as you may guess, while I was present for the early explorative phases and had opportunity to spend time with one of its main proponents, I have my reservations in regards to Western or Cowboy Dressage, never mind Gaited Dressage. But that is another story for another day.

East Meets West
A Groundbreaking Clinic Teaches Dressage Across Disciplines
Published sometime in the fall of 2005

In the multifaceted world of equestrian endeavors, from racing to driving, from English to Western, at first glance one may at times be hard put to find commonalities between disciplines, other than it involving a horse, of course. However, two disciplines from the so-called English and Western worlds respectively, lend themselves easily to comparisons, and are widely regarded as cousin events: 'English' dressage and 'Western' reining. Both require of the horse supreme gymnastic ability and athleticism, coupled with grace and agility, not to mention absolute control, finesse and precision on the part of the rider.

At least, fourteen time World Champion Reining trainer Craig Johnson and I, Susannah Cord, of an infinitely more humble resume but a dressage trainer nonetheless, thought so.

I was raised in Denmark on the classical principles of dressage as a foundation for anything I'd ever want to do on a horse, always mindful of the importance of an independent seat and the positive effects of a solid basic foundation. Again and again I was reminded by my instructors of the importance of a gymnastically fit horse. Little did I or my instructors know that I'd be applying them to western riding one day. But they were right. Dressage has been an excellent foundation for me to spring from. And when Craig and I discuss training, we find we want the same foundation on our horses, we look for the same building blocks. Then we may put it to work in different applications, but basic dressage is basic reining. Basic English, basic Western…basic horsemanship.

In an effort to bring awareness to the common ground between these disciplines as well as highlight the universal usefulness of the principles of dressage, we combined reining and dressage in one clinic, under one roof, and under the tutelage of a one of a kind master of the equestrian arts, Walter Zettl. Of course, I also just really wanted to ride with Herr Zettl again….

I had the great pleasure of riding with Herr Zettl in 2004 in the USDF sponsored Region 9 clinic, and we got to talking about dressage versus western riding in general (since I like to participate in both, I was curious as to Herr Zettl's take on the similarities and differences between dressage and reining in particular).

"I love working with western riders! It is so good to expand the mind and learn from each other!" he exclaimed when I mentioned that I work with a cutting horse trainer in combined clinics, where my dressage seat exercises really help get riders following the horse. (Plus I get to play with cows, never a bad thing.)

Thus, I discovered that Herr Zettl enjoyed teaching western riders and gave the experience of 'crossing over' and value thereof as much significance as I do, if not more. A few weeks later, while mixing feed and ruminating about how to pick Herr Zettl's brain some more, the idea was born to create a clinic around this interest.

With some sixty years of experience, Herr Zettl's knowledge of Classical Dressage and its many applications may justifiably be called supreme, yet he remains curious and enthusiastic about exploring the many nuances and applications of dressage. He readily agreed to the concept, and a date was set.

So now I needed a partner in crime. Craig Johnson seemed the perfect candidate and indeed, he too, readily agreed. We had already spent some time riding together, exchanging ideas and philosophies from different sides of the arena, so to speak. I had also been taking reining lessons from him, and was rather ready for an opportunity to turn the tables on him. However, the challenges in the trade off remained in his favor. At least he was in no danger of turning varying shades of green as I do after each spinning lesson…for someone who avoided any kind of spinning joy rides at the amusement park, small aircraft rides and sailing on less than glassy calm waters, I am proving remarkably resilient, returning time and again for another adventure in holding on to my lunch.

When I asked what made Craig want to co-host this clinic, Craig had a ready answer "Because you asked me to!" As charming as that may be, I didn't believe him for a second. After all, when I came dangerously close to becoming victim to the centrifugal forces of a magnificent spin, he did not help suggest to the horse it slow down. He *clucked* to the horse. So I asked him to dig a little deeper. "Because I believe more in the similarities than the differences between these disciplines. I believe the two worlds have much to offer one another."

Herr Zettl concurred.

The first ever 'East Meets West Clinic' aka 'Dressage and Reining with Dressage Clinic' took place in September 2005 at the magnificent *Stargate Sport Horses* in Bartonville, Texas. Keeping in mind a comment made by Herr Zettl, that too few professionals take the time to ride in clinics themselves, we chose to invite professionals only to ride in the clinic, while open to any and all auditors who were encouraged to attend all lessons.

Four dressage riders and four reiner riders participated, riding in individual lessons. Other than Craig and me, local dressage trainers Audrey Zequeira and Mary Claeys, reiner trainers Brent Loseke and Clint Haverty started off the list when a phone call from Pat and Linda Parelli respectfully requesting an opportunity to ride with Herr Zettl completed the list and brought a whole new aspect to the clinic. Not to mention sparking heated and often rather deploringly erroneous and vicious debates on several internet forums.

The clinic kicked off on a Friday evening with a lecture by Herr Zettl, due to limited space only attended by riders and sponsors of the clinic. Needless to say, I was on pins and needles, wondering how this novel situation with its unusual mix of participants would unfold. I watched and held my breath as Herr Zettl talked about the origins of dressage, going on to the reasons for dressage, how to and what for, all underlined by photos and diagrams.

What I saw as I observed the cowboy hats in particular, was the initial reserve and uncertainty melt into nods and mumbles of agreement and understanding, as well as raised eyebrows as new understanding dawned and heretofore not thought of applications and techniques met with approval. By the end of the lecture, Herr Zettl had not only broken the ice with his humor and charm, but won the respect of, and breathed enthusiasm into, the previously wavering students-to-be. One of my volunteers later told me she overheard Clint Haverty, who had perhaps had the most doubt regarding attending this clinic mumble "This guy really knows what he's talking about…". The next day his wife Liz smiled as she relayed his building excitement at the prospect of riding with Herr Zettl the next day.

The next day arose and if I was on pins and needles the evening before, I was seared through by them that morning. I was the first ride, and though I felt confident our volunteers were well in charge of auditor registration and the clinic schedule, it was difficult to focus on the ride ahead. I kept asking myself "Whose great idea was this anyway?" The first time ever I put on a clinic and this is what I do? Every second another challenge not foreseen arose.

But excitement at the learning opportunities that lay ahead about eclipsed all else. Nonetheless, as I rode in on my, shall we say…*enthusiastic*…Thoroughbred gelding, Major Tom, (soon to be renamed Torchlight,) all I could think about was whether the clinic was unfolding as planned and hoped for. Letting go of the reins of the clinic and picking up the reins of my horse seemed impossible.

It was later remarked that I looked nervous about my ride. My ride? What ride, I was in a panic about the clinic! But soon enough with Herr Zettl's voice in my ear I settled down to the business of riding my horse. We finished in relatively short time, satisfied with having soothed and suppled, calmed, softened and centered both my very nervous horse and my panicked self. With twenty minutes to go, Herr Zettl could so easily have asked us to go on, and try to perform more impressive feats other than quietly circling and transitioning till we came through, but once again we were reminded that it's about the journey not the goal. We had achieved what was feasible that day. We had gained a center and a focus, and it was time well spent. Next please…

As Brent Loseke rode in on his Quarter Horse mare Groovy Chexinic, you could feel the ears prick and the energy shift. What was a Master of Dressage going to ask a cowboy on his reining horse to do? The answer was simple enough. Transitions, leg yields and a solid working trot. Walk trot, trot walk, till the mare was smooth and engaging gymnastically. The western transitions being mainly to a swift stop, tend toward the mechanical with a lack of gymnastic engagement and therefore muscle tone and development. It soon became apparent that preparing the horse through gentle trot/walk transitions built not only control and feel on part of the rider, but engagement, strength and balance in the horse.

Loseke was also asked to post the trot and push his horse's customary jog into a working trot, asking more of her balance and commitment to throughness. At first, you could see both horse and rider hesitate. Is this really what you want? But soon the little mare was swinging softly along on a loose rein with large elastic steps. Their subsequent transitions increased in power and scope.

As Loseke's lesson continued, his confidence in their ability to perform Herr Zettl's requests clearly increased and the work continued in canter with the introduction of canter pirouettes and simple changes. All performed on the lightest of aids, the lightest of contact to the extent of being mainly on a loose rein. As I looked around, I saw nothing but intent and focused faces. It seemed everyone had forgotten it was a dressage trainer teaching dressage to a reining trainer. It had simply become a lesson in horsemanship.

As the day wore on, alternating between dressage and reining riders, this feeling seemed to cement itself. The basic lessons were the same, regardless of horse and equipment. In fact, the only request Herr Zettl had made in regard to equipment was no wire bits. It all came down to the seat, a soft hand, transitions, to gymnastics, to engagement and to being gentle and careful with the horse, always keeping his psychology as a prey animal in mind.

As Herr Zettl would say repeatedly "Ride him like a gorilla behind, and like a baby in front!" Every other word out of the Master's mouth was either "Carefully…" or "Now gently, softly…" The horses all visibly responded to his voice over the speakers, and were drawn to him on the breaks.

Herr Zettl repeatedly pointed out the western horses' ability to stand quietly on a loose rein and he reveled in what was achieved on minimum contact. He often compared this to the tendency in the dressage world, even at world class levels, of skimming past the halt and salute. Why, he asked, should the dressage horses, supposedly trained at higher levels than any other horses in the world, be incapable of something so simple as a quiet halt? Furthermore, Herr Zettl made no bones about his feelings in regard to the trends of modern dressage as opposed to the tenets of Classical Dressage.

In between rides, Herr Zettl fielded questions from the audience, answering with enthusiasm and an obvious deep love and regard for horses. Our carefully planned schedule with fifteen minute breaks between every other ride were thrown to the wind as Herr Zettl plowed on, oblivious to time and the demands on his energy. It was all we could do to interest him in lunch. Rather than wearing out, he seemed increasingly energized as the day wore on, every breakthrough and successful bearing out of his instructions met with outbursts of joy. The faces of the audience opened and laughter and clapping became spontaneous and frequent.

The day ended on a high note, with a benefit dinner and riding exhibition, with proceeds going to The Chisholm Challenge, a Horse Show for Special Riders within the Fort Worth Stock Show and Rodeo. Clinic riders as well as Special Needs Riders representing the Chisholm Challenge performed for an enthusiastic and cheerful crowd, who took all the technical difficulties and mishaps of the evening in stride.

There were dressage demos and reining demos with and without bridles, and of course, the Parelli's with their inspiring liberty work. Even the impromptu and rather technically challenged (our music was reduced to a rather rude noise by the music system, mercilessly loud in the speakers) demo by Craig and myself, was kindly received by the crowd and ended in hysterics when they persuaded us to swap horses, the DQ (Dressage Queen) in white breeches and tall boots on the little Quarter Horse, the cowboy in his hat on my oversized and rather green draft cross. There were bucks and kicks and of course fabulous sliding stops by Craig, but mostly there was a lot of laughter.

But the real thrill for me that evening was when we asked for comments from the audience and Clint Haverty called for the *Second* Annual East Meets West Clinic Thanks to Walter Zettl, Craig Johnson and a host of enthusiastic horse lovers, my little feed room dream had blossomed into a vision beyond my imagination.

Sunday dawned with, if possible, even more enthusiasm on the part of riders and Herr Zettl himself. As we dressage riders continued to build on our foundations and challenge our limitations, the western contingent had now really found their stride and continued to expand their repertoire in leaps and bounds, and Herr Zettl had a ball putting them through established as well as new found paces. The beginnings of a canter pirouette metamorphosed into brilliant, powerful spins, simple changes into screeching, shuddering, dust-flinging sliding stops, and single changes into the first irregular three- and four-tempis.

The grins were from ear to ear as their efforts were met with "YES!" and a fist pumping in the air (Herr Zettl pumping a fist in the air? YES!) and the dialogue that developed between Herr Zettl and the reining riders as the day wore on was everything I had hoped for, and then some. I kept close to the riders as they huddled around Herr Zettl, hanging on his every word, watching every ride with ferocious intensity.

As deeper and more comprehensive understanding took effect, and results became increasingly apparent, one could practically hear the walls come tumbling down and the creativity begin to flow as they discussed applications of technique and exercises within their *speciale*.

Craig Johnson marveled at the newfound power within his already superbly trained horse, simply by elevating his front end through more trot work with greater impulsion and gymnastic transitions.

After grilling me on lateral work shortly before his Sunday ride, Brent Loseke went on to wow us all with his newfound grasp of lateral work and impulsion, not to mention a very respectable first attempt at three and four tempis. Pat Parelli demonstrated how to ride a superbly sensitive, spirited and fine-tuned horse with minimum hand interference and maximum intention and focus, and Clint Haverty simply had a ball doing it all.

Audrey Zequeira showed us what a modern day dressage horse, her gorgeous Hanoverian gelding, Freixenet, should look like as he advanced up the levels toward Fourth Level, and Mary Claeys demonstrated an increasingly soft and harmonious connection as she put her exquisite Baroque stallion, the Andalusian Electrizar, through the paces with Second and Third Level exercises. Linda Parelli finally let us all see what she works on at home behind the scenes, dressage with a touch of Natural Horsemanship (or is it the other way around?) and a great deal of her concept of Fluidity, which allows her to sit her challenging Hanoverian, Remmer, with poise while still allowing him to move freely.

Brent Loseke went on to tie for the win in the Intermediate Open Reining Futurity at The Quarter Horse Congress in Ohio a few weeks later. When congratulated, he said,, "You know I partially credit Walter with that win. I have been spending much more time at the walk and trot and transitions, and the result is my canter work is much better, I have far more control and avoid a lot of problems I would otherwise be dealing with." He and his wife recently joined my husband and me in attending The Spanish Riding School Clinic and Performance in Houston. I think it's fair to say he had a good time. I'd even go so far as to say he is hooked. He mumbled something about wanting more dressage lessons, although he got a little wide eyed when I suggested trying a dressage saddle. And that the Capriole looked like good fun.

Shortly after Loseke's success, I spoke to Craig Johnson who had just returned from another successful show himself. When I congratulated him he said, "Well, you know, I have been using some of those techniques Walter taught us...."

In the end, thanks to the hard work of volunteers, the enthusiasm of Stargate Sport Horses and Craig and Lynn Johnson, the curious minds of horse lovers everywhere and the willingness of a few riders to expose themselves along with the draw and genius of Walter Zettl, we had a clinic and a turnout that far exceeded my hopes and expectations. Over 300 people attended from all over the country. We raised $2500.00 for The Chisholm Challenge. I'd like to think we broke down borders and built bridges. We also confirmed the need for a Second Annual East Meets West Clinic and set the date. September 23-24th, 2006, at Green Valley Ranch in Aubrey, Texas, home to Brent Loseke's training barn. Told you he was hooked.

Premier Equestrian, the company that produce and handle all of Herr Zettl's videos and books were on hand to film the entire clinic, and a DVD has since come out with four rides in their entirety, chosen for the quality and clearness of Herr Zettl's narrative and the subsequent execution of his commands. I make that qualification because I know they didn't choose my ride for its brilliance and superior demonstration of dressage principles. In fact, I challenged the sanity in the choice but was informed that although our ride was mediocre (my words, they were far more diplomatic), Herr Zettl was brilliant and informative.

I can live with that. Being the backdrop for Walter Zettl's brilliance, I mean.

In Retrospect, 2019

…For better or worse, the East Meets West Clinic helped put me on something like a map. The initial reaction and very personal attacks following the announcement of the clinic were more than made up for by the overall effect of the clinic itself, on me, on Walter himself, and on the other riders, in particular the Parelli's and their subsequent work. I was suddenly in receipt of an influx of students from the Natural Horsemanship and western worlds, all of whom contributed greatly to my own education, and informed me of both the possibilities and pitfalls of combining the disciplines.

The second clinic never happened, for reasons I cannot altogether recall, although years later a similar clinic was put on in another part of Texas, using my experience, the name and the format but unfortunately giving no credit.

The DVD of those chosen four rides may still be found in the *Matter of Trust* series of Walter Zettl's work. Sadly, Walter has since passed on, leaving an extraordinary legacy and a world full of mourners who miss his gentle voice, charming spirit and passionate advocacy for the horse. I will be forever proud to have played some small part in bringing his wisdom to a whole new worldwide audience through the Parelli's, for it helped him spread a most worthwhile message, regardless of audience. But most of all, I am grateful for the time I got to spend, in and out of the saddle, listening intently as Walter reminded us to put the horse first, always and foremost.

First Day at School

This is a concept I have used many times with students to get my point across, but the fun of this was getting to go to town with it. It never found the right issue for publication with Horses For LIFE, so I'm delighted to include it here…

I'd like you to imagine that it's your first day at school. Everything is completely new to you. Everything has that foreign, new smell. You haven't been in this building before, though you've walked by with your mom and you've seen the kids at their desks through the window, and known - one day, this would be you… But you really don't know what school is about. You haven't done much else till now, except play at home by yourself or with the neighbor's kids, watch videos and draw stick figures named mom and dad and me. You think you know how to spell your name, but that pesky 's' still kinda gets you. You've heard of the alphabet, and know it's somehow related to your name, but it's still an exotic concept that somehow ties in with that scribbly way mom writes her grocery list.

Now, here you are, your very first day at school, mom just dropped you off and shed a tear as she left you at your desk, which was kind of disturbing, not to say downright scary. Mom doesn't cry, she soothes and kisses your booboos. But today she cried and said, "Bye Baby, look at you, all grown up!" in a way that somehow wasn't at all comforting. Here you are. All of a sudden, all alone for the first time in your life on the first day at school. Some of the kids look familiar, maybe you even know some from the neighborhood.

Maybe you're busy, looking around, waving at Bella from up the road, she's seated by the window, oh, and there's that gap toothed kid, what's his name? He lives three blocks over, by the 7-11. He puked at your birthday party last year, you hope the teacher never puts you next to him. Hey, look at that blackboard, wow, would you love to write on that, run your nails down it, you've heard that's really nasty, and hey, is that colored chalk, wow, they're really big and cool, nothing like the little ones you used on the sidewalk, you wonder what the teacher will be like, she has a funny name, can't remember, oh whatever, isn't this exciting? Isn't this fun!!! Don't you feel all grown up?

Or maybe you're nervous. Maybe this isn't exciting at all. Maybe you don't feel ready, maybe you don't feel prepared. You feel fragile, ready to run for the hills, run home to mommy. How could she just let them take you like that? She cried, said it was time, she had no choice, it's the way of the world. Maybe you're just scared the teacher will ask you something and you won't know the answer and all the kids will laugh at you. Or worse, the teacher will get mad, and yell and call you stupid. You heard about that from your cousin, Sarah, before she went away. She was humiliated and intimidated by her teacher from day one and never got over it. She kept moving from school to school, her nerves getting worse and worse, she'd act out in bigger and badder ways till she just went away and nobody talks about her anymore….they just shake their head and talk about something else. No, you don't feel good about this.

You're just looking at your desk where other kids before you scribbled names and messages you can't read, afraid to even look at your surroundings let alone other kids. What if they talked to you and the teacher came in and got mad because you were talking in class? That happened to Sarah, too, she was just listening to the other kid and she got wacked for it….You're wishing you were home, with mom, listening to her whistle under her breath as she irons daddy's shirts.

Maybe - you feel…ready. You feel like you've been waiting for this your whole life. You've listened to your older siblings and cousins going over their homework and you're confident you get the whole alphabet thing and you know how to spell your name and mom and dad and Pete and Billy and Rascal, coz that's your dog's name. You can do this, and you're ready. You were bored with the toddlers and the games and the daily routine. You're ready for a challenge. Bring it on. You're looking around, a little impatient, when will the teacher show up, will you like her, what will be the first lesson, what you will learn today, who will be your new friends, who will be your BEST friend, coz you're *ready* for a BEST friend, and this is really cool, nothing looks like it does at home, everything smells different, and you're feeling grown up and ready for a whole new life, a big adventure.

Now the door opens and your teacher walks in. You wait with bated as she walks to the big desk at the front of the classroom, puts her bag and books down and turns to look at the class. You're wondering what her first words will be, and will she notice you and will she ask you something and what kind of impression are you going to make today. Now she's looking at you and she seems likes she's about to speak.

But when she speaks, it's in a language you have never heard before. It's gibberish, it's nonsense, it grates your ears. You look at her, eyebrows raised. Excuse me? You politely inquire. Could you repeat that? She does, but this time, a little impatiently, loudly. Still gibberish. You're losing interest. If this is school, you can take it or leave it. Whether you're confident or nervous, this just makes no sense and can't be what everyone was talking about. It must be a mistake, and surely, in a moment, someone will come in and make her go away. You look at her and shrug, hoping she will give up on you and move on to someone who speaks this language she seems to expect you to know. You look out the window, trying to escape her flashing eyes. You look down at the ground because she tapped your desk when you looked out, that was definitely the wrong answer.

But that's the wrong answer, too and frankly, it's getting scary. Because this teacher is now getting agitated, and staring at you, hard, and waving her arms and it seems she really does think you should be understanding her, responding in some way, she pauses now and looks at you. Annoyed, frustrated. She repeats her command, barking, more gibberish, but now she's bigger, angrier, and there's a big stick in her hand. And it looks like, yes, it really looks like, she's about to hit you with that stick…

It's always amusing when you see tourists talking louder and louder, as if that will make more sense of their foreign language to a listener who does not understand it. It's not so amusing when you see this same human tendency applied to horsemanship, where *speaking* louder usually means *spanking* harder. And yet, that is the daily reality of many a horse, whether a young uneducated horse like the one imagined in this metaphoric story, or an older, more seasoned horse that simply still lacks a basic education and struggles to understand what is being asked of him.

When we enter into a relationship with a horse, it is quite likely to them like me meeting a Chinese person and trying to communicate without a common language. I know Chinese people exist, and I know their language is real and I have heard it spoken but I have never learnt a word of it. So if I desire to speak with this Chinese individual and develop some kind of relationship, it would be my responsibility to learn at least parts of their language first, then try to find common ground where there can be a mutually beneficial exchange.

It's not as hard or farfetched now as it once was. There are countless books, videos and learning possibilities for acquiring information on how to communicate better with our horses. It is becoming more and more accepted, even mainstream knowledge, that they do indeed possess a kind of language of their own. A language that we can learn to decipher and apply, however laboriously and clumsily we may do so, since it's very source is one we have become adept at ignoring - the language of the body.

How often do we step back when talking to another person and notice what their posture is telling us? It may be very different from what their words imply, and often this is when we find ourselves distrusting the person without having a rational reason to back it up. Yet, subconsciously we still 'read' them and know how to apply this ancient form of signaling our intentions among ourselves. With horses, we have a unique opportunity to put this ability to work. Almost always kind and generous, they are grateful for the attempt and eager to assist in furthering your education.

Maybe, like me, you are lucky enough to have a challenging horse like Torchlight who has become more like the teacher in this story and me more like the student – though he doesn't get nasty, he does get frustrated and he does have very high expectations of me. But when I make the effort, he rewards me fully and enthusiastically, and I get to go home feeling like I got a big gold star on the blackboard today.

At times daunting, learning a new language is nevertheless an exciting and rewarding experience. And when it involves learning a language spoken in movement that can evolve to a form of dance, it can be outright fantastical and evocative of a whole other world.

A world in which we ultimately meet the horse on common ground and find ourselves speaking plainly and earnestly. Often it turns out your horse has a great sense of humor, or some very sincere suggestions to make. Sometimes you can even, just for a momentous and magical moment, catch a glimpse of that further and elusive place where you find yourselves molded from the same essence, where communication can take on yet another, and entirely unspoken form. Then we speak not only in language and dance, but in spirit.

In Retrospect

...I am beginning to think anyone who sets foot near a horse should be first talked through this as a guided meditation! I continue to be astounded at the expectation of humanity that a horse will and should simply understand what is expected of them and communicated, however poorly, to them. If only Berlitz had a course on Human-Equine Dialogue, it could be mandatory from Pony Club and up!

When One Door Closes...

By the end of 2011, though not quite ready to face it, I felt I had said all I really wanted to say with *Riding By Torchlight*. I hadn't submitted a column in some time; I had only dabbled in a few topics that went nowhere. Somehow, they all ended up sounding like something I had said before. I was fairly disgusted with the horse world at large and had withdrawn from training save for my own horses and a few close friends who were also students. I blissfully continued my studies with Stephanie Grant Millham but wondered what next.

A riding safari in Kenya with renowned safari company, Offbeat Safaris, jumped into focus. Not in my budget I instead thought to offer an article in lieu of payment. A deal was struck and sometime later, I embarked on a ten day journey that would prove to change my life and inspire a book, never mind an article.

The original intent was a one-off article to be presented under the *Riding By Torchlight* banner, and indeed, the first chapter of what would later become *Each Wind That Blows* was published in the magazine sometime in late 2012. The idea grew in scope and imagination into a multi-media production that sadly, never came to pass, while relations between me and the magazine grew tense and finally untenable due to creative and collaborative differences. By the time the magazine and its owner vanished off the internet, I had long since severed connections and struck out on my own.

I would go on to publish *Each Wind That Blows* to critical success, while my personal life underwent a great many changes foretold by the book itself - if one reads well enough between the lines.

The original chapter published under *Riding By Torchlight* has since been re-edited and undergone a great many improvements, and so cannot be authentically reproduced here. Instead, I have decided to include a previously untold story about how Classical Horsemanship brought me full circle from my confusing jumper experiences to finally shine, of all places, on the African Savannah, and a chapter from *Each Wind That Blows* that I thought more suitable to end this anthology with a bit of fun, and give the reader a taste of what it's like when a Danish American Dressage Queen goes on riding safari in the vast wilderness of deepest, darkest Africa...

Classical Horsemanship from Arena to Savannah

The following story is original to this anthology, for I had never thought to put it in writing before. It felt a bit too much like tooting my own horn, and it still does, but at least now it has context, and the real kudos go to the proven strengths of Classical Horsemanship of which I am a product.

As I discussed this book and its contents with Stephanie Grant Millham, she brought up an experience of which I had told her after I came home from my second riding safari in Kenya in 2013. It was an experience that we both felt exemplified the gift, the fruits of the labor, of a concerted practice of Classical Horsemanship; the ability to adapt to the requirements of the ride at hand. It is also a nice book-end, bringing full circle a story I started earlier about form and function, when pretty is as pretty does, pretty well.

I had come home from the first safari in 2012 with a new and healthy dose of confidence in my own riding abilities, completely unaware that it would also cause me to write a book and begin to change my life entirely. Ideas flew between the magazine and myself about all the stories one could tell, and a decision was made that I should return for a second safari with Offbeat Safaris, this time with a photographer and a videographer in tow.

To add to my excitement, the group I was to join turned out to be a group organized by British eventing icon, the delightful Lucinda Green. I was all but beside myself with glee to find myself in the company of a seasoned group of eventers and fox-hunters, including Lucinda herself, all up for anything and everything at any time, which would turn out to include eventually jumping the breakfast table. I may be a Dressage Queen, but these were my kind of people; joyous adventurers and thrill seekers.

Still, I only hoped I could hold my own in such company. Of everyone there, I was probably the least experienced jumper, never mind I had never evented. The one thing I had going for me was that I had been on a riding safari before, and this soon stood me in good stead as I found myself taking in stride experiences that before would have had me quaking in my boots.

As the week wore on, we covered much ground and jumped all the jumps we could find. I took care to watch my fellow riders, in particular Lucinda, of course; analyzing their galloping and jumping form, trying to incorporate whatever I thought I was missing. Whenever they could, Billy and Tom Dodson, the father-son photographer team I had brought with me, took pictures and video we would then enjoy by the campfire later on, often to much hilarity and good natured jibing, as the day and sometimes, mishaps, of the day were remembered.

Towards the end of the week we had opportunity to jump an imposing in-and-out, a massive Maasai thorny brush fence that enclosed their cattle corral. We were, as always, given the option of opting out, but I was determined to be a part of the fun, no matter the prospect and size of the fence terrified me. I was on a super horse, Jack, a black bay Thoroughbred gelding with a keen eye for jumps and a fine form over fences, so I had little doubt he would carry me willingly enough.

In the end, some four or five riders signed up. Lucinda was on a greener horse that she was schooling for Offbeat Safaris, but signed up nonetheless, and in an act that endeared her to me forever, actually expressed concern at the size of the obstacle before us. If she, a six time winner of Badminton Horse Trials, could feel a little intimidated, at least I was in excellent company. Everyone else rode to the other end where the Land Rover with photographers had just parked and were taking aim with eyes and lenses. As we rode a little distance away to gauge our approach, I prayed to everything holy that I would not only survive but have fun and not make a fool of myself.

Our guide Tristan led the way and we followed, speaking for myself only, heart in mouth. As expected, Jack performed admirably and I had only to follow, stay balanced and stay out of his way. He approached confidently and with pert attention, jumping the brush in his powerful, rounded way, carrying me as if I were no more than a child, and providing me with that wonderful arching back that slides the rider's hips back and out of the way as the hands follow the mouth of the horse. We landed neatly and simply cantered with *joie de vivre* (and maybe a little whooping) to the next fence, which gave us no more trouble than the first. It was all over before it had barely begun and left me wanting more, much more.

One of my favorite photos of me from that safari is from right after jumping those two fences, sitting on Jack, head tilted back, eyes shut, grin from ear to ear, the picture of beatific bliss. But there was more to come, though I would have to wait till that evening to find that out.

Back at camp, warm showers, buckets of river water heated over the fire, awaited us. By the time I had my shower and headed to the camp fire, most of the other riders were in evidence, huddled around Billy and Tom's cameras, laughing, giggling and living it up as they relived all the excitement of the day's ride.

As I entered the circle of firelight, Lucinda looked up and called out my name. I stopped short, wondering what would come next. What came next would stun me into speechlessness, though I think I managed to stutter a thank you. Then I simply sat down and scratched my head, and then silently thanked all of my teachers since childhood.

"Susannah!" said Lucinda, *the* Lucinda Green. "I must take lessons from you. Your form is bloody perfect over every fence!"

That night, Lucinda, a class act indeed, not only displayed her incredible generosity of spirit and lack of ego. She not only paid me a tremendous compliment in front of her own students, something few teachers would have the confidence to do. She paid me a compliment I would never forget, and by extension, my teachers of yesteryear as well as the principles of Classical Horsemanship. Principles that have seen me pound the proverbial pavement week after week, year after year, horse after horse, teacher after teacher, in search of that skill and form that would allow me to function as well as the moment required.

I have no illusions that I could in fact teach Lucinda Green anything, or that she was paying me anything other than an incredibly kind compliment in the way that came to her in the spirit of that moment. I am not a skilled jumper, I am not ready for the show jumping ring or cross country course on anything other than a schoolmaster and complete packer like Jack. But one thing I will own, and that is that I have dedicated my life to the pursuit of a horsemanship that prepares the rider for most eventualities as well as some one might never expect. Talent, while I may have some, only goes so far. With the riding safaris I truly tested my mettle for the first time and found my journey in Classical Horsemanship well rewarded, dovetailing beautifully with such an extravagant adventure.

I was taught a horsemanship where dressage lays down a foundation for both horse and rider; the dressage seat a fundamentally secure position of which the jumping and galloping positions are extensions with modifications. Where the balance and organization of the dressage seat are folded up and rebalanced for speed and obstacles, but the required foundation, the stability of core and leg, remain the same.

My position over jumps, on a good day, on a day when the sun is shining and I am turned loose on a good horse to gallop at a fence without thinking too hard, when I can just go along with the spirit of the moment and let my body respond without interference, is not the result of any particular skill as a jumper, for I can claim none. It is the result of a solid and pragmatic philosophy and set of principles practiced diligently, that we have come to call Classical Horsemanship. I only hope I may always be able to set as positive an example as I did, unwittingly, one fine day in Africa.

Blood, Mud and Mayonnaise

An excerpt from *Each Wind That Blows*

It's a long, hot walk through dun grass covered in the bristling Whistling Thorn Bushes. Named for their black-brown seedpods that pop open in the brush-fires that sweep the plains, the subsequent heat induced cracks in the shell whistle in the Savannah wind. Before this roasting, however, they are homes to stinging ants that drill holes in the shell and move in. They are right at thigh height and Tristan warns us to keep from brushing against the bushes. The vibration of a touch will bring on a swarming ant attack.

We are weaving through the jutting traps of bare, black branches covered in masses of white thorns and ant-filled seedpods, lifting legs, leaning and crouching in the saddle for what seems like hours. Finally, just in time as the day is heating up with no breeze to fan our bodies, we come across more stony plains that keep us in the lower gears, but at least we can trot and cool off a little in a breeze of our own making. We are doubly pleased when we come upon another vast and flat, rock free plain sporting a good sized herd of some ten or twelve giraffe in the dusty distance.

I feel a gallop coming on and my heart pounds in my chest when Tristan turns and offers the customary…trot. Yes! I know what this is really about. It's on my bucket list. The giraffe are about a half mile away in a long single file, blurry in the heated haze, but we set off in what is soon to become a hand gallop. By the time we are half way there, the horses are good and ready for more.

Only a few hundred yards ahead of me the giraffe are running, their long, gangly legs flinging up dust into the veiled sky. Lest it become a chase, Tristan is careful to stay at oblique angles to the game, following on a parallel path rather than running them down from behind. The giraffe are to my left and Tristan to my right, I am sandwiched between them with nowhere to go but forward, with sand in my teeth and water leaking from my eyes behind my sunglasses. Libra is getting stronger and stronger, making it difficult to keep him behind Tristan's line of travel when we pull level with the back of the herd of giraffe, my arms and back working in unison to keep Libra in check without having an outright fight.

I am not sure how many more gears Libra has but it feels like we are just a few short of runaway. Also not certain is what feels better, the speed, the thrill or the fear. "I am an adrenalin junkie!" Yells my inside voice, something suspected but not fully known now affirmed, but there is little time to savor this newfound glee in inner revelation. We are side by side with the giraffe, loping in their paradoxically lingering gallop just some fifty feet to my left, and Libra is having second thoughts.

He can't seem to decide if he wants to outrun or escape them, and while I am trying to slow him down enough to duck behind Tristan to switch sides, Libra decides to try both, all at once. He all but has the bit as he switches gears, drops out from under me in a sudden veer to the right, straight into Tristan and Cape to Cairo. Thank Heavens for their training and Cape to Cairo's lead mare grit, because she doesn't give an inch. For a moment we grapple like polo riders in a heated match, swaying, mashing and running together, Tristan yelling for me to get the horse away from the giraffe. Well, yes, I nod energetically, yelling: "I am trying!"

Then the loss of balance and Cape To Cairo's influence slows Libra down just enough for me to regain some semblance of control. Apparently what we do is duck behind Tristan and Anita on a flat out Mary to reemerge on their right, but the move is too fast to register and the memory of it lost in the chaos. I just know that suddenly we are on their right with horses between us, the dust and the giraffe. Libra is still going, pulling ahead of the other horses and heading for the giraffe that are following the bend of the river to pull in front of us. I am trying all known methods to rein him in with little effect as the giraffes loom ever closer. A flash of Libra and I tangled up in six foot giraffe legs flashes through my mind, settling like ice in my belly.

The other horses are slowing down and falling behind us. Finally, Libra begins to flick his ears back at them so they no longer point at the still thundering giraffe. Stopping is suddenly within the realm of possibilities now that the other horses stop behind us. We ease to a not so graceful stop, the ice in my belly melting at once. I start laughing my head off. Nothing like a little terror to tickle the funny bone.

Everyone is laughing and coughing, bursting with excitement. I am elated, patting Libra, telling him he is brilliant, high-speed spook and belly ice notwithstanding. All is well that ends well. I am so, damn, happy I can barely stand it. I have galloped with giraffe and though it can now be crossed off my bucket list, I decide not to, just in case we have another opportunity. Wouldn't want to jinx it.

We are close to our picnic site as we set off on a loose rein walk through the green bush of the nearby meandering creek. The now calm horses walk like old hands, picking their way through the landscape. We've barely caught our breath before Tristan calls for another gallop. We are so close to break time, the land ahead is opening once more, and here come zebra and wildebeest in wild disarray, running and leaping brought on by our sudden rude appearance in their pristine world. We soon learn that just like horses, wild herd animals will use almost any excuse to have a run, buck and a fart.

We pick up the reins and the horses have neither curbed their enthusiasm nor relinquished the remains of adrenalin from our previous run. Soon we are thundering along again, mingling with hunchbacked wildebeest and honking zebra, their curious call of warning an odd combination of a short bray segueing into a harsh bark as they tear around in front of us, beside us, behind us. Libra is all for the running and I am laughing, whooping, gasping and hanging on for dear life, coursing the not so elegant edge between control and its utter abdication. My legs are tiring, feeling a little loose and wobbly, but there are some dredges of reserves left. I call on them just as Tristan calls for a walk, so we may let the horses walk off the heat and sweat before arriving at our picnic.

We water the horses in a muddy creek, and after getting thoroughly, refreshingly drenched by Mary's insistent and enthusiastic water pawing, we are met in the shade of scattered trees on the hill above by our grooms.

Right behind them come Amy, Norma and Archie and behind them can be spotted some very welcome chairs and lunch. I gratefully hand over Libra to Stephen with a pat and words of appreciation in both Libra and Stephen's general direction, then stumble to the shade where Betty and I grab matching pairs of ginger ale and collapse into blissful sighing and moaning.

We barely conjure up the energy to engage in some tearing off of half chaps and boots, then we are putting up our feet on the little tables arrayed around us and sinking deep into our seats. We sit quietly for a few minutes, inhaling the shade and our sodas, a rare indulgence, but I dearly need the sugar and salts right now.

We catch ourselves in a duet of deeply felt exhalations and burst into laughter. Anita joins in, standing before us in a once white shirt now splattered in various stains which she names for us. Blood, mud and mayonnaise, she declares. Blood from a scratch courtesy of a thorn bush, mud from Mary's water antics, mayonnaise from the sandwich in her hand. I find this unreasonably funny. It sticks in my mind.

Blood, mud and mayonnaise. It's been that kind of a ride. We are tired but in high spirits, ready for the respite after almost five hours in the saddle, and with miles still to go.

A Window Opens...

It is only now, as I look back over all these stories, that I truly realize the profound impact writing *Riding By Torchlight* has had on my own life. The column was a place for me to process, study and recalibrate my own experiences and learning, a place to grow and shape my very character, and not just in relation to the equestrian world. As always, the horses provide a mirror in which we may gaze fully at ourselves and the world we live in, be that for better or for worse, but hopefully, always for the sake of growth.

Riding by Torchlight provided me with the proving ground I needed as a writer, before I ever knew I was a writer. While I had always enjoyed writing and filled dozens of journals with my scribbles since childhood, I had never fully thought to apply myself to the endeavor in a more concerted fashion. Because of the column, I discovered I had a voice, and that such a voice could mean something to others as well. By the time *Riding By Torchlight* came to a close, I *felt* like a writer and had begun to embrace the idea that I could do more, write more, and be more than just a frustrated horse trainer.

It was a gift that grew from unexpected places, and sparked unexpected journeys, a gift that kept on giving as I happily embraced a new paradigm as a happy, part-time horsewoman, full-time writer with all that entails. Because of *Riding By Torchlight*, I had the courage to start my own blog, *The Torchlight Chronicles*, a daily blog that I wrote religiously for the better part of a year as an exercise in writing. I wrote on whatever popped into my head on any given day, with precious little to do with horses, and it ended up being read by readers around the world.

When I tired of that idea, and once *Each Wind That Blows* was written, I used my newfound confidence to jump on an unexpected opportunity to write for an online developing lifestyle and luxury magazine, *Art Chateau*. For *Art Chateau* I have researched and written articles on anything from luxury travel, ancient archaeology and Marlene Dietrich to Tesla's plans for Mars. I can't wait for the magazine to go public and require another quota of articles, they were just that much fun to do.

Because of those ideas, and my passion for travel, I began to develop a travel blog, *Torchlight Travel*, where I play with different styles and ideas, the intent being to help promote some of the very special places, particularly in Africa, that I have had the pleasure of visiting. They are ideas that keep growing and expanding, and I always wonder where they will take me next, for my bucket list spans the globe.

Indeed, *Riding By Torchlight* has proven to be the gift that keeps on giving. One idea planted by a friend was the thought that *Each Wind That Blows* had more to offer in the way of teachings. Seeking to give such an undertaking a firm foundation has led me to my most recent pursuit, undergoing certification as a DreamBuilder Life Coach, a program I enjoyed as a client and now seek to put to ever better use as a coach myself, in ways still being discovered. I was halfway through the program when I realized the reason it resonated with me so deeply, is because it echoes the life lessons I learned in *Riding By Torchlight*, on my safari and in writing *Each Wind That Blows*, as well as the many teachings of all the people and horses I have encountered in my life as a horsewoman.

Now, with this book, I am profoundly grateful to come to another full circle of sorts, bringing the best of *Riding By Torchlight*, the writings that started it all, together in one book even as I finally fully comprehend how they ultimately sent me down a very different path. These are the stories that were instrumental in making my life what it is now, and to some degree, helped spark and shape discussions still ongoing in the equestrian sphere. It is both sad and fascinating to realize that this column remains relevant still today, some ten years later, but then, when it comes to horses, the wheel is forever turning and pretending to reinvent itself.

Ultimately, *Riding By Torchlight* has been a lesson in following your bliss, for when it comes right down to it, it all started with a few paragraphs of equestrian passion written down in some long ago Classical Dressage chatroom…

About This Book

Spanning the better part of a decade, *Riding by Torchlight, A Grass Roots Advocacy for Classical Horsemanship from Arena to Savannah*, is a collection of columns and stories written by Susannah West Cord during a tumultuous time in the recent history of modern Dressage. Addressing anything from the challenges of rehabilitating an off-the-track-Thoroughbred to the Rollkur controversies haunting the competitive world of dressage, the collection also includes essays on the finer points of Classical Horsemanship as applied on a mad dash with giraffes across the African savannah, and what to do when a horse gets his hoof stuck in his mouth.

While most of the compositions were previously published and read worldwide, *Riding By Torchlight* includes several stories original to this collection, as well as excerpts from other works by the author, making for an eclectic, thought-provoking and entertaining read.

At times intensely personal and introspective, *Riding by Torchlight* is by turns philosophical, humorous, adventurous, moving, fierce and inspiring. Whether it's a heartfelt tribute to an extraordinary horse, or a scathing commentary on the vagaries of the ruling equestrian bodies when faced with issues of equine welfare, the author holds nothing back and leaves no stone unturned in speaking her mind and from her heart. Honest and revealing, the collection as a whole serves as a look inside the heart and mind of a devoted horsewoman trying to make sense of all she's been taught and felt, searching for answers and hope in the face of a swiftly changing equestrian landscape of shape-shifting principles and beliefs. Ultimately, *Riding by Torchlight, A Grass Roots Advocacy for Classical Horsemanship from Arena to Savannah*, carries a torch for a Classical Horsemanship developed over centuries of trial and error, while shining a light on its countless applications and benefits with a touch of humor and a great deal of devotion.

About The Author

Raised in Denmark, Kenya and Zimbabwe, Susannah West Cord is a lifelong horsewoman as well as a life coach, speaker and writer now living in the USA. For over twenty years, Susannah has devoted herself to serving fellow seekers wishing to achieve a healthy and mutually beneficial relationship with their horses, while enjoying the fruits of a systematic training program focused on the physical, mental and spiritual wellbeing of the horse. While her studies took her down paths that included Natural Horsemanship and Western riding, Classical Horsemanship is the spark and the center around which Susannah's journey of horsemanship has revolved, and to which it has always returned.

Building on the traditional, cavalry based foundation of horsemanship she received growing up in Denmark, Susannah went on to study with Jane McLoud and her mentor, Liz Searle, in California, a study much informed by the teachings of Baron Hans von Blixen-Finecke. From there, Susannah went on to train independently in California and Texas, and more recently, North Carolina, while always seeking to further her own education in any way possible. Her teachers and clinicians have included Walter Zettl and his protégé, Eddo Hoekstra, as well as Carol McArdle and Manolo Mendez. Since 2010, Susannah has been mentored by Stephanie Grant Millham, a long time student of Nuno Oliveira.

When not writing or traveling, Susannah can be found training horses, speaking, coaching, teaching workshops and enjoying photography in the foothills of the Blue Ridge Mountains of North Carolina, where she pursues her passion for Classical Horsemanship, life, travel and all good things in between.

For more information: https://www.torchlighttraining.net and https://www.susannahcord.com

Xenophon Press Library

www.XenophonPress.com

Xenophon Press is dedicated to the preservation of classical equestrian literature. We bring both new and old works to English-speaking riders.

30 Years with Master Nuno Oliveira, Henriquet 2011
A New Method to Dress Horses, Cavendish 2019
A Rider's Survival from Tyranny, de Kunffy 2012
Another Horsemanship, Racinet 1994
Austrian Art of Riding, Poscharnigg 2015
Classic Show Jumping: the de Nemethy Method, de Nemethy 2016
Divide and Conquer Book 1, Lemaire de Ruffieu 2016
Divide and Conquer Book 2, Lemaire de Ruffieu 2017
Dressage for the 21st Century, Belasik 2001
Dressage in the French Tradition, Diogo de Bragança 2011
Dressage Principles and Techniques: A Blueprint for the Serious Rider, Tavora 2018
Dressage Principles Illuminated, Expanded Edition, de Kunffy 2019
Dressage Sabbatical: A Year of Riding with Classical Master Paul Belasik, Caslar 2016
École de Cavalerie Part II, Robichon de la Guérinière 1992, 2015
Equine Osteopathy: What the Horses Have Told Me, Giniaux 2014
Fragments from the writings of Max Ritter von Weyrother, Fane 2017
François Baucher: The Man and His Method, Baucher/Nelson 2013
General Chamberlin: America's Equestrian Genius, Matha 2019
Great Horsewomen of the 19th Century in the Circus, Nelson 2015
Gymnastic Exercises for Horses Volume II, Eleanor Russell 2013
H. Dv. 12 German Cavalry Manual of Horsemanship, Reinhold 2014
Handbook of Jumping Essentials, Lemaire de Ruffieu 2015

Handbook of Riding Essentials, Lemaire de Ruffieu 2015
Healing Hands, Giniaux, DVM 1998
Horse Training: Outdoors and High School, Beudant 2014
I, Siglavy, Asay 2018
Learning to Ride, Santini 2016
Legacy of Master Nuno Oliveira, Millham 2013
Lessons in Lightness: The Art of Educating the Horse, Mark Russell 2016
Lessons in Lightness Expanded Edition, With Contributions by Jillian Kreinbring M.S., Mark Russell 2019
Methodical Dressage of the Riding Horse, Faverot de Kerbrech 2010
Military Equitation: or, A Method of Breaking Horses, and Teaching Soldiers to Ride, Pembroke, and *A Treatise on Military Equitation*, Tyndale, edited by Charles Caramello, 2018
Principles of Dressage and Equitation, a.k.a. Breaking and Riding, Fillis 2017
Racinet Explains Baucher, Racinet 1997
Riding and Schooling Horses, Chamberlin 2019
Riding by Torchlight, West 2019
Science and Art of Riding in Lightness, Stodulka 2015
The Art of Riding a Horse or Description of Modern Manège in Its Perfection, D'Eisenberg 2015
The Art of Traditional Dressage, Volume I DVD, de Kunffy 2013
The Ethics and Passions of Dressage Expanded Edition, de Kunffy 2013
The Forward Impulse, Santini 2016
The Gymnasium of the Horse, Steinbrecht 2011
The Horses, a novel, Elaine Walker 2015
The Italian Tradition of Equestrian Art, Tomassini 2014
The Maneige Royal, de Pluvinel 2010, 2015
The Portuguese School of Equestrian Art, de Oliveira/da Costa 2012
The Spanish Riding School & Piaffe and Passage, Decarpentry 2013
To Amaze the People with Pleasure and Delight, Walker 2015
Total Horsemanship, Racinet 1999
Training Hunters, Jumpers and Hacks, Chamberlin 2019
Training with Master Nuno Oliveira 2-DVD set, Eleanor Russell 2016
Truth in the Teaching of Master Nuno Oliveira, Eleanor Russell 2015
Wisdom of Master Nuno Oliveira, de Coux 2012

www.ingramcontent.com/pod-product-compliance
Lightning Source LLC
Chambersburg PA
CBHW060504240426

43661CB00007B/915